The Politics of AGRICULTURE in Tropical AFRICA

Volume 9
SAGE SERIES ON AFRICAN MODERNIZATION AND DEVELOPMENT

Jonathan BARKER
Editor

The Politics of
AGRICULTURE
in Tropical AFRICA

SAGE PUBLICATIONS
Beverly Hills   London   New Delhi

For information address:

SAGE Publications, Inc.
275 South Beverly Drive
Beverly Hills, California 90212

SAGE Publications India Pvt. Ltd.
C-236 Defence Colony
New Delhi 110 024, India

SAGE Publications Ltd
28 Banner Street
London EC1Y 8QE, England

Printed in the United States of America

Library of Congress Cataloging in Publication Data

Main entry under title:

The politics of agriculture in tropical Africa.

(Sage series on African modernization and development ; v. 9)
Bibliography: p.
1. Agriculture and state—Africa, Sub-Saharan.
I. Barker, Jonathan, 1938-   . II. Series.
HD2118.P64   1984   338.1'866   84-2013
ISBN 0-8039-2295-7

FIRST PRINTING

Contents

Preface

As Africans in villages and towns take what steps they can to find their way through hard times, intellectuals can try to clarify why and how times are hard. This book pays particular attention to the interconnections among conditions and struggles at local, national, and transnational levels in the belief that obstacles to the improvement of the living conditions of low-income Africans are found at all three levels and that obstacles at different levels may reinforce one another. The authors of the different chapters have their own perspectives on the nature of the interconnections and they use a variety of concepts to further the analysis. The exchange of views among the authors in the course of preparing the book helped many of us to clarify our own understanding of the political economy of agricultural change in Africa. I hope the resulting book can contribute to the dialogue in Africa and elsewhere about how politics and policies of progressive change can be engaged.

The book is truly a collective effort. As editor and author, I was helped at every turn by the other contributors to the volume; they shared ideas and offered advice from the workshop at the University of Toronto in May 1982 where drafts of most of the chapters were subjected to collegial criticism, to the working out of final versions late in 1983. The Social Sciences and Humanities Research Council of Canada helped my thinking and learning about politics and agriculture in Africa with travel and research assistance under grants 451–82–2501, 410–82–0813, 410–80–0648. A visiting fellowship at the Institute of Development Studies at the University of Sussex in 1982–1983 gave me the milieu and the technical support to complete the editing and writing. Pat Lacey, in particular, coordinated the typing, and typed herself with such speed and skill that I was the only bottleneck in the production of a final typescript. Peter Gutkind, the series editor, gave me the right combination of freedom and help. Colleagues at the University of Toronto, friends, and family were consistently supportive.

To all these helping hands, I express gratitude while claiming for the authors responsibility for the text as it herein appears.

—Jonathan Barker
University of Toronto

INTRODUCTION

1

POLITICS AND PRODUCTION

JONATHAN BARKER

For tropical Africa, the word "crisis" is heard with increasing frequency and stridency to describe the situation of the region's economies and the particular state of individual countries. Statistics amply show that stagnating production is widespread and that many social groups in many regions are unable to meet their basic needs. Poor economic performance and widespread deprivation, however, do not make a crisis. In its full meaning, the word refers to much more than a situation of pain and suffering. It suggests that key institutions are at risk: The system of authority is in question and the networks of communication and exchange threaten to unravel. The perception of a crisis in tropical Africa is the assertion of the close linkage between economic conditions and political stability. It implies a venture into the science of political economy. To point to a generalized crisis is to claim that a decisive change for better or for worse is imminent, a claim that implies an understanding of the political economy of change.

The chapters in this volume contribute to the creation of a more adequate political economy of change in African agriculture. There are several pretenders to the throne of master-science of crisis in Africa; some of them will be criticized in the pages to follow. The more important task of this introduction, however, is to draw together the main strands of the political economic analysis that inhabits the case studies in the volume. In combination, they explore the local, national, and transnational dimensions of the politics of agriculture in tropical Africa and they explore them in historical depth as well as in vignettes of immediate situations. Consistently they explore the relationship between production and politics. It is a two-way relationship: Political motives—for staying in power and for rewarding regions and classes of loyal support—and political means—such as the use of administrative coercion—influence agricultural policy and shape patterns of production. Patterns of production, for their part, create social and economic interests that influence and shape politics. In many countries of Africa, politics in the 1980s still bear the impress of interests and tendencies created by the interaction of indigenous and transnational forces in the colonial systems of agricultural production. In this book, each case study of a country or of an institution is also a study in how to reason about the political-economic equation in a period of deep and rapid change. The studies do not all use the same concepts, nor do they contain the same emphases, but they do share a common task of analyzing the interaction of politics and production in concrete and specific circumstances.

CRISIS AND ANALYSIS

Poor economic performance has brought most governments in Africa under severe economic strain as they try to balance the maintenance of government organizations and programs against falling revenue, and as they reduce imports even of essential goods in line with the falling purchasing power of export sales. The strain draws governments closer to private and public institutions of lending and assistance. Many governments have faced powerful intervention into their economic policy by international creditors led by the International Monetary Fund and the World Bank. Transnational firms also feel the economic pinch and make representations and take actions to ensure the maximum protection of their vital interests. In a typical adjustment loan, the IMF will require policies like raising the price for foreign exchange (devaluation), ending food price subsidies, reducing government spending, and raising producer prices for agricultural exports and marketed food crops. Such a package can turn a situation of economic strain into a crisis of stability as the real incomes and employment of urban salaried classes are squeezed. In contemplating this and other scenarios of economic strain in Africa, before echoing the cries of crisis, some discrimination is in order. The suffering and the threat to communities and institutions affect different regions, classes, and groups differently. The crisis is an uneven one.

Chronic unemployment, malnutrition, sickness, frequent police coercion, and routine denial of political rights do not in themselves raise crisis alarms. They are the all-too-easily accepted banalities of underdevelopment. For a deeper understanding, a good question to ask is, crisis for whom? For which people and for which institutions? The stream of migrants from villages to towns and cities is fed by a multitude of personal and family crises as groups and individuals face the implications of poor prices, loss of land, loss of soil fertility, absence of food and tools and seed to start the farming season, or other obstacles to making a living in the countryside. Government institutions, mining companies, crop exporting firms, and construction companies may continue to operate smoothly and routinely in the midst of such crises, especially if one or two good crops, oil, copper, or foreign loans grease the national economic gears. Much crisis in Africa is contained within disfavored regions and disinherited classes and hardly gains national attention, let alone international publicity.

A deeper form of crisis occurs when the economic pressures become general, but even here governments can adapt to falling revenues and the economy can adjust to a fall in foreign exchange. Popular rising expectations can give way to falling ones. Where opinion does not move spontaneously, government repression can encourage it as repression of the many keeps peace for the few. More prosperous regions or classes may thrive even when disfavored ones are suffering miserably. Even if there is less business, there can be much business as usual. The powerful can try to manipulate crisis to their advantage, or at least to minimize the damage to themselves.

Often, those who proclaim a crisis claim also to know what set of actions would prevent the worst or achieve the best in a situation where decisive change is likely. The World Bank's (1981) report Accelerated Development in Sub-Saharan Africa—An Agenda for Action, which is analyzed in Chapter 3—presents its recommendations as if they were verified applications of an established economic science to a well-understood situation. When it is seen how often the mistaken policies of the past that the bank now wants to see scrapped and replaced are the very policies the World Bank helped to install a decade or so ago, the baselessness of the report's attitude of certainty is patent (Bulletin, 1981; Africa Development, 1982; Payer, 1982). Its use of "crisis" seems calculated to induce a sense of urgent acceptance of its particular partisan analysis rather than to contribute to a sorely needed debate.

This volume seeks to bring into that debate a proper appreciation of the transnational and local as well as the national forces in the politics of agriculture in tropical Africa, and the complex crises it is undergoing.

THE CENTRALITY OF AGRICULTURE

For the countries of tropical Africa it is impossible to imagine a durable improving trend in the basic standard of living without consistent growth in agricultural production. The connections between agriculture and living standard are strong. A majority of the population of the region grow a large part of the food they eat; for them, increase or decline in the production of crops grown for local use is immediately registered in levels of consumption and nutrition. Agriculture also supplies a growing home market in towns and cities and among rural workers, traders, artisans, and specialized farmers who do not grow their own food. One of the conditions necessary for supplying the increasing home market from home production is a growing surplus of production beyond local rural needs. The rapidly increasing imports of food grains to tropical Africa reflect inadequate growth in food production.

Supply of food, however, is only one of the ways agriculture contributes to living standard. Much of the foreign exchange of tropical Africa is earned by the sale of agricultural products abroad. Income from coffee, tea, cocoa, peanuts, palm products, tobacco, cotton, sisal, cashews, pyrethrum, and many lesser crops like pineapples, rubber, bananas, flowers, and fresh vegetables is used to import industrial machinery, technicians, petroleum products, and transportation and communications equipment as well as luxury goods and food. There are strong arguments for the importance of developing industry in tropical Africa, especially industry that is linked to agricultural production. But the weight of agriculture in self-provisioning of the farming population, in supplying the home market, and in earning foreign exchange in export markets is so great that rising agricultural production is essential for any broad increase in living standards. Except possibly for a few mineral-exporting countries, rising agricultural production is essential for industrialization as well.

In the 1980s, the issue of agricultural development in tropical Africa has taken on a new urgency. While other regions of the Third World began to show a small per capita growth in agricultural output in the 1970s, tropical Africa registered a significant drop in agricultural production in the 1970s and overall stagnation in the two decades since the independence watershed of 1960. The oil shocks, the downturn in commodity prices, and the world recession mark out the period since the mid-1970s as a new and difficult economic phase for Africa. The trends since 1980 are especially alarming.

At the time of independence, the subcontinent had known a decade of significant increase in agricultural exports and that growth continued until about 1965. Then began a period of declining exports; in the decade of the 1970s, exports shrank almost 20% in volume, about the same amount they had grown in the previous 10 years. According to estimates credited by the World Bank, food production for local consumption followed a similar pattern. It increased in step with the increase of population in the 1960s, while in the 1970s the rate of increase of food production dropped below the rate of increase of population: Per capita food production declined. In the period 1969-1971 to 1977-1979, the volume of agricultural production (food and nonfood) per capita increased in only seven countries: Upper Volta, Burundi, Malawi, Rwanda, Cameroon, Swaziland, and Mauritius. For tropical Africa as a whole, it dropped by 1.4%. Since by all the conventional indicators this is one of the poorest regions of the world, stagnation and decline of the basic productive activity must dim hopes for rapid economic progress; worse, it means widespread and growing material hardship (World Bank, 1981: 2, 3, 167).

Recognition of the poor performance of African agriculture and of the importance of improved performance for development is far from understanding why there is agricultural stagnation, what its social and political consequences are, and what might be done and by whom to improve the situation. There are three important debates about how to approach the political economy of African agriculture. First is the dispute about how much weight to give to transnational forces as opposed to internal ones—the debate about dependency. The second is the question of whether to stress production or exchange—the debate about which tradition of political economy to follow. The third is the discussion about the relative strength and autonomy of the state in relation to class and economic forces—the state debate. What follows sets forth the most pertinent aspects of the debates and draws from them a perspective on the political economy of African agriculture.

Dependency and Agriculture

The perspective of dependency and underdevelopment, inspired and influenced by Latin American thinking, has focused on the way in which underdeveloped political economies are integrated into the evolving system of world capitalism, arguing that external forces block, truncate, and distort the development of production. Applied to Africa, the perspective convincingly showed that Europe-centered capital shaped regional production specialties in peasant export crops, settler farming, or supply of cheap labor to plantations and mines (Amin, 1976; Arrighi and Saul, 1973; Rodney, 1972; Shivji, 1976). A large number of case studies have shown in detail the variety of ways in which Africa's rural population has been subordinated to transnational capital and "peasantized" in the sense of being made vulnerable to the extraction of wealth and power by merchants and states tied to the development of capitalist industry in Europe and North America (Amin, 1975; Saul and Woods, 1971; Klein, 1980; Palmer and Parsons, 1977; Heyer et al, 1981). These studies also reveal, however, a basic shortcoming in the dependency argument. There has been an important dynamic of class formation and peasant political action within Africa that has influenced the terms of connection with transnational capital (Laclau, 1977; Brenner, 1977; Leys, 1977).

As a whole, the collection of studies in this volume confirms the need to go beyond a crude notion of the determining power of external forces in African agricultural change. The chapters on transnational firms, the World Bank, the United States Agency for International Development, and the Canadian International Development Agency confirm the continuing direct influence of transnational interests on African rural production. They also document some of the limits to that power as rural producers strive to maintain some food autonomy, as rural and urban classes use external resources in their own bids for wealth and power, and as governments and ruling classes seek to defend the interests they hold dear. The World Bank and the IMF, even with the leverage they hold as gatekeepers for private lending, encounter great resistance to wholesale acceptance of their requirements in a country like Tanzania. USAID tries to propagate its own conception of modernization, but its trainees often follow policies quite different from the ones it recommends. CIDA funds state farms even when it would prefer to use its influence to promote private enterprise. The chapter on transnational business finds that, in its task of extending and consolidating its African presence, transnational capital is more and more led to invest in joint ventures and management contracts that give some control, even if it is imperfect and limited, to African institutions and classes.

The country and local studies give an even more dynamic picture of the interaction between transnational and internal forces. Some of these will be noted in the next section on the local dynamics of change in production systems, but several larger-scale conflicts and adjustments can be noted. In Upper Volta, Ivory Coast, and Sudan transnational cotton interests have a large stake in the evolution of production and processing of their favorite crop. Yet the pattern of investment and production is influenced as well by the interests of the state and its regional ties in Upper Volta, its connections with manufacturing capital in Ivory Coast, and indigenous trading and agricultural capital in Sudan. Moreover, in all three cases the action of the producing peasants and tenants and farm laborers is also felt in the pattern of production and change, sometimes with explosive force, as in the case of the Jouda incident in Sudan, but usually in a more quietly persistent and indirect way as in the resistance to controls demonstrated by cotton growers in Ivory Coast and Upper Volta. In Nigeria, the regional patterning of agricultural production and trade shaped political conflict in a regional-ist pattern and contributed to the civil war.

The debate about dependency is sometimes looked upon as an academic discussion, but the evidence of this volume is that the conflict and tension between transnational forces and localized ones is an ongoing reality. Since yesterday's transnational influences are behind some of the power of local classes today, the line between internal and external can be seen to shift over time. At most moments, however, the distinction remains politically meaningful and dependency questions can become live political issues. The question is seldom one of autonomy or autarchy versus dependency; it is one of the terms of the interaction. Who will set the agenda for action in African agriculture? This is a question that will be raised again once the other debates about perspective have been canvassed.

Modes of Production and Forms of Struggle

As in the case of the dependency debate, the divisions of opinion about peasant production and its integration in the larger economy point to places in the social structure where ambiguity and contestation are frequently found. It is not easy to sort out the arguments and positions because peasants, ruling classes, and the nature of the relationship between the two are all the subject of differing views. Three extreme positions, while mistaken, reveal some of the important features of peasants and capitalism in Africa. One view is that production operates according to its own values and rules distinct from those of capitalist enterprises, and has a powerful ability to survive and even to penetrate organs of government and business and subvert their modernizing drive. Goren Hyden (1980) has given a most vigorous statement of the peasant "economy of affection" rooted in the values of reciprocity emphasizing how strongly it resists capitalist values and incentives. Peasants, in this argument, are strong with a negative power of resistance, but helpless to expand production. There is abundant evidence that this view, like its equivalent predecessor, the tradition-bound peasant, is badly off the mark. Rural producers do respond to income incentives by expanding production as the rapid growth of Africa's export and home economies has shown (Helleiner, 1975). But the resistant peasant viewpoint does bear upon an important truth. Peasants do not always easily and naturally join into the capitalist market. The change can be a traumatic one, laden with moral conflicts about family and community obligations and with practical dilemmas about the allocation of land and labor.

The symmetrical opposite to the resistant peasant myth is also to be rejected. Some writers assume that peasant farmers are pure petty commodity producers looking to maximize income without having to measure impact upon family or community. Robert Bates (1980) takes this view, seemingly without asking why land and labor all over tropical Africa have only imperfectly entered the market as commodities, and why farmers often maintain food crops even when it costs something in short-run disposable income. Again, an erroneous extreme standpoint illuminates an aspect of reality: Producers do on the average respond to market incentives, and some of them have become quite complete petty commodity producers, and even small capitalist farmers. But the change in production relations that these responses embody is played out through conflict over authority in the household, control of land and labor, and imposition of marketing and administrative institutions. The conflicts reflect class struggle and resistance to class formation. They respond to and also cause the unevenness of incorporation and expansion within the market.

A third and final extreme argument holds that farmers have been so subordinated to capital that they have lost all meaningful economic autonomy and therefore they are no longer independent producers responding to market signals. They are tantamount to wage workers, totally vulnerable to capital that exploits them through the low wages and the low agricultural prices it pays. Once again, there are examples of peasantries whose self-provisioning ability has been destroyed or gravely damaged (as the studies of Ivory Coast and Sudan show clearly) and examples of producers brought under direct control by capital (as the discussion of contract farming reveals in the next chapter). As a general statement about African agriculture, however, the model misses the crucial dimension of variation and ambiguity, and therefore contestation and conflict in the partial and uneven subordination of peasant farming to capital and market relations.

The studies in this book show that the three mistaken models express real but incomplete and varying tendencies that are usually subject to some countervailing forces. The chapter on Sudan shows how two different villages reach very different ways of living with the power of the market, one going so far as to adopt a system of wages-for-housework while the other holds family and community relations partially distinct from market transactions. The cotton projects in Upper Volta and Ivory Coast go to great lengths to control peasant farming, but resistance is real and the results for productivity are mixed. The case of the Limpopo Valley in southern Mozambique brings out the special vulnerability of a peasant economy that has become dependent on the outmigration of labor, in this case to the mines of South Africa, when both labor circuits and agricultural circuits are disrupted. The chapter on Zambia details two very different patterns of struggle between peasant farmers and the state for economic opportunity and political power in the commercial market for maize.

The authors in the volume grapple with the relation between capital and peasantry with the help of rather different terms and theoretical perspectives. Several of them employ the idea of reproduction of the domestic production unit to express the process by which family producers maintain the family as a living and producing entity. With integration into capitalist circuits, the process of reproduction may become dependent upon capitalist circuits as well as domestic self-provisioning. A critical factor is the degree to which peasant labor is integrated into a wider labor market. The studies of Sudan and Upper Volta are especially informative about the impact of labor markets and labor control on peasant production. The need to sell crops can also become fundamental to survival of the economy, just as the need to sell labor can. As the cases of Nigeria and Zaire show, control of land is also vital to the reproduction of peasant farming units; markets or other transactions in land can vitally affect peasant reproduction. As markets for labor, crops, and land become fundamental to the process of reproduction, the relationship between production (for the market to make money) and reproduction changes. The case studies explore several aspects of that change: the growing vulnerability of peasant producers to exploitation, the capacity of capital to derive more surplus value from agriculture, the ability of peasants to resist exploitation politically and economically, the role of contingent crises like the Sahel drought (Franke and Chasin, 1980) or the oil price shocks for the strength and strategy of peasants and capital, and the role of market institutions. The logic of these complex and contested relationships has been explored in the literature of articulation of modes of production (Foster-Canter, 1978; Wolpe, 1980) and the problematic status of the peasantry become dependent on capitalist circuits for its reproduction has been well captured in Bernstein's (1977) idea of "simple reproduction squeeze." The studies in this volume emphasize the political as well as the economic nature of the relationship and the need to subject it to empirical as well as theoretical scrutiny. The ideas of family-local and agro-industrial systems are intended to facilitate that empirical exploration.

The purpose of distinguishing these two systems of agricultural production, processing, and distribution is to clarify the present-day dynamics of African political economies. But the distinction also reflects the history of agricultural change in tropical Africa, and it can best be understood in schematic historical terms. Before the imposition of colonial rule in Africa, most production was for use within the family, the village, or the local area. There was also long distance trade, some of it in important products of everyday consumption such as salt, cola nuts, and iron tools; in West Africa, a considerable bulk of material entered the long distance trade. Yet, the fact remains that most needs were met from local production, and most production was carried out within groups of kin. Lower-status dependents were sometimes members of households or formed separate households within the residential unit.

Labor was often organized on the basis of more than one principle: kinship, gender, age, slavery, caste-guilds and so forth. Probably most production was structured by household relationships under the formal direction of the head of household, usually the senior man. He, his wives, children, and other dependents divided up the work of feeding the household, with the women doing most of the day-to-day work. However, there was sometimes scope for individual production for use or for trade by the individual producer. Age groups not defined by kinship and divided by sex sometimes had fields of their own. Kinship groups not united in a household or in a residential unit could also cultivate a field or manage a herd of cattle. The point is that individuals often produced useful goods within more than one kind of group. Since complex and crisscrossing production groups are still the rule in much of Africa, terms like "the household production unit" or "the primary production unit" must be read as convenient, but sometimes misleading, simplifications.

The colonial imposition quickly brought a much larger system of long distance trade into connection with the family-local system. The reordering and expansion of the long distance economy took place, more often than not, under conditions of social disorder caused by the slave trade, the ending of the slave trade, epidemics, ecological disruption, wars of conquest, and the establishment of institutions of colonial rule. Individuals, families, communities, and regions were creating new ways of livelihood, building on the traditions they knew, but responding to new economic and political realities. It was a time as well of moral and cultural renewal as religious movements developed and spread.

The new colonial long distance trade was a forerunner of what is now being called the world agro-industrial system or the world agribusiness and commodities system (George, 1981; Goldberg, 1974). The products of Africa were palm fruit, rubber, peanuts, cocoa, sisal, cotton, coffee, and tea. The three main forms of production were small-scale cultivation by Africans, larger-scale settler farming, and large-scale corporate plantations. Settler farms and corporate plantations (and some African producers of cash crops) depended upon labor drawn from the African smaller-scale farming population. Therefore, African small-scale production was part and parcel of plantation and settler farming systems as an upstream supplier of labor. Among the most important effects of settler and plantation agriculture have been their withdrawal of labor from family production.

The three forms of production were integrated into the worldwide agro-industrial system in somewhat different ways. For plantations and settler farms, there were other upstream suppliers of inputs to agriculture: companies selling machinery, fertilizer, selected seeds; governments doing research and building transportation routes. For African production there were few inputs (except for seasonal labor in some cases) from outside the locality. Downstream from production, plantations typically included mechanical processing that greatly diminished the bulk of the product or that had to be quickly done for the product to retain its value. For sisal, fibers were extracted; for tea, the leaves were dried; for arabica coffee, the berries were hulled, fermented, and dried; for rubber, the latex was processed; and for palm fruits, the oil was expressed. Settler and African farms also engaged in some immediate processing: drying robusta coffee, sun drying tea, cleaning peanuts. Sometimes a local plant did essential processing like ginning cotton. But in all cases, the crop left the continent in a relatively raw state; the industrial transformation of the product, and its distribution and retail sale, took place in Europe.

The agents that organized and maintained this transcontinental agro-industrial system were, in addition to the producers described above, large trading companies, shipping lines, food processing companies, and the colonial states. As the chapter on transnational corporations explains, oligopolies formed in the major agro-industrial activities, and there was also a tendency toward vertical integration, most thoroughly in the case of Unilever with its chain of production from palm plantations in the Belgian Congo to the manufacture of soap and margarine in Britain and Europe.

The role of the colonial state was to see to the construction of the necessary transportation infrastructure, to help determine the strategy of agro-industrial development (whether it would be based on African smallholders, European settlers, or plantation firms), to reconcile Africans to the needs of the agro-industrial system for all or part of their land and their labor, and to mediate differences among different kinds of capital (traders versus settlers versus plantations versus shippers; French versus English; Europeans versus "Asians" or "Lebanese").

Governments since independence have continued the process begun at the end of the colonial period and seized many of the economic levers formerly controlled by transnational firms. Governments are now in charge of the purchase of agricultural exports from producers. In many cases, they also manage transport, some processing, and sale on the world market. Governments have expanded their supply of inputs, credits, and advice to farmers and, as the cases studied illustrate, they have invariably sponsored a few large-scale production schemes either for export or to meet domestic demand. Finally, in countries without valuable mineral exports (the cases of the Ivory Coast, Upper Volta, and Sudan in this volume), the governments are dependent upon the export of agricultural products for the bulk of their revenue. Where mineral exports are the major source of revenues (the cases of Zambia, Zaire, and Nigeria in later chapters), agriculture still must support the vast majority of the population, produce food for the nonfarming miners, workers, traders, and civil servants. The failure of agriculture means crippling bills for food imports, rapid urban migration, and a difficult problem of income distribution. Therefore, even mineral states are pushed to pay some attention to agriculture, although they can ignore the stagnation of agriculture rather longer than the agricultural export dependent governments can.

Independent governments are an active part of the agro-industrial system. At the same time they are subject to the tensions and demands that agro-industrial activities cause for family and local production and distribution. They are also faced with the claims for an expanding economic role for the national private sector, sometimes in collaboration, sometimes in competition with state agencies.

The State Debate

The third great debate in African political economy, after the dependency debate and the modes of production debate, deals specifically with the question of government: it is the state debate (Goulbourne, 1979). The debate itself has not been engaged in a very effective manner. At one extreme is the view exemplified by the report of the World Bank (1981) on "Accelerated Development for Sub-Saharan Africa: An Agenda for Action." The report argues that most government intervention in agricultural production has been damaging to the economy and recommends that governments turn marketing over to the private sector and reduce their role in subsidizing inputs and holding food prices down. Whatever the merit of the recommendations, they are in no way informed by analysis of why governments do what they do or of the implications of following the report's recommendations. During one of its campaigns for rural reform, the party leadership in Tanzania coined the slogan "siasa ni kilimo"—"politics is agriculture"; there is enough truth in the slogan to reveal a huge gap in the case made by the World Bank report.

Marxist analysis has posed the question of whether class power is exercised by an African economic bourgeoisie, an institutional African bourgeoisie lodged in the state, by transnational capital, or by an alliance of two or more of the above. On what class forces is the state most dependent? Is it relatively autonomous from those forces? Is there a potential for a radical break in the direction of state action toward socialism or is the apparatus and are the holders of power closely tied to the existing line of policy? These questions do require clarity about the definition of classes, autonomy, state apparatus, but they can only be resolved through a method of study that separately identifies class forces and state actions and that tries to see how closely the two are related in particular cases and how they evolve over time.

A recent analysis (Bates, 1982) applying marginalist economic reasoning to the agricultural policies of states shows that some of their most systematic policy biases are consistent with giving priority to industrial development, pacifying the urban wage earners and the urban unemployed, and enlarging the patronage available to state officials. Governments tax agriculture and subsidize industry, whether owned by indigenous or foreign capital. They keep food prices low and foreign exchange cheap, thus encouraging the importation of food and discouraging its internal production. They subsidize wealthier farmers in order to gain some support in rural areas. They promote huge and often unproductive agricultural schemes because the schemes generate contracts for urban business and establish farmers who are certainly dependent and possibly grateful.

This kind of middle-level analysis of the economic and political logic of state interventions in markets, their use of patronage and coercion, and the industrial or agricultural emphasis of their investment policies is useful as far as it goes. It is necessary to go further and look beneath the assumptions about the industrial emphasis of African governments to the class interests and ideological formulations that support and justify the emphasis. The studies in this book show that the interests of foreign investors in import-substituting industries like textiles and sugar (chapters on Ivory Coast and TNCs) can attract subsidies and pricing policies favorable to industry. In Sudan, the preference of the state for large public and private schemes is founded in the political influence of the class of landowners and pump scheme licensees, and influence working to the detriment of tenants, laborers, peasant farmers, and pastoralists. Generally, "merchant" states, dependent for their own revenue upon a share of export crop earnings, are likely to bear a different relationship to agriculture than are the "rentier" states gaining income from the export of copper (Zambia and Zaire) or oil (Nigeria) (Kitching, 1980).

Some recent analysis (Hart, 1982; Bates, 1982) argues that the most likely way in which agriculture will get more favorable prices and investment from governments is for rural class formation to proceed to the point of creating a strong rural landowning class. It will favor policies biased toward the interest of large producers, but these will be less unfavorable to small producers than the present policies are. The basic argument is that rural producers are fragmented and politically weak and defensive. Taken singly, their best strategy is to seek protection from the worst eventualities from a patron. The result is manipulable clientelism.

In fact, there are often significant institutions of rural solidarity. Moreover, the new efforts by states to bring agriculture under tighter control may be changing the situation of farming people toward greater organization and less fragmentation. The very controls of crop authorities and outgrower schemes are forms of organization of producers in their common subordination to price-setting and production-controlling agencies. These are conditions that may stimulate political organization of producers in defense of their own interests. At this point, the economic analysis of politics needs to give way to a more political analysis: What are the traditions of political organization in a particular country and locality? What kinds of supportive organization and leadership are available? The Sudan chapter shows the importance of wider political support for farmer organization, including some urban and worker support. The possibilities for political organization require specific case analysis in their full national and political context. Some general comments about the tensions that occur in the process of agricultural change are relevant to such analyses.

TENSIONS AND CHANGE
IN AGRICULTURAL PRODUCTION

Historically and in a continuing process there is a many-sided interaction between the agro-industrial system and the family-local system. The main agencies of the agro-industrial system—governments, transnational firms, and international development agencies and small independent production groups—act to increase the production of export commodities. The main agencies of the family-local system—kinship production groups, women producers, local small-scale traders, and family consumption groups—act to maintain the family-local system. Of particular interest are the small-scale producers who participate directly in both systems. Their production is a zone of tension and stress. Researchers have discovered several distinct processes of change in small-scale production deriving from the interaction between producing for the agro-industrial system and producing for the family-local system. In any particular case, the pattern of change may reflect one or more of these tensions in different degrees.

One widely noted change is the growing tension within small-scale production units between production for the agro-industrial system and production for family and local use. The tension is most apparent where there is direct competition for land and labor between the two systems. As the studies of Upper Volta and Ivory Coast show, such competition is greater in the savanna zones and dry plateaux where millet and maize are the main food crops and cotton and peanuts are the main cash crops. Because cash and food crops require intensive labor at about the same time, careful attention to one kind of crop damages the other. Food and cash crops also grow on the same kind of land; where land is in short supply, producers have to choose which kind of crop to favor. In the case of tree crops—coffee, tea, and cocoa—the competition with food crops is less marked. Periods of peak need for agricultural labor do not overlap very much. There can, however, be competition for land, recently a significant problem in some areas. The cost of uprooting tree crops makes rapid conversion from cash to food crops difficult.

The competition for labor affects many activities, not only agricultural production. Historically the extra labor required for new cash crops came at the expense of the social and military activity of local men, off-season work and social activity of men and women from other regions with a different agricultural calendar who were employed on sharecropping or labor rental terms, and increased agricultural labor by women (often under the direction of senior men). When these sources of labor are exhausted, economic competition between production for use and production for sale is heightened, as the analyses of Nigeria, Upper Volta, and Ivory Coast demonstrate. In some areas, production for sale has displaced production for local use to the extent that most people buy most of their food with the money they earn from crop sales. The Nigeria, Zambia, and Sudan studies find competition between wage labor and both food and cash crop production can draw labor from small-scale agriculture to large schemes (in Sudan) or to urban employment (in Nigeria and Zambia). The way in which government policies bias the incentives between cash crops and food crops and between own account production and wage labor will be discussed below.

Class formation is a second tendency observed in many rural areas. The production of cash crops and the whole downstream train of activities—marketing, transporting, processing—offer opportunities for increasing wealth. Some people use their increasing wealth to employ or attract more workers so as to further increase their economic activity. In this process, a rural class accumulates increased command over productive resources and another class loses its economic power; some people give up command over some part of their own labor in return for a wage or the probability of paternalistic protection. The accumulating class may have one or more of different origins. They may be small farmers who had the skill, luck, and means to take advantage more rapidly and more thoroughly than their neighbors of the cash crop opportunity (Zambia chapter). They may be traders, transporters, politicians, chiefs, or religious leaders who parley their function as economic and political intermediaries into an expanding base of economic and social power (Sudan, Upper Volta, and Ivory Coast cases). They may be people based outside the rural area—government officials, military officers, or business people—with funds to invest (Nigeria and Zaire chapters). The political-economic consequences of the different kinds of class formation can be very different, as will be discussed in a later section. None of these kinds of class formation guarantees improvement in the productivity of either labor or land.

A third process of change, already noted, is the primary reproduction squeeze or marginalization (Bernstein, 1977). It often combines the first two processes. Producers who have lost their capacity for self-provisioning may also lose their capacity to survive on cash crop earnings. Several mechanisms can result in production groups that are no longer viable. Land may be lost through sale or seizure or through division among a growing number of heirs. Overcropping or new forms of cropping, sometimes related to the rapid rise of population in an area, may damage the fertility of the land. Drought and flooding may suddenly bring the production crisis to a head for many people in an affected region. The only alternatives for the people affected is to search for land or employment elsewhere on a temporary or permanent basis or else to wait for gifts of food. Almost any wage or any terms of settlement appear attractive. Marginalization is a process that produces inexpensive labor for rural and urban wage employment. It also produces unemployment and destitution.

A fourth process of interaction between agro-industrial and family local production is the growing control of agencies in the agro-industrial system over the whole of the production activity of groups of small-scale producers. In an effort to improve productivity and to increase their own rate of return, government agencies, international agencies, and transnational firms attempt to direct the productive activity of producing groups. Examples are cited in all chapters in this book. The means of control include agricultural extension advice; control of access to land or water; regulations sanctioned by refusal of credit, supply, or marketing facilities; and direct police coercion.

In a fifth process, the local-family production system is almost completely displaced. In collaboration with international development agencies or with private capital, the state creates a sector of state farms or centralized schemes in which production is centrally managed and large-scale technology is employed. The instruments of control over production vary: direct wage employment, tenancy contracts, conditional membership terms. Sometimes the centrally managed schemes coordinate the production and marketing of more independent "outgrowers". These schemes compete for land, labor, and markets with the local production systems, and even within them there is a tendency for local systems to reappear on small family plots.

All five of these processes increase the control of capital over production; they are part of the process Marx called the subsumption of labor by capital. What is critical, however, is less subsumption itself than who is carrying it out (an emerging class of local or national capitalists, transnational firms, the state, international development agencies) and the way they are doing so (how centralized, with what organized controls, and with what technology). The way the control of capital is increasing determines the rate of rise in rural productivity, but its effects are much wider than that. It influences the distribution of wealth and power, including the power to increase productivity further; shapes the autonomy and political strength of different categories of rural people; and affects social relations in families and in local communities. Subsumption is a reversible process, but when the grip of agro-industrial capital is loosened, not likely is a return to the preexisting reality.

It cannot be assumed that greater control by capital over production will lead to greater productivity. The goal of those who gain greater control may be to gain some other objective. Governments may establish and use control over rural production to maximize political support in the short run. Other goals may be to prevent some other class or group from establishing control or to maximize the extraction of surplus without improving productivity. Second, an agency that seeks to raise productivity may fail to do so because of inadequate technical and organizational methods or capacities. Since World War II colonial governments, independent governments, private transnational firms, and private indigenous firms have asserted greater control over production and implemented purposeful schemes for increasing productivity of land and labor, often without success. Sometimes the project failed not because other purposes intervened, but because they used inappropriate techniques. Third, efforts to increase productivity can be brought low by market fluctuations. Often, the agency that is claiming greater control over production is responding to market signals and calculating that changed production will win profits. If the signals change as the investments are beginning to bear fruit, then the whole effort may be damaged.

Finally, changes in the ecological and political climate can savage the best performing scheme for subordinating production to new control. Such changes may have their own roots in economic history, but they arrive as apparently independent events. Several years of drought, a civil war, a flood can alter social and economic conditions fundamentally, destroying production systems and changing the available instruments of control.

Despite the obstacles, it is almost certain that increased agricultural productivity will be realized in Africa. How soon? Reflecting what pattern of class and regional forces? The two questions are important ones, for some countries in Africa may fall behind by a generation or two of unnecessary penury, and the forms of agricultural progress established in the next several years will shape decisively many aspects of community life and political custom.

In this time of stagnation, the pressures for production are so great that all other considerations are likely to be cast aside. Nevertheless, questions of distribution and quality of community life, questions that interest many African producers, need also to be considered. This is the place to return to the question of, whose agenda for action? It is clear from the studies in this book that transnational capital and external donor agencies have great influence on African agriculture, but they have far from a free hand. Partly under the impact of new forms of agricultural organization such as contract farming, collective villages, large, centrally managed schemes and partly as a result of the expectation of significant government services and price-setting action, peasant farmers are likely to become more active in politics. Over the long run, that is the likelihood. Governments stricken with falling revenues become more disposed to listen. The other sources of conflict in African societies grounded in class differences, regional ties, external influences, and urban-rural tensions will also determine what kind of political coalition dominates government. Peasant farmers and farm workers and those who want to place their interests on the agenda for political action have their work cut out for them. Africa's multiple crises mean that there is hope for change.

REFERENCES

Africa Development (1982) Special Double Issue on the Berg Report and the Lagos Plan of Action. 7 (1/2) Codesria, Dakar.

AMIN, S. (1975) L'agriculture africaine et le capitalisme. Paris: Anthropos.

AMIN, S. (1976) Unequal Development: An Essay on the Social Formations of Peripheral Capitalism. New York: Monthly Review Press.

ARRIGHI, G. and J. SAUL (1973) Essays on the Political Economy of Africa. New York: Monthly Review Press.

BATES, R. (1981) Markets and States in Tropical Africa: The Political Basis of Agricultural Policies. Berkeley: Univ. of California Press.

BERNSTEIN, H. (1977) "Notes on capital and peasantry." Review of African Political Economy 10:60–73.

BRENNER, R. (1977) "The origins of capitalist development: a critique of neo-Smithian Marxism." New Left Review 104:25–92.

Bulletin (1983) Accelerated Development in Sub-Saharan Africa, 14(1). Institute of Development Studies, Sussex, England.

COQUERY-VIDROVITCH, C. (1980) "Les paysans africains: Permanances et mutations," pp. 25–40 in C. Coquery-Vidrovitch (ed.) Sociétiés paysannes du tiers-monde. Lille: Presses universitaire de Lille.

DUPRIEZ, H. (1980) Paysans d'Afrique noire. Nivelles, Belgium: Terre et Vie, Imprimerie Havaux.

FANON, F. (1963) The Wretched of the Earth. New York: Grove Press.

FOSTER-CARTER, A. (1978) "The modes of production controversy." New Left Review 107:47–77.

FRANKE, R. and B. CHASIN (1980) The Seeds of Famine: Ecological Destruction and the West African Sahel. Montclair, NJ: Allenheld, Osmun.

GASTELLU, J.-M. (1980) "Mais, où sont donc ces unités économiques que nos amis cherchent tant en Afrique?" Cahiers Orstom, Série Sciences Humaines 17(1–2):3–13.

GEORGE, S. (1981) Les stratèges de la faim. Geneva: Grounauer, 1981.

GOLDBERG, R. (1974) Agribusiness Management for Developing Countries—Latin America. Cambridge, MA: Ballinger.

HASWELL, M. (1975) The Nature of Poverty. London: Macmillan.

HELLEINER, G. (1975) "Smallholder decision making: tropical African evidence," pp. 27–52 in L. G. Reynolds (ed.) Agriculture in Development Theory. New Haven, CT: Yale Univ. Press.

HEYER, J., P. ROBERTS and G. WILLIAMS [eds.] (1981) Rural Development in Tropical Africa. New York: St. Martin's Press.

HILL, P. (1977) Population, Prosperity and Poverty: Rural Kano, 1900 and 1970. Cambridge: Cambridge Univ. Press.

HYDEN, G. (1980) Beyond Ujamaa in Tanzania: Underdevelopment and an Uncaptured Peasantry. London: Heinemann.

ILIFFE, J. (1972) Agricultural Change in Modern Tanganyika: An Outline History. Dar es Salaam: Tanzanian Historical Society.

KITCHING, G. (1980) Class and Economic Development in Kenya: The Making of an African Petite-Bourgeoisie. New Haven, CT: Yale Univ. Press.

KLEIN, M. [ed.] (1980) Peasants in Africa: Historical and Contemporary Perspectives. Beverly Hills, CA: Sage.

LACLAU, E. (1977) Politics and Ideology in Marxist Theory. London: New Left Books.

LEYS, C. (1977) "Underdevelopment and dependency: critical notes." Journal of Contemporary Asia 7(1): 92–107.

PALMER, R. and N. PARSONS [eds.] (1977) The Roots of Rural Poverty in Central and Southern Africa. London: Heinemann.

PAYER, C. (1982) "Tanzania and the World Bank." Working paper A285 C.H.R. Michelson Institute, Fantoft, Norway.

RODNEY, W. (1972) How Europe Underdeveloped Africa. London: Bogle L'Ouverture Publications.

SHIVJI, I. (1976) Class Struggles in Tanzania. New York: Monthly Review Press.

SWAINSON, N. (1980) The Development of Corporate Capitalism in Kenya. Nairobi: Heinemann.

WOLPE, H. [ed.] (1980) The Articulation of Modes of Production. London: Routledge & Kegan Paul.

World Bank (1981) Accelerated Development in Sub-Saharan Africa: An Agenda for Action. Washington, DC: Author.

**TRANSNATIONAL AGENCIES
AND AGRICULTURAL CHANGE**

2

AGRIBUSINESS AND
AGRARIAN CHANGE

MOHAMED S. HALFANI and
JONATHAN BARKER

The rising demand for wheat flour to make bread for Zaire's swelling cities is being met by Continental Grain Company, one of the American giants in the grain trade. Continental negotiated with the Zaire government the right to decide whether any other firms could import wheat. With the only large flour mill in the country, Continental also has a monopoly on flour production (Morgan, 1979: 226–231). In the Ivory Coast and Upper Volta, the Compagnie Française pour le Développement de Fibres Textiles was instrumental in organizing expansion and modernization of cotton production (Campbell and Gervais, this volume). Also in the Ivory Coast, Nestle's has built a factory for the manufacture of soluble coffee to sell in the growing internal market and in the expanding markets in Africa and the Arabian Gulf (Masini et al., 1979: 113–135). The same company was hired by Tanzania to manage a nationalized instant coffee factory. In Sudan, the government's great emphasis on mechanized farming schemes has opened a significant market for Massey-Ferguson to sell tractors and other farm machinery (Johnson, 1979). In Kenya, Del Monte is growing pineapples on a large new plantation, canning them, and selling them on the European market. The dozen or more multipurpose river basin development projects in some state of implementation in Africa all must employ equipment, technology, and expertise of transnational agribusiness firms to develop and maintain their agricultural production aspect.

The examples are typical of the worldwide growth of an agro-industrial system structured in large part by transnational firms. The clumsy phrase, agro-industrial system, is needed to describe the connected chain of activity: manufacture and supply of agricultural inputs such as fertilizer, chemicals, seed, machinery; farming itself; marketing and transporting crops; and processing and distributing food products. In this growth, tropical Africa has been less attractive to transnational businesses, including agro-food business, than other parts of the world. Agribusiness looks for economies with large and growing markets, ample raw materials, an appropriately skilled labor force, and an extensive and reliable infrastructure. It looks for governments that are stable with effective and helpful administration. It wants favorable investment codes, fiscal regimes, and customs regulations. Making a rough composite score on all these factors and ordering all countries in the world by their rank would reveal many African countries in the lower part of the ranking. Countries with socialist governments that reject transnational private investment and countries with sparse populations, rudimentary transportation systems, and poor drought-ridden economies rank near the bottom. Thus, Mozambique, Angola, Tanzania, Niger, Chad, Mali, and Gambia are not prime TNC targets. Politically unstable countries are also far down the list, countries like Uganda and Zaire. Highest on the African list are Nigeria, Ivory Coast, and Kenya. Yet the role of TNCs is a significant topic for study even in hostile, poor, and unstable environments because a few TNCs under such conditions can have an important impact.

The new expansion of agribusiness into the underdeveloped world has stimulated contrasting evaluations. The case *for* transnationals is that they bring to regions where the productivity of farming is low several elements necessary for the institution of higher productivity. TNCs provide access to new and more profitable markets in the developed world.

They can deliver a package of technological and managerial skills for growing, processing, and marketing produce, and they are willing to apply their expertise and even train local nationals as their successors. Properly organized experienced companies can thus substantially increase the productivity of the Third World's agriculture [Vol. 1, 1980: 140].

The firms, it is claimed, can adapt to farming by smallholders and cooperatives, or they can organize production more directly. The profits a TNC may export are the necessary price for instituting agricultural improvement from which the country and the farmers also benefit (Goldberg, 1980; Lipton, 1977).

The case *against* transnational firms in third world agriculture is critical of their role in production, accumulation, and consumption; it is claimed that they structure the agro-food system in a way that increases inequality, dependency, and poverty. In production, the TNCs, it is argued, favor export crops over food crops, diminishing the self-reliance of the economy and of small producers. They favor large centralized projects with heavy capital requirements and high import needs when labor, not capital, is abundant and foreign exchange is in very short supply. TNCs, it is held, promote inappropriate luxury consumption models for meat and processed foods. Even the mass diet is adversely influenced by advertising for beer, soft drinks, tobacco, white bread, and infant bottle formula. The promoted tastes require imported foods, high-priced brand names and imported processing technology. With respect to accumulation, the case against the TNCs holds that they export profits and revenues for research and investment in other places and with no relevance to underdeveloped countries. Moreover, they block accumulation by smallholder producers or by the larger progressive farmers who could otherwise become active and effective engines for agricultural growth. More generally, they draw the national ruling groups toward a dependent and inegalitarian slow model of change. Other charges brought against the transnationals are that they introduce ecologically damaging methods of farming and that they further regional inequalities and the exploitation of women (Franke and Chasin, 1980; George, 1979; Lappé and Collins, 1979; Dinham and Hines, 1983).

Several important issues are raised by the conflicting evaluations. The first is the nature of the participation of transnationals in tropical African countries in the evolving world agro-food system. Second is the effect of transnational firms on production itself. Third is the effect upon the community and society in which production takes place. Fourth are the relations transnationals establish with states.

TRANSNATIONAL FIRMS AND COLONIAL RULE

The pattern of TNC presence in tropical Africa owes much of its shape to the structure of the colonial economies. Almost all the features of the transnational presence in tropical Africa today have their counterparts in the colonial period. Even the poorest, the most socialist, and the least stable of the countries of tropical Africa have a small armature of transnational agro-food firms as a legacy of the colonial political economy. In those countries, more attractive to business since independence, the inherited colonial firms often remain an active and crucial part of the economy. After the political partition of Africa in 1885, European capitalists opened the continent's colonial era by raiding it for easily seized export goods—tapping wild rubber trees (often with forced labor), shipping out hardwood cut near waterways, taking valuable minerals from surface mines already worked by Africans. By the 1920s, the advancing firms covered the continent; they began to merge, coordinate, and organize among themselves. The "second partition of Africa" by transnational corporations was completed and consolidated between the wars as the well-known colonial oligopolies and giant integrated firms expanded their volume of business until the depression plunged many regions and many companies into crisis (Hopkins, 1976). Another period of business change accompanied the worldwide expansion of trade and multinational investment in the 1950s. Yet the colonial pattern remained and remains powerful, channeling new activity even as it changes.

Colonial rule guaranteed metropolitan firms all the political conditions for profitable investment: stability, helpful administration, and favorable tax and investment rules. Colonial governments also did much to construct necessary infrastructure and to supply cheap labor by tax and administrative pressures. The colonial offices in London, Paris, Brussels, and Lisbon did the higher planning in the colonial system, directing the flow of settlers and specifying crop specializations in the interests of cheap administration and metropolitan industry (Wolff, 1974: 86). Colonial transnationals took part in the experimentation, economic pressuring, and political maneuvering out of which the colonial design emerged.

VARIATIONS IN COLONIAL AGRO-INDUSTRY

Agriculture and agricultural trade were secondary lures for capital in colonial Africa. By far the greatest attraction for transnational firms was mining. Measured in terms of capital invested and profits realized, mining was far ahead of agriculture in the amount of transnational activity (Frankel, 1938: 210ff.). However, the indirect effects on agriculture of mining investment were very large. Men left farming for shorter or longer periods to work in mines and mine labor created a market for local food crops as well as for imported food. The withdrawal of labor from agriculture often damaged productivity and altered family relations, including the organization of work on the land (Palmer and Parsons, 1977). Returning mine workers might also invest a part of their earnings in tools, labor, and other farming inputs. Large-scale mining creates powerful interests pressing for cheap food, often exerting a powerful influence on agricultural pricing and investment (Cowie and Momba, this volume).

Although less transnational capital was invested in the agro-industrial system, the value of agricultural exports was much greater than the value of mineral exports, as it remains today if petroleum exports are excluded. The breadth and depth of the effect upon African society was very great.

In West Africa, the initial involvement of foreign companies in agriculture was undertaken by merchant firms. The changing demands of Western capital from slaves to agricultural raw materials and minerals led to a proliferation of Europe-based trading firms, specializing in tropical exports and supported by banks and shipping companies. At the end of the nineteenth century, dozens of firms operated in West Africa. Among the larger were the Royal Niger Co., G. L. Gaiser, John Holt, the Compagnie Française de l'Afrique Occidentale, and the Société Commerciale de l'Ouest Africain. Shipping to and from West Africa was dominated by Elder Dempster and Woermann Shipping Companies and financial operations were handled by the Bank of British West Africa and the Banque de l'Afrique Occidentale. Traders, shippers, and bankers collaborated in the purchase of peanuts, cocoa, and palm products for shipment to Europe where they were manufactured into salad oil, margarine, chocolate, and other products which in turn were sold on European and world markets (Hopkins, 1976: 275). TNCs adapted themselves to peasant production by integrating all kinds of import and export trade over a wide geographical area in a process of horizontal expansion.

In Central and East Africa, there typically developed a greater degree of vertical integration. Companies with a base of operations in India (Smith MacKenzie) or South Africa (British South Africa Co.) moved into the field backed by banks (National Bank of India, Standard Bank) and by shipping companies (British and India Steam Navigation, Union Steamship Co.) (Hopkins, 1976: 275). The presence of European settler farmers and Asian traders and the absence of restrictions on direct production influenced the way transnationals entered agriculture. There was a strong integration between trading activities and agriculture production. For example, Mitchell Cotts, a London firm with shipping and trading interests in South Africa, entered East Africa in 1926. It soon added the export of wheat and maize together with the supply of agricultural inputs to its businesses, becoming the sole agent buying and selling for the Kenya Farmers' Association. By 1938 it was involved in the production of grains and sisal. Foreign companies could directly engage in farming; provide financial assistance, technical inputs, and marketing facilities to white settlers; or work with African producers (Hopkins, 1976: 49, 277).

The impulse for colonial development in Africa came from the need of Europe's burgeoning industries for new resources and new markets. By the second decade of the twentieth century, the predominance of exclusively merchant firms was gradually being eroded. Even in West Africa, trading branches of industrial companies were absorbing and taking over the activities of merchant firms. For example, between 1910 and 1929, one of the world's giant vegetable oil processing firms, Lever Brothers, brought out a whole series of trading companies operating in Nigeria, Sierra Leone, Liberia, Gambia, Cameroon, Ivory Coast, and Ghana. In 1929, Lever's Niger Company merged with its greatest rival, the African and Eastern Trade Corporation (AETC), forming the United Africa Company, which in Nigeria, Ghana, Sierra Leone, and Gambia controlled the majority of trade in palm products, ground nuts, and cocoa (Unilever's World, n.d.: 65).

In East and Central Africa where there were few restrictions, the main trading and engineering firms such as the British East Africa Company, Smith Mackenzie, Gailey Roberts, A. Bauman & Company, and Mitchell Cotts began to invest directly in the production and processing of sisal, cotton, coffee, tea, and pyrethrum. Companies like British American Tobacco (BAT), Brooke Bond, and Unilever, whose initial involvements were mainly in processing and marketing their products, began to assume an active interest in production (Swainson, 1980: 58–65). The condition that generated this trend was the intense competition among manufacturing companies to control raw material supplies and to influence input prices.

There were some variations in the manner in which the companies organized their agricultural activities. While some companies like Unilever had a vertically integrated system with plantations, processing plants, and import/export activities, and Brooke Bond supplemented its plantation output with the marketing of smallholders' production, other companies like BAT depended entirely on independent producers.

Three Colonial Firms

The fear of being squeezed out by the middlemen who were supplying the basic raw materials for the Lever companies, plus increasing competition from the margarine and soap firms Van den Berghs and Jurgens forced Lever Brothers to establish their own sources of raw materials. In 1911, Lever acquired concessions from the Belgian government to exploit natural oil palm in a radius of sixty kilometers of each of five points in five different regions of the Belgian Congo, with a future promise of 750,000 hectares of freehold land for plantations. The Lever company, HCB (for Huileries du Congo Belge) was to establish its exploitation in stages, fulfilling given production targets within stipulated periods of time (Fieldhouse, 1978: 503–504).

While the conventions purported to guard the indigenous people's right of land ownership and also to promote their social welfare, the major task the people were to perform was to provide labor to the plantations and to sell their palm kernel to the monopoly buyer— Unilever. Since cutting fruit was hated work and since low labor cost was the key to profitability, the Belgian colonial state ensured that the Lever company had adequate supply of labor and kernels through the establishment of a capitation tax and a supplementary tax (based on the number of wives a man had), and by stiff administrative pressure. During the 1930s' depression, the price paid for palm fruit was reduced; the pressures brought about by the fiscal policies and backed by physical force led to a series of uprisings that were crushed by the Belgian state with "extraordinary savagery" (Fieldhouse, 1978: 509–516). The establishment of the plantations later in the 1930s and the signing of tripartite agreements between Unilever, the colonial state, and African authorities enabled the company to have a more regular supply of palm fruit with less repressive mobilization of labor, and also permitted the company to operate in a wider area. Furthermore, through the above agreement, Unilever acquired a monopoly of buying all the palm fruit harvested by the Africans (Fieldhouse, 1978: 517ff.).

Unilever constructed plants in Africa for extracting and processing palm oil and manufacturing soap and margarine in Nigeria and Zaire in the 1930s; Zimbabwe, Zambia and Malawi in the 1940s; Kenya in 1953; Ghana in 1963; and Uganda in the 1970s. By the end of the 1950s, the company had managed to integrate a part of its vegetable fat industry in several of the African economies, from production or raw fruit purchase to sale of a consumer product. Its main business in Africa (excepting its UAC operations) remained exporting large amounts of vegetable fats for manufacture and sale in Europe (Fieldhouse, 1978: Ch. 6; Wilson, 1968; Unilever's World, n.d.).

Brooke Bond, until the 1920s, operated mainly in India where it had tea plantations. It was compelled to diversify its sources of production, especially after the emergence of nationalism in India, to compete more effectively with other tea-trading firms such as Lipton's (now a Unilever subsidiary), Twining, and James Finlay. The companies established large tea plantations and also marketed tea grown by independent producers, mainly European settlers. As a result, there was an intense competition for both land and markets. In the second half of the 1930s, Brooke Bond entered into an arrangement with East African tea growers to give them access to its financial and sales organization, and to provide them with its goodwill, trademarks, and patents in return for 7.5% of the gross-selling proceeds of the tea it handled (Swainson, 1980: 78–92).

The British American Tobacco Company in the early twentieth century established trading branches to purchase tobacco grown by African smallholders for shipment to Britain for processing. However, to compete effectively, especially with other tobacco companies like Rothmans, BAT needed to process the leaf within the producing area. In East Africa, it established its first plant in Uganda in 1934, with another in Kenya in 1954 after obtaining an agreement with the colonial state that it would be the only buyer of smallholder tobacco. BAT did not undertake any production activities; instead, through the supply of inputs, extension, services, credit, marketing, and quality control, the company was able to direct smallholder tobacco production and to integrate it with manufacturing and distributing cigarettes in the continent (Morss et al., 1976: Vol. 1: 203–211; Swainson, 1975: 132).

The Role of the Colonial State

At a political level in this early period, the role of the colonial state was to reconcile the indigenous people to the interests of the metropolitan companies and, where settlers were present, to sort out differences that might arise between companies and settlers.

A conflict of this nature occurred in the 1930s when the International Tea Committee—a body created by the large tea corporations—agreed to restrict the expansion of tea production and tea sales in the world market in an attempt to contain the low prices caused by market oversupply during the depression period. Such an agreement would have retarded the tea industry in East Africa and was therefore strongly opposed by settler farmers. The three East African governments initially sided with the big corporations (which also dominated the local growers' association). However, political pressures from the settlers led to a change of position and the colonial governments in consultation with the metropolitan state agreed to excuse East African growers from the restrictions (Swainson, 1980: 86–92). Conflicts between the two non-indigenous forces were not very common, however, and therefore the major role of the colonial state was to ensure that the companies and the settlers obtained labor, land, and favorable pricing policies.

Colonial governments maintained close consultation with business both on a formal and an informal basis (Bauer, 1954: 147). There were business advisory bodies in each colony, and in the metropoles the main business interests were organized to inform and pressure the colonial ministries. Where there were sizeable plantation companies, they often retained quasi-governmental functions in providing community services and maintaining public order.

In the case of Zaire, for example, the Belgian colonial state had the responsibility of maintaining Africans' land rights and also promoting their social welfare. At the same time, it had to ensure that the Unilever enterprise had adequate supplies of labor and raw materials. It therefore asked the company to build a few schools and hospitals, and in return, the state provided its repressive and regulative instruments to facilitate the company's surplus accumulation (Fieldhouse, 1978), an exchange of services of which there are familiar echoes in the Zaire of Mobutu.

Typically, the government's tasks in the colonial agro-industrial system were to organize the financing and construction of the basic transportation infrastructure (ports, roads, railways, telegraph); to conduct research in tropical agriculture, to provide certain services to farmers (supply of seeds on credit, construction of crops storage depots, agricultural extension services); to regulate marketing from producer to trading company by establishing marketplaces and enforcing contracts; and to encourage the required flow of labor to plantations, European estates, or African cash crop zones by taxation and administrative pressures. The degree of institutional integration between government and business varied considerably, but the basic coordination of firms and governments in the creation and evolution of the colonial agro-industrial system was a common feature of all the colonial regimes in Africa. Of course, these services and investments were financed for the most part by taxes and earnings derived directly or indirectly from the labor of African peasant-farmers, miners, plantation workers, artisans, and traders.

Extensive coordination is also apparent in the higher planning that went into the construction of the colonial systems and again in their transition to independence. In the creation of the system there was coordination in the choice of crops, the major form of production (African, European, or plantation), and the modernization and extension of the system once established. Again, during decolonization, there was considerable central direction aiming to maintain the agro-industrial system by adapting it to a new political phase. Of course, much of the coordination in both these historical projects was in reaction to events that could not be controlled fully: the actions of European and African farmers, the agricultural limitations of regions, the failure of certain forms of organization, and competition from other regions of the world all had their influence. Yet, it is accurate to say that the colonial agro-industrial systems were joint ventures between government and business in the fullest sense.

The Transition to Independence

On the whole, the independence decade (1955–1965) corresponded to a period of relatively high prices and expanding markets for African export products. It was also a period of growing public investment in infrastructure and in agricultural projects. It corresponded as well to the initial formation of a worldwide agro-industrial system centered in the United States. For tropical Africa, it was a period of rapid expansion and deepening participation of transnational firms in the local branches of the agro-industrial system. Except for one decisive change, there was great continuity with the colonial period proper. The change was the demise of settler agriculture. The few settlers in the Ivory Coast were the first to leave, then Zaire. Tanzania made a slower transition, but settler power was early extinguished as a viable alternative. In Kenya, the transition was made with important transnational assistance in the form of massive settlement schemes and the retention of a significant sector of large-scale farming, some of it by white settlers (Wasserman, 1976). Zambia retained a few European farms and Zimbabwe, as of 1983, was trying to keep the sector viable for the time being. In Angola and Mozambique, virtually the entire population of Portuguese settlers fled as African liberation movements won independence. For those countries with large and economically significant sectors of settler agriculture, the task of transition to other forms of commercial agricultural organization was a difficult and important one.

After World War II, with the rise of nationalist movements and the booming commodity markets, the colonial states began to play a much wider economic and political role. Since in this period Britain was suffering from a severe dollar crisis, the state encouraged and promoted private capital investments in the colonies. British firms were encouraged to increase agricultural production so as to cater for Britain's food needs as well as assist in creating financial services. The Colonial Development Corporation and the Overseas Food Corporation were formed to work jointly with private capital in establishing large agricultural schemes.

To exploit the boom, Brooke Bond tea company, for example, undertook major innovations in tea planting and manufacturing techniques. Between 1947 and 1960, it expanded its plantations, introduced vegetative propagation of high-yielding varieties, and replaced random plucking with a technique of plucking the top three leaves together with the bud. During the same period, the manufacturing process was made more capital intensive.

Under guise of ensuring quality control, Brooke Bond and the other tea companies provided extension sources and technical inputs and dominated the institutions that catered for smallholders. The companies also connected British machinery suppliers with smallholder tea factories and trained Africans to run the factories. The metropolitan companies were able to shape the conditions under which smallholder tea cultivation developed from production, processing, to marketing and also to link the industry to the global system that they dominated (Swainson, 1980: 251–264).

The fact that British American Tobacco Company was operating right from the beginning through contractual arrangement with producers made the transition to the post-independence situation a bit easier. For over 25 years, the company had operated a production system that effectively integrated smallholder production with the company needs. At the end of the 1950s, smallholder farmers were not only growing the crop, but they were also organizing their own subcontractors to build curing barns and they were curing the tobacco leaves, all under the close guidance of BAT. In the years preceding independence, the company concentrated on increasing productivity and establishing more branches to supply the expanding local market (Morss et al., 1976).

Unilever had a more complex adjustment task. By the 1950s, the company had established a vast enterprise in the continent: plantations in Zaire, Nigeria, and Cameroon; diverse trading operations throughout sub-Saharan Africa; and soap and margarine factories in Zaire, Ghana, Nigeria, and Kenya. While there was some kind of vertical integration among linked activities, many subsidiaries were relatively independent and occasionally even competed with one another. Therefore, the changes that took place with the transition to independence have to be examined separately.

By the 1950s in the Belgian Congo, the company had broken away from monoculture activities and diversified into rubber, cocoa, coffee, tea, and cattle. Just on the eve of independence (1958/1959) the company's subsidiary—HCB (Huileries du Congo Belge)—had succeeded in renewing its tripartite agreement for 10 more years. This meant the company was able to maintain for over 30 years its land concessions as well as its monopoly position in palm oil marketing in exchange for the provision of a few welfare services. Probably with the acquisition of political power by the indigenous people in mind, Unilever also agreed to the allotment of 5,000 shares (in money equivalents) to the Congo government. To appease nationalist sentiment, Unilever began in 1959 to bring Africans into its plantation management. Eighteen senior positions were to be gradually allocated to Africans, but only as a consequence of normal wastage. Here, as in the political realm, gradualism failed as the turmoil of the early 1960s caused a massive departure of European personnel and forced a rapid Africanization (Fieldhouse, 1978: 536–541).

In the processing plants, Unilever undertook measures to preempt interventions by the new governments. In Nigeria, for example, the measures taken included "the merging of Van den Berghs (Nigeria) Ltd. with LB (N); establishing a service fee agreement with Unilever," and putting agreements with other Unilever companies "on 'an arms length basis'—that is, ensuring that, if the Nigerian government acquired a share in LB (N) Ltd. it did not thereby acquire legal title to any of the trademarks used by . . . other Unilever companies" (Fieldhouse, 1978: 366). Unilever also diversified its manufacturing activities and included toothpastes, edible oils, shampoos, and face creams among its products. At the same time, the trading subsidiary of the company—the United Africa Company (UAC)—began to cede its direct trade with African consumers and producers to local traders, assisting them with credit arrangements to serve as middlemen in collecting peasants' products and distributing imported goods. The UAC itself concentrated on the importation of durable consumer goods like refrigerators, bicycles, automobiles, and farm machinery (Fieldhouse, 1978: 372–373; Unilever's World, n.d.: 70–71; Bauer, 1954: 127).

By the end of the colonial period, TNCs had effectively penetrated the agricultural sector and established horizontal and vertical linkages in regions across the continent. With the assistance of the colonial state, TNCs had initiated and promoted the cultivation, marketing, and first stage processing of crops demanded by the metropolitan industries. They had established important links with government agencies, traders, and producers and their influence ramified right through rural society.

TNCs IN INDEPENDENT TROPICAL AFRICA

In a few countries, independence meant TNCs had to adapt to the abrupt nationalization of primary trade marketing of export commodities and in the settler colonies, as the example of Kenya shows, companies came to terms with the rapid replacement of settlers by some combination of state firms, large private African farms, and African smallholder production. At first, new investment was slight as both governments and TNCs felt their way to new policies and to a new balance in the relationship among government, TNCs, and the national private sector.

In a few years, TNCs new to the continent began to invest, and old firms tried new tactics. New methods of entrance included management contracts and consultancy, joint ventures, and the supply of business and logistical services. The companies were attracted to invest in Africa, depending on the country, by the liberal investment climate, the nearness to a potential export market, cheap resources in good demand, and the possibility of serving an expanding external or internal market. The modernization programs undertaken by African governments and international development agencies in the rural sector have also raised the demand for goods and services from transnational agribusiness. Thus, through the supply of farm machinery, fertilizers, seeds, and processing equipment, TNCs have managed to establish new linkages in African economies and to expand old ones.

NEW EXPORTS AND NEW ORGANIZATION

Worldwide growth of TNC investment in what is called "nontraditional exports" has been an important part of the development of the agro-industrial system. Geographically, the new investment has concentrated on Mexico and Central America for the North American market and North Africa for the European market. In tropical Africa, TNCs have invested, for example, in pineapple production in the Ivory Coast and Kenya, fresh vegetables in Senegal, alfalfa in Ethiopia, and flowers in Kenya. This kind of agricultural development has had some importance in Kenya and the Ivory Coast, but even in these countries, the great increase in the value of exports has come from the expansion of traditional export crops like coffee, tea, and cocoa.

Another realm of TNC innovation has been to establish what can be called nontraditional methods of organization that give TNCs a strong grip on production without displacing smallholders or interfering with their rights in land and other means of production. Most common are two very closely related arrangements: contracting with smallholders, and outgrower or associated producer schemes. In the former system, a company makes arrangements with the producers to buy given quantities of crops with particular specifications, in return for modern inputs, extension services, and a fixed price. Under such an arrangement, the peasants retain ownership of the land but are compelled to abide by the conditions set by TNCs with regard to cultivation, marketing, and pricing. BAT is an old hand at contract farming. Other examples include that of Cadbury Schweppes and a tomato paste factory in Nigeria, "Tea Importers Inc." with its tea project in Rwanda (George, 1979: 49), Bud Antle's Senegold project in Senegal (Franke and Chasin, 1980: 186), SODEPALM's palm oil development in the Ivory Coast (Amagou and Gleizes, 1975), and Unilever and palm fruit in Zaire (Lamarchand, 1979: 245).

Often, the state enters the contract through government agencies established to coordinate and promote agricultural production as well as to facilitate the export process. The TNCs contract with the agencies to obtain the raw materials they need. Nestle's dealings in the Ivory Coast is a good illustration of this relationship. The Fund for the Stabilisation and Maintenance of Prices of Agricultural Products (Caisse de stabilisation et de soutien des prix de production agricole, or CSSPPA) is a state corporation that markets coffee, cocoa, cotton, and palm oil products. The fund guarantees a minimum farm-gate price, giving what the fund considers a satisfactory return to the producer. It adds a differential calculated to cover the cost of delivery to the factory or to the export depot at the port. The minimum purchase price plus the differential becomes the "local shop price" paid by Nestle's subsidiary CAPRAL, which does not fluctuate with raw coffee prices on the world market. Thus, coffee producers operate with a guaranteed sale price and CAPRAL has negotiated from the government authorization to buy at a low price broken beans unfit for export. Selling in the

Ivorian market and in other markets outside the International Coffee Agreement (Greece, Africa, Middle East), CAPRAL does not have to pay the fund the difference between the international price and the internal price when the international price is higher as exporters of raw coffee do. It thus has a cost advantage over competing firms that pay the world price for their raw coffee. In addition, CAPRAL has been saved FCFA 1 billion in taxes over 12 years because of the government's generous tax concessions.

CAPRAL cooperates with national organs to assist planters in improving and increasing the quality and quantity of crops. It works with the French Institute for Coffee and Cocoa (IFCC), and the Society for Technical Assistance for the Modernisation of Agriculture in the Ivory Coast (SATMACI) to produce a new coffee variety—Arabusta—which has the physical qualities of Robusta plus the aroma of Arabica (Masini et al., 1979: 113–130).

For some companies, the total reliance upon independent producers is considered to be risky, and therefore the alternative arrangement of outgrower schemes is used. In this system, a company uses independent producers to supplement output from its own plantations. In some of these schemes, part of the company land can be leased to farmers who are also provided with other factory facilities on credit arrangements.

The Mumias sugar project in Kenya illustrates several of the features common to many contract farming schemes. The aim of the transnational firms is control rather than ownership. Only after pressure from the government of Kenya did Booker McConnell take 5% ownership in the Mumias Sugar Company. The Kenya government took 70%, while the remaining shares were divided among the Commonwealth Development Corporation, the Kenya Commercial Finance Company, and the East African Development Bank. Booker McConnell, however, was awarded the management contract and its subsidiary, Fletcher and Stewart, supplied the factory (Mulaa, 1981; Hansen and Marcussen, 1982).

The Mumias Sugar Company maintains tight control over the operations. The sugar factory went into production in 1973 with a nucleus estate of almost 4,000 hectares and 6,000 contracted farmers. By 1979, there were about 13,000 outgrowers and only 13% of the farmers in the contract area had no contract. Farmers were not, in this case, forced to take contracts; they competed with one another to sign up. The farmers' work includes clearing the land, and later planting the cane, weeding, and applying fertilizer. The company ploughs and harrows the cleared land, supplies planting stock and fertilizer, monitors the progress of the crop, organizes the labor teams that harvest the cane, and transports the cane to the mill. If the farmer fails to carry out his tasks, the company will hire them done, and charge him for the work at the time the crop is delivered. Ordinarily, the services supplied by the company are valued at about half the price of the cane; farmer and company share the proceeds fifty-fifty (Mulaa, 1981; Hansen and Marcussen, 1982).

Most farmers come out with a cash income considerably larger than they had previously and significantly greater than noncontract growers of cane. There were some who suffered from the expropriation of the land for the nucleus estate and in the early years of the project the stories of wild spending sprees circulated freely. But, as the scheme has settled into a pattern, the more enduring effects are beginning to become clear.

In 1978, an estimated K sh 70–75 million in gross income was paid to 11,000 contract farmers and to permanent and casual wage workers. About 10% of the farmers have expanding economic activities, often in other cash crops and in trade and transport, supported in many cases by salaried employment as well as by sugar income. The opportunity to expand in sugar production itself is very sharply limited by the centralized control of the company. A second much larger group of outgrowers use their enhanced income to improve their standard of living and to invest in education for their children, but not to generate an expansion of their own economic activity. They continue to reproduce themselves, but at a higher level of consumption. A third group has difficulty maintaining itself for many different reasons. One common reason is overcommitment of limited land to cane and difficulty in managing with a much reduced supply of homegrown food (Mulaa, 1981; Hansen and Marcussen 1982).

The wider and deeper effects of the new market relationships will only appear with changes in the international and national economic cycle. Ecological change would also have serious consequences. Any crisis of price or production would cast many of the expanding and presently self-sufficient farmers into the category of struggling and often failing producers. Recognition of this danger as well as the more immediate experience of central controls are probably behind the sparks of self-organization and spontaneous resistance by outgrowers that have already taken place at Mumias. The larger farmers in particular are irked by the blockage to their expansion inherent in the outgrower company structure. There is provision for some farmer representation on matters of credit given by the company to growers. One man tried to use election within the scheme as a springboard to a wider political career (Mulaa, 1981).

In most of tropical Africa contract farming is a minor sideline, but in Kenya and the Ivory Coast it has become a movement of wide significance. It is estimated that "in 1981 about 12% of Kenyan smallholdings will produce cash crops on contract to agro-industries, amounting to some 30% of total marketed output from smallholdings, or about one-sixth of total marketed agricultural output of agriculture in Kenya" (Hansen and Marcussen, 1982: 21). Outgrower schemes and contract farming in which governments, transnational development agencies, and agribusiness firms collaborate is certainly one avenue of growing influence by transnational corporations in African agriculture.

Import-Substitution Agro-Industries

For governments, the increasing food shortage in the continent, coupled with foreign exchange constraints have enhanced the importance of establishing import-substitution agro-industries. TNCs have made good use of the opportunity to set up enterprises that cater for the internal market while at the same time enjoying a high tariff protection. In Senegal, for example, a syndicate of banks, engineering firms, government agencies, and development organizations have established a high technology, heavily financed scheme for the provision of rice to Senegal's urban population. The project was boosted by a $30 million loan arranged by Citibank and funds from Saudi Arabia. The 30,000 hectares enterprise in eastern Casamance was planned and organized by International Control and Systems of Houston, Texas, a firm that deals with farm implements and agro-industries. The official development agency responsible for the project—SODAGRI—was to be 50% owned by private American capital (Franke and Chasin, 1980: 191–192).

Other companies producing for the local market include Cadbury Schweppes Ltd., which has wholly owned principal subsidiaries in Ghana and Kenya, and 40% holdings in Cadbury Nigeria Ltd. (Stopford et al., 1980: Vol. 1, 195–197). Through the latter subsidiary, Cadbury was invited into the Zaria tomato project that involved organizing farmers cultivating 300 acres of tomatoes in order to supply a tomato paste factory (Morss et al., 1976: Vol. 2, 213–221). Similarly the market factor was among the major reasons that influenced Unilever to establish soap and edible oil plants in Nigeria, Zaire, and Kenya. Nigeria's large economy and Nairobi's position in the eastern

African market attracted the company to locate the plants in the two countries. Nestle's coffee factory in the Ivory Coast, noted above, is another example of an import substituting agro-industry. Connected with it is a factory for manufacturing metal containers for packaging the coffee and other products. Nestle also makes Maggi cubes, which it has successfully promoted as a mass consumption item (Masini et al, 1979).

By far the largest import substituting agro-industry has been sugar production and processing. It can replace a large volume of imports in a rapidly expanding internal market and in some cases promises export earnings. Transnational firms possess highly specialized technology for sugar production. As a plantation crop processed locally, sugar gives government and company tight control over production and earnings. The high world market price for the crop in the early 1970s was an additional factor that attracted some governments to establish sugar industries. Below are described a few of those ventures.

In May 1977, a contract was signed between ABR Engineering, a Belgian company, and the Société Sucrière de Save, a company owned jointly by the governments of Benin (49%), Nigeria (46%), and Lonhro (5%), to set up an agro-industrial complex in Save in the People's Republic of Benin. The total investment involved U.S. $120 million for infrastructure, irrigation, supply of equipment, and factory commissioning. Lonhro has a contract to provide technical assistance (Licht's International, 1978: E 3; Europe-Outremer, 1982: 20). In the same year, Tate and Lyle Technical Services in association with Redpath Sugars (a Canadian Subsidiary of Tate and Lyle) conducted a feasibility study for a 50,000 ton sugar project in the Benoué valley in northern Cameroon. It would be the country's third sugar complex; the other two produced about 68,000 tons of sugar in 1982–1983.

Tate and Lyle was given a 5-year management contract in 1976 worth "several millions" of dollars in a sugar project for the Ivory Coast. Redpath Sugars is responsible for all construction and management from land preparation to product shipment including the development of a sugar plantation; the construction of the irrigation system; the supply of agricultural machinery and equipment; and the establishment of a sugar factory with an initial output of 60,000 tons, a marine sugar and molasses terminal, 850 housing units, roads, and a rail spur. The financing of this U.S. $171.6 million project came from a consortium of Western banks (50%), the Canadian Export Development Corporation (30%), CIDA (5%), and the Ivory Coast government (15%) (Gatt-flyer No. 4, 1977).

The Ivory Coast already has a production capacity of about 270,000 tons a year although actual production was 166,000 tons in 1981–1982. Consumption in the country was an estimated 75,000 tons in 1981. The financial pressure to maximize production and exports is very great because of the high debt service payments, reaching FCFA 40,000 million in 1981, of Sodésucre, the parastatal responsible for the six operating sugar complexes. To assure export markets in a time of world and EEC surplus, the Ivory Coast requested a quota for selling to the EEC at a guaranteed price. The report of a committee of the French National Assembly that visited the Ivory Coast in 1982 to examine the quota question, reveals some of the implications of sugar development:

> The difficulties of the sugar program cannot leave France and the European Economic Community indifferent. European companies built four of the six complexes, and other European firms were involved in the sugar program through sales of agricultural equipment, irrigation equipment, or transport vehicles. It is therefore desirable that the EEC be more open to the request of the Ivory Coast and that France contribute to a change in the Community position. . . . The Community quota would create the financial stability needed for the formulation of more ambitious economic development projects and the implementation of true transfers of technology, to the mutual benefit of all partners [Europe-Outremer, 1982: 24].

Other examples of management and technical contracts could be described for Kenya, Somalia, Sudan, Cameroon, and other countries (Licht's International, 1978; Europe-Outremer, 1982: 629–630; Dinham and Hines, 1983: 71–90).

Investment Climate and Government Policy

The different development strategies adopted by African countries have affected the extent and form of the penetration of TNCs. Countries like Kenya and the Ivory Coast offer tax holidays, establish infrastructural systems that are suitable for foreign investments, regulate wages and prices and even relax foreign exchange controls in order to capture foreign investors. With 68% of the economy under foreign control, the Ivory Coast has one of the least restrictive investment codes; it includes the right to repatriate virtually all profits, plus the granting of tax holidays of up to 7 years (Masini et al., 1979: 11–28).

In a country like the Ivory Coast, the petty-bourgeoisie and foreign capital are in an agro-industrial alliance in which the state and middle-sized private farms take care of the farming activities, and foreign capital in cooperation with the state handles marketing and processing. The Ivory Coast state is a very active intermediary in facilitating the entry of foreign capital and the exit of payments to foreign investors, with detrimental effects for the internal integration of the economy (Masini et al., 1979). The Kenyan case with Brooke Bond shows that the petty-bourgeoisie sometimes can use its political power to take over control from a TNC (Swainson, 1980: 257–264). The alliance does not preclude jockeying for advantage.

On their side, the TNCs have attempted to gain maximum control over production, processing and profits with a minimum outlay of capital. This has been accomplished in part by undertaking horizontal and vertical diversification. Another device has been to obtain a management contract. The giant tobacco company BAT, which has 60% interest in BAT Kenya Ltd., 57% in the Monrovia Tobacco Corporation, 75% in BAT Malawi, 60% in Nigeria Tobacco Co. Ltd., 86% in Aureol Tobacco Co. Ltd. (Sierra Leone), and also shares in BAT Zaire and BAT Zambia, also has management contracts in most of these subsidiaries (Stopford et al., 1980: Vol. 1, 111–115).

Often, TNCs forgo and even relinquish ownership of the means of production while maintaining or strengthening control of the production process in order to reduce the risks of nationalizations and to shift the risks of failure to the local participants. TNCs limit their investment risk by minimizing their share capital while expanding the business connections between the venture and the TNC's parent company or subsidiaries in the metropole. Investment partners are found among local capitalists or government institutions and foreign private banks or multilateral agencies. The TNC parent company and other subsidiaries supply the technology, trademarks, and expertise. Thus, in the Mumias sugar scheme in Kenya, Booker McConnell's equity share is only 5%; however, the company supplied the technology for the factory and is also managing the entire project. In 1976, it was given the responsibility of increasing sugar production to 160,000 tons by 1981 at a cost of £38 million. The bulk of this latter amount went to Booker's coffers (Stobough, 1976: 68–83). Similarly, in the huge Kenana sugar project of Sudan, Lonrho put in 12% equity in the sugar venture and at the same time acquired a management contract to run the enterprise (Cronje et al., 1976). In the Ivory Coast sugar project where a consortium of TNCs organized for a $171 million loan to the African country, 64% of the value of purchases was to benefit Tate & Lyle and its subsidiaries (Gatt-flyer, No. 4 1977). This excluded the management contract that one subsidiary (Redpath) acquired.

An American fruit canning company (unnamed, but probably Del Monte) managed to strike a deal in reviving a fruit canning factory in an East African country in which it acquired management control and ownership of 80% of the equity in an operation with total assets of over $1.5 million, all for an investment of $152,000. The rest came about equally from local government and private loans. Within four years, the American company had repatriated its initial investment capital and from then on it was getting profits (Stobough 1976: 68–83).

At a second level, TNCs are also getting the assistance of multilateral public agencies such as the World Bank, UNDP, FAO, and of other bilateral institutions. The World Bank, to mention only two examples, gave crucial support to the smallholder program of the Kenya Tea Development Authority, and it also provided some money to Unilever despite the fact that it refused to lend money to the Zairean government for developing the nationalized palm-oil industry (New African, February 1981: 90). In addition, the composition of some organs of multilateral agencies that cater for Africa exhibit a strong alliance with TNCs. The membership of the farm mechanization working group within the UN's FAO had representations from Caterpillar, John Deere, Fiat, IHC, Massey-Ferguson, Mitsui, BP, and Shell. Similarly the pesticide working group has members from BASF, Bayer, Borden, BP, Ciba Ceigy, Roche, Imperial Chemicals, Linguigas, Mark Phillips, Sandoz, Shell, Stanffer, and Wellcome Foundations (New African, Sept. 1980). Projects ratified by such committees need to have some kind of business potential.

The system of management and technical assistance has proved to be a most effective way for TNCs to penetrate African countries that have restricted the entry of foreign capital. Countries like Tanzania, Guinea, Mali, and Mozambique have established crop authorities and parastatals, land control measures, and strict investment policies. They have also nationalized foreign enterprises, limited equity control for new ones, and regulated profit repatriation. However, capital constraints, the lack of skills and technology, and the difficulties of selling their semiprocessed agricultural goods are forcing these countries to seek the assistance of transnational agribusiness. In Tanzania, the body that coordinates the nationalized agro-industries had to invite foreign TNCs to manage 62% of the enterprises that had been taken over (Hall, 1979: 196). For example, inability of the original parastatal management to penetrate export markets culminated in the invitation to Nestle to run the instant coffee factory at Bukoba (Tanzania Coffee Project, n.d.).

The companies are often in a position to expand their involvements in these economies or to generate more profit out of their limited involvement (sometimes through devious means such as overpricing, transfer pricing, technological lock-ins, cheap inputs for subsidiaries elsewhere). In Tanzania, for example, Mitchell Cotts (UK), which has 51% of shares in a company that extracts liquid pyrethrum from pyrethrum flowers (Tanganyika Extract Co.), together with Erhnberg of Sweden, which has a 25% share in Tanzania Tanneries, have succeeded in directing most of the sales of the semiprocessed products to their respective parent companies for final manufacture (Packard, 1979).

TNCs AND THE AGRO-INDUSTRIAL SYSTEM

The nature of TNC involvement in the agro-industrial system has changed since independence. First, there has been a significant movement downstream toward the establishment of relatively advanced processing and manufacturing industries. During the colonial period, the major activity by the TNCs was marketing and farming, with a little processing for the removal of waste to facilitate transportation. That pattern still stands, but in the last three decades there has been a noticeable increase in locally processed crops (and imports) for domestic consumption, and, in some cases, for export markets. Presently, in tropical Africa, there are numerous factories for sugar, cigarettes, soft drinks, beer, instant coffee, textiles, canned fruit, canned fish, tomato paste, soaps, and detergents. However, the proportion of agricultural products processed by these factories is relatively very small and the colonial pattern is still powerful. Although groundnuts are processed and exported as oil, the bulk of the coffee, palm oil, tea, tobacco, cotton, and cocoa is still exported in its raw form to be processed in industrial countries.

A related conspicuous feature is the increasing involvement by TNCs in the supply of food for consumption in Africa. Since the late 1960s, foreign companies have been actively involved in ventures dealing with sugar, vegetables, maize, fruits, rice, tomatoes, and meat, reflecting the growth in the urban population and in non-self-provisioning rural producers. They are also suppliers of the swelling flow of food imports.

Upstream from production on the land, TNCs supply growing fertilizer use through imports or through the construction and management of fertilizer plants. They supply chemicals and implements. For example, through the agricultural mechanization program in Sudan, between 1963 and 1973, the country imported a total of 7143 tractors, 935 disc plows, 2561 seeders, 3087 ridgers, and 635 combines, thus providing lucrative business and locking farm technology to Massey-Ferguson, Ford, International Harvester, Zeltod, and Allis-Chalmers (Johnson, 1979). The many river-basin development projects and the large integrated agro-industrial schemes like those for sugar production are sources of numerous valuable contracts for construction, equipment supply, consultant reports, and management.

TNCs have brought agricultural production in Africa more tightly within the worldwide organized agro-industrial system. But they have done so with crucial assistance from African governments and transnational agencies of technical and financial assistance for development. Whether following socialist or capitalist policies, the state has taken the role of directing and organizing many economic activities. While there is significant variation in the degree and manner of involvement by TNCs, there are particular functions the state has to perform in order to facilitate the activities of agribusiness. The necessary infrastructure has to be built, and where direct production by the company is agreed, the state makes land available, often virtually free of charge. Where smallholder production is preferred, the state undertakes the task of organizing peasants so as to make their labor accessible: "agricultural development programs" in Nigeria, "settlement schemes" in Tanzania and Zambia, or "outgrower schemes" in Kenya. A rhetoric of rural development is often adopted in these programs so as to legitimize the connection with TNCs.

The state also helps the TNC with investment funds for the project from the government itself, from the local financial market, or very frequently from bilateral and multilateral agencies. The local state serves as guarantor in case of a loan and assumes the main responsibility if it is bilateral or multilateral assistance, but the planning and conception of the project may be importantly influenced by international finance and development agencies.

The agro-food system is a chain of influence through which TNCs pursue their interests and promote their ideologies. It can be expected that they will use their resources to create climates of policy and opinion that will maximize their profitable participation in Africa's agricultural change, maximize the control they can exercise, and minimize the risks they face. How successful they are and how far their activities can be made consistent with the needs of poorer classes and improving productivity in Africa depends crucially upon the activity of African states and African producers.

Social Consequences

The consequences of TNC activity go beyond the agro-food system itself to farming communities, national economies, social relations, and ecology. At the farm level, the most important development that has taken place since the 1960s is change in the mode of intervention by TNCs—from operating through market relations to establishing, by themselves or in cooperation with government agencies, more direct control of production at the farm level. Transnational agribusinesses do not merely buy what the peasants are producing; they have introduced variants of contract farming and outgrower schemes and directly influence the choice of crops, scale of production, method of farming, and the entire farm schedule.

The utilization of the technological packages offered by TNCs has made it possible to increase total yield and raises the question of how the benefits are distributed and what the other consequences are. Often, the cost has been increasing producer indebtedness, loss of independence, and reliance on imported inputs. Peasants have found themselves producing only to pay back loans they have acquired in order to obtain hybrid seeds, fertilizers, tractors, and sometimes transportation. Because government agencies usually mediate the link between producers and TNCs, it is generally governments or mixed agencies that act as debt collectors and marketing agencies, taking some share of the surplus for themselves through taxes or appropriate pricing while defending the fees or profits of the TNCs. But in many cases, TNCs still monopolize the external marketing of crops and they continue to serve the producers' consumer needs through trading subsidiaries and the manufacture and sale of cigarettes, tea, sugar, beverages, and other items of mass consumption. TNCs are still often in a position to pass low prices of African exports back to the producer and to pass high prices for manufactured goods and imports forward to the consumers.

Yet there is no doubt that the incomes of a significant number of small-scale producers in Africa have been very substantially raised by their contracts with TNCs or mixed TNC-public crop development agencies. Just as many of the cash crop growers in colonial Ghana, Nigeria, Tanzania, Uganda, and so on gained considerable real income advantages from growing and selling cocoa, groundnuts, coffee, and cotton and so do many of the tea growers for KTDA, the sugar growers for Mumias, the palm kernel producers for SODEPALM gain. These latter-day progressive farmers are more closely tied to a system of technological change than their colonial predecessors and they have less control over their own social and economic organization. But some of them have become accumulators of capital and investors in new productive activity in their own right. It is unwarranted to conclude that producers never benefit from association with TNCs.

Even when some producers benefit, there are other important social consequences. In a few cases, TNCs have forced the eviction of peasants from land wanted by the company for plantations. Again, it is the government that mediates the transfer of control, usually making the land available at very low cost. The land in question may be the main source of livelihood for the local people. The Italian firm MAESCO has produced alfalfa for feeding animals in Japan in an Ethiopian region where thousands of people and their cattle, camels, sheep, and goats had to be evicted; some of the people subsequently faced starvation (Bondestam, 1975: 138). In Kenya, once it had established plantation production of pineapples, the fruit company Del Monte demanded the phasing out of smallholder production of the crop, a request the government promptly granted.

Among the social repercussions of TNC activities is the exacerbation of differentiation in the rural areas. The increase in productivity that the TNCs foster affects directly only the few farmers who have sufficient collateral to qualify for credit, who are rich enough to afford the risks of innovations, and who happen to live in the right region. Since the poor farmers cannot get credit for investment and are normally hesitant to innovate, their level of productivity remains low. Forced to borrow simply to eat or to plant, the poorest farmers may eventually be forced to work for richer farmers and perhaps even to sell or abandon their plots (Franke and Chasin, 1980: 191–192).

Even where producers benefit, outgrower schemes and contract farming are mechanisms by which TNCs use the labor of peasants without proletarianizing them. Some observers have argued that the conditions of contract farmers are little different from those of factory labor. The contract farmer, however, usually has nominal land rights and some capacity for production of food and other crops, and (perhaps) the option of abandoning the contract and growing noncontract crops. In the case of a crop that is in high demand in the local market (such as a food crop), the producer may have more leverage over the TNC, as the situation of Cadbury Schweppes in Nigeria shows. At times, when the company was offering 2 cts per pound of tomatoes to the producer, at the local market the tomatoes were selling as high as 5 cts per pound. As a result, the producers directed most of their tomatoes to the local market causing severe shortages to the factory (Morss et al., 1976: F28). Nevertheless, such an outlet is temporary; the fact that the producer is forced to go back to the agency to acquire the inputs for the next season binds him or her to the marketing contract. The peasants' alternatives are more restricted when the crop cultivated is a perennial one like tobacco, coffee, cocoa, or tea sold for export through monopoly buyers. The difficulty of substituting either crops or markets when the terms offered are bad puts the producers in a permanently weaker position.

A possible effect of the unequal power is worth closer attention: more effective organization of the producers. Like factory workers, closely supervised peasant farmers have strong incentives, a clear target, and improved means to impel organization and representation of their interests vis-à-vis the TNC or government agency with power over them. Both for their effects on production and for their political impact, the new supervised grower schemes bear watching.

Agricultural Transition

It can be argued that despite the rural inequality, the loss of producers' autonomy, and the outflow of purchasing power fostered by TNCs, the firms do introduce modern technology and organization to African agriculture and help to raise productivity essential for increasing domestic food supplies and for generating foreign exchange, both of which are badly needed by these economies. The multiplier effect of agro-industries helps expand the industrial base in Africa. Furthermore, African producers benefit by having assured buyers for their crops and by seeing their goods penetrate Western markets. All these can be considered positive contributions of transnational agribusinesses.

On the other hand, most high technology large-scale projects have failed and many seeming successes are in fact receiving subsidies from small producers. Where they do succeed, the technology transferred may be so complex that for a long time it will require foreign servicing and spare parts, draining foreign exchange and prolonging dependency. Worse still, the technology often has a low employment generating effect. Furthermore, the worldwide nature of the agro-industrial system leads many agribusiness firms to focus on luxury and specialized export crops for European and American markets. Where they produce for African markets, they favor luxury products like coffee and nonessential mass consumption goods like beer and cigarettes. In technology, organization, and inclination, they are poorly adapted to improve productivity of many crops where it is most needed: cassava, plantains, millet, pulses. Nor are the dry lands, steep slopes, and tropical wet zones where so many Africans work the land the environments where the experience and technologies of TNCs are appropriate. No doubt production-raising technologies for each kind of environment will one day be found. It seems unlikely in the extreme, however, that TNCs on their own will develop, perfect, and adapt the technologies for any but a few high-value export crops. Other agencies, especially African governments, have to take the lead in Africa's agricultural transition.

REFERENCES

AMAGOU, V. and G. GLEIZES, (1975) "Le groupe SODEPALM et l'agro-industrie du palmier à huile en Côte-d'Ivoire." Economies et Sociétés 9 (9–10, Sept.-Oct.): 1485–1524.

BATES, R. (1980) "Pressure groups, public policy and agricultural development: a study of divergent outcomes," in R. Bates and M. Lofchie (eds.) Agricultural Development in Africa: Issues of Public Policy. New York: Praeger.

BAUER, P. (1954) West African Trade. London: Routledge & Kegan Paul.

BONDESTAM, L. (1975) "Notes on MNCs in Ethiopia." African Review 5: 535–549.

CRONJE, S., M. LONG, and G. CRONJE, (1976) Lonrho: Portrait of a Multinational. London: Penguin.

DINHAM, B. and C. HINES, (1983) Agribusiness in Africa. London: Earth Resources Research Ltd.

Europe-Outremer (1982)

FIELDHOUSE, D. (1978) Unilever Overseas: The Anatomy of a Multinational 1895–1965. London: Croom Helm.

FRANKE, R. and B. CHASIN, (1980) Seeds of Famine, Ecological Destruction and the Development Dilemma in the West African Sahel. Montclair, NJ: Allanheld, Osmun.

FRANKEL, S. (1938) Capital Investment in Africa: Its Course and Effects. London: Oxford Univ. Press.

Gatt-Flyer No. 4 (1977) Toronto: Gatt-fly, January.

GEORGE, S. (1981) Les stratèges de la faim. Geneva: Editions Grounauer.

——— (1979) Feeding the Few: Corporate Control of Food. Washington, DC: Institute for Policy Studies.

——— (1976) How the Other Half Dies. England: Penguin.

GHERSI, G. and J.-L. RASTOIN, (1981) Multinational Firms and Agro-Food Systems in Developing Countries: A Bibliographic Review. Paris: Development Centre of the Organization for Economic Cooperation and Development.

GOLDBERG, R. (1980) "International arrangements within and between developed and developing food economies," pp. 169–198 in R. Goldberg (ed.) Research on Domestic and International Agribusiness Management: A Research Annual, Vol. 1. Greenwich, CT: Jai Press.

GOLDBERG, R. et al. (1974) Agribusiness Management for Developing Countries: Latin America. Cambridge, MA: Ballinger.

HALL, L. (1979) "Transfer pricing: the issue for Tanzania," in A. Coulson (ed.) African Socialism in Practice. London: Spokesman.

HANSEN, M. and M. MARCUSSEN, (1982) "Contract farming and the peasantry: cases from western Kenya." Review of African Political Economy 23 (January-April): 9–36.

HOPKINS, A. (1976) "Imperial business in Africa." Journal of African History, 17: 29–48; 18: 267–290.

HORST, T. (1974) At Home Abroad: A Study of the Domestic and Foreign Operations of the American Food-Processing Industry. Cambridge, MA: Ballinger.

ILIFFE, J. (1979) A Modern History of Tanganyika. Cambridge: Cambridge University Press.

JOHNSON, R. (1979) "The politics of mechanization in Sudanese agriculture." Presented at the annual meeting of the Canadian Association of African Studies, Winnipeg.

JORGENSON, J. (1975) "Multinational corporations and the indigenization of the Kenyan economy." African Review 5(4): 429–450.

LAMARCHAND, R. (1979) "The politics of penury in rural Zaire," in G. Gran, (ed.) Zaire: The Political Economy of Under-development. New York: Praeger.

LAPPE, F. and J. COLLINS, (1979) Food First. New York: Ballantine.

Licht's International (1978) Sugar Report. Special edition.

LIPTON, M. [ed.] (1977) "Rural poverty and agribusiness." Discussion paper No. 104. Institute of Development Studies, University of Sussex, England.

MASINI, J. et al. (1979) Multinationals and Development in Black Africa: A Case Study in the Ivory Coast. Westmead, England: Saxon House for European Centre for Study and Information on Multinational Corporations in Brussels.

MORGAN, D. (1979) Merchants of Grain. London: Weidenfeld and Nicolson.

MORSS, E. et al. (1976) Strategies for Small Farmer Development. 2 volumes. Boulder: Westview.

MULAA, J. (1981) "The politics of a changing society: Mumias." Review of African Political Economy 20, (January-April): 89–107

New African

PACKARD, P. (1979) "Corporate structure in agriculture and socialist development in Tanzania: a study of the national agricultural and food corporation," in A. Coulson (ed.), African Socialism in Practice. Nottingham: Spokesman.

PALMER, R. and N. PARSONS, [eds.] (1977) Roots of Rural Poverty. London: Heinemann.

STOBOUGH, R. (1976) Nine Investments Abroad. Boston: Harvard Univ. Press.

STOPFORD, J. et al. (1980) The World Directory of Multinational Enterprises. 2 volumes. New York: Macmillan.

SWAINSON, N. (1980) The Development of Corporate Capitalism in Kenya. Nairobi: Heinemann.

Tanzania Coffee Project (n.d.) The Coffee Crunch.

Unilever's World (n.d.) CIS Anti report No. 11.

VOLL, S. (1980) A Plough in Field Arable: Western Agribusiness in the Third World. Hanover, NH: University Press of New England.

WASSERMAN, G. (1976) The Politics of Decolonization: Kenya, Europeans and the Land Issue, 1960–1965. Cambridge: Cambridge Univ. Press.

WILSON, C. (1968) Unilever 1945–1965. London: Cassel.

WOLFF, R. (1974) The Economics of Colonialism: Britain and Kenya, 1870–1930. New Haven: Yale Univ. Press.

World Bank (1981) Accelerated Development in Sub-Saharan Africa: An Agenda for Action. Washington, DC: Author.

3

THE WORLD BANK
AND THE MODEL OF
ACCUMULATION

JOHN LOXLEY

CRISIS IN AFRICA—
BERG'S DIAGNOSIS AND PRESCRIPTION

In 1981, the World Bank published "Accelerated Development in Sub-Saharan Africa:—An Agenda for Action" (popularly "the Berg Report"), which sought to analyze the reasons for the widespread economic crisis being experienced by that region in the late 1970s and to prescribe a future course of action to "accelerate" development there. This document, prepared under the supervision of Elliot Berg, one of the bank's principal ideologues, can be taken to represent the view of the bank on these issues and, accordingly, one can expect that bank policies and programs in this region will be guided by it in the near future. Also, the report is likely to have a considerable influence on the thinking and actions of bilateral donors, many of whom look to the IBRD for guidance on economic analysis and policy direction. Given the acute dependence of sub-Saharan Africa on economic aid and foreign advisors, there is a strong possibility that the Berg report will be influential in shaping views *in* Africa about the causes of economic crisis and, more importantly, in molding future economic policy. Certainly, it has not been taken lightly in the 45 states that it covers. In Tanzania, for instance, President Nyerere is reported to have insisted that all his cabinet ministers read it even though (perhaps because) it is highly critical of that country's policies and performance. It is also the subject of discussions at the international level between African states. For all these reasons the report is an important one that merits careful consideration. The purpose of this chapter is to review its contents and to assess the nature, appropriateness, and desirability of its recommendations.

It is no easy matter to summarize the report given the wealth of material it covers but, at the risk of oversimplification, it can be said that its central theme is that "domestic policy issues are at the heart of the crisis in sub-Saharan Africa"(p. 121). In support of this position, it argues that "past trends in the terms of trade cannot explain the slow economic growth of Africa in the 1970's because for most countries . . . the terms of trade were favorable or neutral" (p. 19). The principal reason for widespread crises in the current account of the balance of payments experienced by many African countries in the 1970s was the slow growth in export volume. This slow growth reflected domestic policy biases against agriculture and against exports in favor of industrialization based on import substitution that was misguided, high cost, and inefficient. These biases were propagated and reinforced by inappropriate policies in the areas of exchange rates, taxation, urban wages and prices, and other direct controls. Growth was also retarded by the replacement or restriction of the private sector by the state in all major sectors of the economy to the point where the state sector, in either its government or parastatal form, had overreached its administrative and management capabilities. The acute fiscal crises being experienced by many African states are symptoms of this overexpansion that takes the form of the provision, without user charges, of extensive education, health and water supply facilities, the growth of expenditures on administration and defense, and the emergence of parastatal deficits that must be met from the budget. Finally, poor export growth and per capita income growth were partly caused by excessive population growth.

From this diagnosis of the problems follow the policy prescriptions of the report that focus on stimulating agricultural exports, encouraging private sector activities and allowing market forces to operate more pervasively as state controls over economic activity are dismantled. The key to accelerated development in the future would be the expansion of agricultural exports produced largely by peasant farmers, whose activities would be encouraged by a significant increase in their real net returns, achieved by reducing state controls over the prices and distribution of farm inputs and farm outputs, and by the depreciation of the exchange rate. Investment strategies in this sector would be "production-focused," concentrating on "regions with relatively high potential" and using larger farmers "to spearhead the introduction of new methods"(p. 52). Private enterprise would be encouraged to replace the state in most sectors and the relief that this would provide to the budget would be heightened by the imposition of user charges on public services currently being provided free of charge. Industrial development would be clearly subordinate to agricultural growth and would again be oriented toward export expansion on the grounds that the next logical phase of import substitution in Africa, into intermediate goods production, is not feasible due to the small size of the domestic market. To enable countries to export manufactured goods successfully, exchange rate devaluation would again be needed, as would be other measures designed to reduce the real wages of urban workers. Parastatal industrial enterprises would operate on commercial lines and the state would encourage the activities of indigenous entrepreneurs.

The report concludes that foreign aid flows to the region should be doubled in real terms by the end of the 1980s. Aid should be more flexible than in the past, and should be coordinated more closely by donors themselves. The report emphasizes that aid flows of the size and quality recommended are not likely to materialize unless recipient countries adopt structural adjustment programs along the lines proposed, including more aggressive family planning programs. If they do, and if aid targets are realized, then GDP growth per capita can be expected to reach 1% p.a. maximum in the 1980s.

ASSESSMENT OF BERG

At the level of detailed specifics, there is much that one can agree with in the Berg Report, but it is not the purpose of this chapter to draw up a scoreboard of individual points of agreement or disagreement. Instead, the intention is to focus on the validity of the report's view of the historical origins of the crisis in Africa and on the nature and viability of the alternative model of accumulation it is seeking to promote in this part of the world. It will be argued that Berg seriously underestimates the importance of "external" factors in shaping policy and performance in sub-Saharan Africa over the last decade and, equally, overestimates what is likely to be achieved by integrating African economies even more firmly into the world system as it currently operates. Successful implementation of the "Agenda for Action" would entail abrupt and far-reaching realignments of class interests and require a degree of state coercion unprecedented in much of Africa.

There is a certain irony in the fact that the release of the Berg Report coincided with the worst crisis in the global economy since the Great Depression. The collapse in the terms of trade for African countries since 1978 has been dramatic and is not captured in data available to Berg. For low-income countries south of the Sahara, the average deterioration between 1978 and 1981 was 19% (27% for Ethiopia, 26% for Madagascar); for middle-income countries it was 13% (36% for Ghana, 30% for Ivory Coast) (World Bank, 1982a: 30). The terms of trade have continued to decline since then so that any gains made in the 1970 to 1978 period have been more than offset. In this situation, African governments are likely to receive with justified skepticism the argument that their balance of payments problems are the result of domestic policy shortcomings or that the way forward is to produce more for the world market.

While members of the World Bank team can hardly be blamed for not being clairvoyant, they can be faulted for inadequately treating the impact of instability of the global economy on domestic policy and performance over the period they reviewed. Fluctuations in terms of trade can be at least as, if not more, important to producers as trend movements and for many African exports it is much easier to restrict output in response to falls in net returns that it is to reverse the process when net returns rise. Thus, in the early 1970s, deliberate steps were taken to reduce the production of such crops as coffee and sisal in the face of deteriorating market prospects. Reversing that process involves production lags of 3 to 5 years not counting the lead time needed to convince producers of the stability of medium/long-term prospects. Likewise, the impact of the 1973-1974 oil and food price increases is totally downplayed in the Berg Report, which assesses terms of trade movements by reference to the years of 1970, 1975, and 1979 only. The implicit assumption that African economies can adjust smoothly and quickly to such profound external shocks is a highly questionable one. For many African countries, the increased fuel bill, even after significant reduction in fuel usage, has seriously eroded their ability to purchase essential imports for the agricultural and industrial sectors, thus creating production bottlenecks that are difficult to break without a significant increment in available foreign exchange.

The report also greatly understates the importance of external advice and of external aid generally in the formulation of domestic policy in Africa. It is as if the IBRD, in particular, has no collective memory of its own advice and certainly no interest in introspection or self-criticism. Yet the bank and other aid donors have themselves been responsible for promoting many of the structural characteristics that they find so objectionable. Thus, the bank has actively participated in creating an industrial structure that is highly dependent on imported inputs and on scarce skilled technical and managerial personnel (Payer, 1982: Ch. 5). The bank also participated actively in various aspects of agricultural planning including, in many countries, advising on crop price formulation—yet nowhere in the report is there any evaluation of its record in these areas.

In the past, the IBRD has been guilty of the fallacy of composition: It advised countries to diversify agricultural production without adequately forecasting the decline in prices that would inevitably follow widespread acceptance of that advice. Thus, as the output of tea and tobacco has increased significantly over the past 10 years stimulated by IBRD/IDA programs, world prices have in consequence fallen. It appears from the Berg Report that the bank is in danger of committing the same error again, but this time on a much grander scale. It projects that world prices of 5 out of 9 of Africa's major food exports are likely to decline in the 1980s even before implementation of its proposals for promoting agricultural exports, and while it admits that Africa's "dependence on exports of slowly growing primary products is a disadvantage," it then glibly asserts that "exports can be diversified" and that "Africa's share of world trade in most commodities could be increased with relatively small effects on prices" (p. 23). Yet Africa is important in the world production of cocoa, coffee, tea, sisal, groundnuts, groundnut oil, palm products, and cotton, and a doubling of their export growth rates (as Berg assumes, from the worst aid case with no policy changes at one extreme, to the best aid case with complete acceptance of the Action package at the other) would undoubtedly have a negative impact on world prices. More to the point, African countries would do well to check out the kind of advice the bank is giving to primary producers elsewhere in the world before blithely accepting its price projections or its exhortations to diversify production.

Similar objections could be raised about the possibility of the export of manufactured goods becoming an important part of an African development strategy in the current decade. The economic crisis in industrialized capitalist countries has thrown the dozen or so newly industrialized countries (NICs) into economic disarray. In 1981, their growth rates were negative and the stagnation of their export markets made it impossible for most of them to service the massive international debts that had been so central in financing the development of their export capacity (IMF, 1982). The resulting financial crisis, which threatens the whole international banking system, is being met by the adoption of harsh austerity programs in these countries designed to drastically reduce demand for local and imported goods.[1] The resort to large and frequent devaluations is an attempt to reinforce domestic austerity and to make exports more attractive by reducing the real wages of workers relative to those of competitors. Each NIC is desperately trying to retain or increase its share of a market that is no longer growing.

Even when their market was growing steadily, as it was in earlier years, serious reservations were expressed about the possibility of this type of industrialization being generalized among underdeveloped countries without provoking a strong protectionist reaction from Europe and North America (Cline, 1982). How much less generalizable is the model when the industrialized capitalist countries themselves are in crisis?

The current global crisis, therefore, highlights very vividly the shortcomings of the export-oriented model of accumulation that is being peddled by the World Bank; but even if world markets were more buoyant, there would be other serious objections to this model. Principal among these is the overtly regressive distribution of income and wealth that it implies. In this respect, the Berg Report drops any pretence at addressing "basic needs," which has featured prominently in World Bank rhetoric in recent years. Instead, it proposes to cut urban wages and to levy user fees for government services such as health, education, and water supply. Rural investment is to be concentrated on the most productive areas and on larger, "progressive" farmers; whole areas of the economy are to be thrown open to the private sector, both domestic and foreign, under the stimulus of government incentives. There is nothing nuanced about this; the unbridled forces of the market are to be allowed to operate, and narrowly defined "efficiency" and "growth" are to become the central objectives of economic policy.

It could be said that the Berg Report is, in this area, a more honest document than many to emanate from the bank, for there can be no denying that while the IBRD has talked piously of the importance of meeting basic needs, the weight of its advice and of its programming has always tended to favor promotion of private enterprise and of "progressive" farmers and to encourage free markets and production for the market as opposed to self-consumption. In a report (World

Bank, 1982b: 7) published shortly after the Berg Report, the bank admitted that its rural development programs "have provided few direct benefits for the landless, for tenants unable to offer collateral for loans, and for the 'near-landless' farmer who finds it hard to borrow, acquire inputs, and take risks," yet these are the very sections of rural society least able to meet the basic needs. This particular report then goes on to recommend that in the future, bank activities should have a more explicitly poverty-focused orientation. But the recommendations of the Berg Report swing in an entirely opposite direction.

The bank's concern with "basic needs" has been largely rhetorical because of its failure to address the problem of the necessity to transform the social relations of production that create and perpetuate poverty. The model of accumulation proposed by the Berg Report would also require a radical restructuring of the balance of class forces in African societies, albeit in a different direction, yet the report does not address the political ramifications of this. While existing models of accumulation may be losing their legitimacy in the face of sustained crisis, the alternative model proposed by Berg is likely to prove even more difficult to legitimate as it undermines the position of workers relative to that of capital, as it seeks to weaken the position of the bureaucratic and managerial elite (in many countries now unambiguously a class) in the state sector relative to that of domestic and foreign capitalists, and as it strengthens inequalities in the rural areas. Its implementation would probably generate such widespread political tensions that it would require significant state repression of one sort or another to see it through.[2] This has certainly been the pattern elsewhere where states have moved rapidly toward export and market-oriented models of accumulation.

The success of the NICs, especially, owes a great deal to political repression often involving direct military intervention. Military dictatorships are particularly suited to the task of restructuring the economy along these lines because, on seizing power, the military usually has no clearly defined class interest in one model of accumulation or another. At the same time, it has the ability to impose its will on those sections of society resisting abandonment of the old model of accumulation thereby ending, at least temporarily, the political crisis emanating from the contradictions inherent in that model. The new model cannot, however, be sustained indefinitely by political repression; sooner or later it must be legitimated by generating a degree of social harmony (Thorpe and Whitehead, 1979). This will not happen if its very essence is dependent, for instance, upon a level of workers' real wages that can be maintained only by political repression. Nor can it achieve legitimacy if it is wracked by crisis. The current political crises in such countries as Chile, Argentina, Brazil, and the Philippines are as much the product of a failure to legitimize their export/market-oriented models of development internally, as they are of the global economic crisis and market collapse, though the latter have served to sharpen domestic tensions that have hitherto been tightly controlled. It remains to be seen whether this model will still be a viable one once military juntas are replaced by more liberal regimes.

One does not, however, need to leave the continent of Africa for confirmation of the political dimensions of the export-oriented model of accumulation. The Republic of South Africa has been pursuing a Berg-like strategy for some years and its emergence as an NIC can be traced directly to the institutionalised repression of its Black population under the system of apartheid. It is upon this foundation, of the super-exploitation of labor, that South Africa has attracted Western direct investment and huge bank loans (Loxley, 1983). Well before the onset of the global crisis, the fascist state was finding it increasingly difficult to contain the liberation struggle and internal pressures can be expected to mount as the economic crisis deepens (Saul and Gelb, 1981).

The struggle against apartheid and minority white rule has had far-reaching implications for all the front line states in Southern Africa. Liberation struggles in Angola, Mozambique, Rhodesia, Namibia, and South Africa have placed an enormous burden on neighboring independent African states, and significantly influenced their economic performance. At the present time, there is a state of war between South Africa and Angola and Mozambique that dominates the political economy of the whole region of Southern Africa. Yet, the Berg Report (pp. 10–11) pays no attention to this whatsoever, cursorily dismissing the struggles for independence as being "in general . . . remarkably peaceful" and concentrating instead on post-independence political and social turmoils without, of course, searching for the contribution that "external" or historical factors might have made to these unfortunate upheavals.

The Berg Report had little option but to ignore South Africa and Namibia entirely for introducing them would not only have raised awkward questions about the nature of the model of accumulation it is advocating; it would also have made it difficult to sustain the argument that economic crisis, in this part of Africa at least, is the result of purely domestic mismanagement. Further, acknowledging the economic stranglehold that South Africa has over this region would have required the report to qualify its bland exhortations in favor of regional cooperation, and to recognize both the urgency for such cooperation and the enormous structural and political difficulties that the front line states through their Southern Africa Development Coordination Committee (SADCC) face in making it a reality. For, paralleling its military offensive, South Africa has launched an equally determined economic offensive to strengthen its economic ties with neighboring African countries in a bid to forestall the development of alternative economic unions.

African governments seem to be well aware of the political implications of rushing headlong into the export-oriented model of accumulation and, so far, the Berg Report has received a cool reception in Africa.[3] Yet Africa is in the midst of crisis and the import substitution/primary export model has more or less run its course, raising the question of what happens next. Increasingly, African governments are being left with no choice but to seek emergency financial support from the International Monetary Fund and, to a lesser extent, from the IBRD in the form of structural adjustment loans. It is at this point that pressure is being applied on governments to *move in the direction* of implementing the recommendations of the Berg Report. The report itself blatantly exhorts aid donors to make their assistance conditional upon economic reforms along the lines it suggests, and these reforms are entirely consistent with the "conditionality" attached to IMF and IBRD balance of payment loans. Thus, what can be expected in the future is that more and more African countries will be pressured by external agencies to adapt Berg-type proposals in piece-meal fashion. The gradual adoption of the model in this way would still be no easy task as the failure rate of African governments to meet IMF and IBRD performance criteria is very high indeed (Helleiner, 1982; Payer, 1982: 154); an indication of the political difficulties involved in managing the "shock treatment" by which the IMF in particular prefers to introduce this model, and of the inherent contradictions within the model itself. Indeed, a reasonable case could be made that IMF "assistance" is as likely to generate political crisis as it is to forestall it. From this perspective the future of sub-Saharan Africa looks to be a very bleak one.

There are, however, alternative models to which Africa might turn, which are more auto centered in character. Of these, the Thomas (1974) convergence model is by far the most promising. In this model, production is geared first and foremost to utilizing local resources to meet democratically defined needs and foreign trade is simply an extension of domestic production, not its determinant. The emphasis is

on centering production around a range of *basic goods* or goods that
figure prominently in the production of other goods and that, therefore,
have extensive forward and backward linkages and that have a high
income elasticity of value added. Thomas argues that cost efficient
scales of production can be much smaller than the optimal scale and
this also facilitates democratic control and greater regional balance.
Where local needs are still much smaller than the cost efficient scale of
production, the excess can be exported, so the model is not autarkic.
The need for foreign aid is acknowledged provided it is consistent with
the convergence strategy.

This model presupposes the collective ownership of the means of
production, economic planning in physical terms, and the desire to
build a socialist society. Unlike the World Bank approach, it addresses
directly the class impediments to the eradication of poverty and the
interrelationship between class structure, income and wealth distribution, and the structure of production.

The political prerequisites for implementing this model are obviously
very demanding, but to a degree could be met by countries such as
Angola and Mozambique were it not for the state of siege in which they
find themselves at the present time. The rate at which the strategy could
be implemented would still be conditioned by the global crisis as the
surplus would need to come, for many years into the future, from the
very sectors one is attempting to transform. Thus, phasing in convergent production would still be constrained by the world demand for
traditional exports, by the price of imports, and by the quantity and
quality of available aid, but these constraints would ease as the
convergent structure began to dominate. Countries would still have an
interest in improving the efficiency of traditional agricultural and
industrial sectors and in this area some of the *specific* proposals of the
Berg Report might be found to be of value provided they did not run
counter to the principles of equity and medium- and long-run
convergence. Countries pursuing convergent strategies would also have
a stake in a reformed international order that widened or stabilized
markets for their production surpluses or made available greater
amounts of cheaper or more flexible aid, for these would, in their case,
support the strategy of convergence.

Thus, countries adopting Thomas-type models of accumulation
would not be opting out of the international system but rather altering,
in a fundamental way, the terms of their participation in it. To the
extent that a number of countries were pursuing convergence strategies
they could greatly reinforce each other's efforts. A liberated socialist

South Africa and Namibia would, from this point of view, radically transform the possibilities for socialist accumulation in the whole African region.

The crisis in Africa is not likely to be short lived and, over time, governments will come under increasing pressure to adopt strategies similar to those proposed in the Berg Report. It is important that, in the political struggles that will inevitably ensue, the left in Africa be seen to be offering a viable, equitable alternative that puts the needs of the people to the forefront. The convergence strategy would seem to be such an alternative around which people might be mobilized.

NOTES

1. For example, in 1982–1983, Brazil took a series of austerity measures designed to reduce its imports by no less than $3.5 billion (Toronto Globe and Mail, October 28, 1982).
2. A similar criticism of the Berg Report has been raised by Charles Harvey in a review written for African Contemporary Record (forthcoming) and, apparently, by Stephany Griffith-Jones in the IDS Bulletin, Sussex, England, for January 1983, but this latter was not available to the author at the time of writing.
3. See "World Bank Survey," Africa Now, September 1982, pp. 48–49, in which it is reported that the UN Economic Commission for Africa was "scathing" about the report. The President of the World Bank maintains that African governors of the World Bank support its recommendations.

REFERENCES

Africa Now
Africa Contemporary Record
Institute of Development Studies, Sussex. (1983) "Accelerated development in Sub-Saharan Africa: what agenda for action?" Bulletin 14, (January).
CLINE, W. R. (1982) "Can the East Asian model of development be generalised?" World Development 10/2.
HELLEINER, G. K. (1982) "The IMF and Africa in the 1980s," Paper presented at the Africa Studies Association, Washington DC, November 1982.
International Monetary Fund (1982) World Economic Outlook. Washington, DC: Author.
LOXLEY, J. (1983) "Labour migration and the liberation struggle in southern Africa." Paper to be published in 1983 by Centre for Developing Area Studies, McGill University as part of the proceedings of their 1980 Seminar and Colloquium Series, "International Labour Issues."
PAYER, C. (1982) The World Bank: A Critical Analysis. New York: Monthly Review Press.

SAUL, J. S. and GELB, S. (1981) The Crisis in South Africa: Class Defence, Class Revolution. New York: Monthly Review Press.

THOMAS, C. Y. (1974) Dependence and Transformation: The Economics of the Transition to Socialism. New York: Monthly Review Press.

THORPE, R. and WHITEHEAD, L. (1979) "Introduction," in R. Thorpe and L. Whitehead (eds.) Inflation and Stabilisation in Latin America. London: Macmillan.

World Bank (1981) Accelerated Development in Sub-Saharan Africa: An Agenda for Action. Washington, DC: Author.

World Bank (1982a) Annual Report. Washington, DC: Author

World Bank (1982b) Focus on Poverty: A Report by a Task Force of the World Bank. Washington, DC: Author.

4

USAID IN THE SAHEL
Development and Poverty

WILLIAM DERMAN

The Sahel Development Program is the last humanitarian economic assistance program run by AID [Unidentified AID official; Douglas, 1981].

. . .whether these projects succeed or not, the conditions of the peasantry will deteriorate. Even if their material conditions were to improve, they will lose their economic independence and thus their strongest guarantee of some measure of political freedom [Goren Hyden, 1980: 17–18].

The United States government responded to the West African drought and famine of 1968–1974 with a policy that aimed to make the Sahel[1] a showcase for development assistance. It would demonstrate how the resources of the world's wealthiest nation could be used to stop the spreading Saharan desert and to raise the "poorest of the poor" to standards of living appropriate to the modern world. In addition, United States programs would clearly be seen to be based upon humanitarian concerns since there appears (on the surface) to be little in the Sahel of direct strategic, economic, and political significance to the United States. The development of the Sahel was no longer to be a matter of simple economic rate of return; it would include environmental and social assessments of proposed activities, and greater attention to meeting the needs of women. In the 1960s, emphasis was upon roads, ports, power generation, dams, and irrigation. In the 1970s, emphasis was to be given to education, health, population, smallholder agriculture, and agricultural research. Unlike earlier efforts, it was to be a long-term commitment designed to help the poorest nations and it would be carried out in coordination with the rest of the West in a part of Africa that had been previously a French zone.

The Sahel "crisis" was an occasion for USAID to elaborate its conception of development aid in an atmosphere relatively free of the pressures of urgent military, political, or business influences. The U.S. profile was low because it was part of a multilateral effort. The World Bank and ILO ideas about helping the poor gave new currency to humanitarian arguments. The academic critique of modernization theory and the Latin American presentation of dependency views had loosened up the intellectual atmosphere among the academic clients and reference groups of USAID. In the Foreign Assistance Act of December 1973, Congress had sanctioned significant "new directions" in development strategy. What *new* kinds of analysis, projects, and policies did the agency come up with?

THE MULTILATERAL FRAMEWORK

The initial responses to the drought and famine of 1968–1974 were emergency food aid and relief supplies. These relatively short-term efforts were transformed into a long-range strategy and organization for studying and then resolving the environmental and food issues of the Sahel (Sheets and Morris, 1974; Glantz, 1976; Faure and Gac, 1981). The major donor organizations in the Sahel place their emphasis not upon desertification (in fact their neglect of environmental issues is astonishing given their earlier emphasis upon the degradation of the environment), but on socioeconomic development (Lofchie, 1975; Comité Information Sahel, 1974; Copans, 1975; Raynaut, 1977). As Franke and Chasin (1980: 145) comment,

> In a few short years since the massive drought and famine of 1968–74, the Sahel has gone from an unknown desert fringe to a region in which hundreds of millions of dollars, major scientific resources, and enormous administrative efforts have been concentrated to develop what is said to be a major new model for development planning.

In 1973, six nations of the region (Chad, Mali, Mauritania, Niger, Senegal, and Upper Volta) established the Permanent Inter-State Committee for the Struggle against Drought in the Sahel (CILSS). The group was concerned with emergency assistance and long-term planning for the region. Subsequently, Gambia and Cape Verde Islands joined CILSS. The western donor nations formed a coordinating body known as the Club du Sahel, where the representatives of donor nations could harmonize interests and policies with each other and with CILSS nations.

New Directions for U.S. Assistance

As part of the Foreign Assistance Act of December 17, 1973 (Section 639B), the United States Congress supported the initiative for a long-term Sahelian development program. The president was directed to submit a proposal to Congress for budget action by April 30, 1976. USAID, as the U.S. development arm, was to prepare the report. The report was also to be consistent with the strategy of the newly formed Club du Sahel. The Foreign Assistance Act of 1973 has been termed the New Directions congressional mandate because it emphasized income distribution as well as growth, the participation of intended beneficiaries in decision making, the use of appropriate technology, labor intensive activities, and the adapting of programs to local conditions (Hoben, 1980). In addition, Congress later added an emphasis upon basic needs, such as nutrition, shelter, clothing, health, and education. The Sahel Development Program was part, if not the centerpiece, of this new congressional mandate with its emphasis upon directly assisting the poor. The rather broad participation by United States academics and universities in the Sahel has an economic base in the contracts available from USAID, but it also has an intellectual and moral base in a perceived shift in how aid is to be given and whose interests it will serve.

The strategy, most commonly referred to as the Sahel Development Program, was adopted in April 1977 by CILSS Council of Ministers and in May 1977 by the Club du Sahel at Ottawa. The primary goal of the strategy is for the Sahel to attain food self-sufficiency by diminishing food imports and increasing agricultural production dramatically. The strategy early emphasized rainfed agriculture, but later stressed irrigation, the expansion and extension of the transportation network, increased storage of crops, increased marketing, increased water supply, increased training, and education for Sahelians combined with a variety of animal and human health programs (see Tables 4.1 and 4.2).

The Sahel Development Program differs substantially from other development programs because it is taking place within a rather complicated multilateral framework. Aside from the Club and CILSS,

TABLE 4.1 Sahel Development Program: First Generation Program (1978–1982)

Categories (Sectors)	% of aid to be allocated for this sector
Dry land farming	22.0
Irrigated agriculture	29.6
Village & pastoral water supply	2.4
Livestock	10.6
Fisheries	2.4
Crop protection	2.3
Environment & forestry	5.9
Marketing	0.9
Transport & infrastructure	12.4
Human resources (health, education, training)	
	100.0

The total allocation is $3,060 million U.S. dollars

SOURCE: CILSS—Club du Sahel. 1978: 9.

TABLE 4.2 Recent Agricultural Production and Future Targets*

Product	Average 1969–1970	Target 2000
Maize, millet sorghum	4,000	8,450
Wheat	8	560
Paddy rice	380	1,800
Sugar cane	270	4,700
Cattle	265	590
Sheep and goats	115	300
Fish	370	700

SOURCE: Stratégie et Programme de Lutte Contre la Sécheresse et Développement dans le Sahel. Paris, 1977, p. 13. The estimates were derived from FAO and extended by the Club du Sahel.
*Thousands of metric tons.

also involved are the Organisation pour la Mise en Valeur du Fleuve Senegal (OMVS), the Niger River Commission, the Lake Chad Basin Commission, the Gambia River Basin Development Organisation, and the West African Rice Development Association, inter alia. Within the multilateral context, USAID has had to adopt its own strategy. For example, the early reluctance of USAID to support the dams wanted by the governments of Senegal, Mauritania, and Mali on the Senegal River gradually shifted and the agency prepared documents to show how large infrastructural projects will benefit the poor.

Within the multilateral flow of aid, the relatively low percentage of U.S. assistance to these Sahelian programs is notable (see Table 4.3). In general, the contribution of USAID funding to CILSS nations has been only 5% to 7% of the total (compared with 16% to 20% for France). However, because of the relatively large U.S. contribution to the World Bank, actual United States spending in the Sahel is greater than that reflected in Official Development Assistance figures. In addition, the amount is much greater than it was before 1974. The perceived power of the United States combined with its influence with the World Bank, the OPEC states, and the other Western powers lend a greater weight to what the United States does than can be deduced from its actual dollar contribution (shown in Table 4.4).

The multilateral framework does not shield the Sahel aid program from domestic United States political forces. In fact, USAID is a highly political instrument (despite claims to the contrary by its employees) and is subject to shifts in United States foreign policy as the changes in the Sahel program under the Reagan administration testify.

Why Aid Is Important

The goals of USAID for the Sahel set out in its Proposal for a Long-Term Comprehensive Development Program for the Sahel in 1976 are those developed by CILSS and the Club: food self-sufficiency in the context of accelerated economic and social development. As to means, the proposal claims donors and recipients accept (1) "That without a fundamental alteration in their systems of production, the people of the Sahel, just to survive, will require even greater quantities of international donations" (USAID, 1976: Part I.6); (2) That, given the potential for increased productivity in dry land farming and in the long-term development of the major river basins, "such a transformation of the area's productive capacities is indeed possible—provided that adequate infusions of international development assistance are forthcoming" (USAID, 1976: 6–7). Development, in the perspective of USAID, is clearly something that the Sahelian nations cannot undertake on their own part. The weakness of the nations and peoples of the Sahel is so grave that disaster would befall them without the generous assistance of their Western friends.

TABLE 4.3 Commitments to the Sahelian Countries by Donor*

Rank	1976 $	1976 %	1977	1977 $	1977 %	1978	1978 $	1978 %	1979**	1979 $	1979 %
France	209	20	France	184	19	France	236	19	France	260	16
EDF	133	13	S. Arabia	122	12	EDF	169	13	EDF	204	13
IDA/IBRD	134	13	EDF	119	12	Canada	115	09	Germany	127	08
S. Arabia	130	13	Germany	90	09	IDA/IBRD	103	08	S. Arabia	117	07
Germany	68	07	Canada	69	07	Germany	94	07	IDA/IBRD	110	07
ADF	46	05	IDA/IBRD	64	06	USA	94	07	USA	85	05
Canada	45	04	UNDP	63	06	ADF/ADB	73	06	Kuwait	85	05
AFESD	42	05	USA	59	06	Netherlands	61	05	UNDP	78	05
Netherlands	37	04	Netherlands	38	04	S. Arabia	52	04	ADF/ADB	76	05
USA	35	03	OPEC Sp. Fund	26	03	UNDP	51	04	Netherlands	57	04
Total	879	87	Total	834	84	Total	1,051	82	Total	1,199	75
Other Donors	129.8	13	Other Donors	155	16	Other Donors	214	18	Other Donors	399	25
Total	1,008.8	100	Total	989	100	Total	1,266	100	Total	1,598	100

SOURCE: ODA Assistance to CILSS Member Countries CILSS/Club du Sahel, Vol. 1, Oct. 1980.
* In millions of U.S. dollars. Food aid excluded.
** Canada's final budget must not have been available.

TABLE 4.4 United States Aid to Sahel Countries*

Sahel	Development Assistance			PL 480 Title II			Total Assistance		
	1980	1981	1982	1980	1981	1982	1980	1981	1982
Cape Verde	3.1	3.0	3.6	2.0	.4	.2	5.1	3.1	3.7
Chad	.2	—	—	1.2	—	—	1.4	—	—
Gambia	4.7	6.2	5.0	1.6	1.2	1.0	6.3	7.4	6.0[a]
Mali	15.5	13.0	9.9	.5	—	—	16.1	13.3	10.0[a]
Mauritania	2.7	8.0	9.2	7.0	3.3	3.1	9.7	11.3	12.3
Niger	9.5	13.0	14.2	1.1	1.7	.5	10.6	14.9	15.1[b]
Senegal	10.0	13.8	18.0	8.8	7.3	7.8	26.0	28.8	35.2[c]
Upper Volta	9.2	14.1	18.2	11.5	17.0	11.0	20.8	31.2	29.3[d]
Sahel Region	21.6	24.6	29.5				21.6	24.6	29.5[e]
Total							117.6	134.6	141.1

* In millions of U.S. dollars.

a. Total assistance includes International and Military and Educational Training (IMET around $100,000 per year).

b. Total assistance includes IMET funds of $205,000 for 1981 and $400,000 for 1982.

c. Total assistance includes $7 million a year for Title I and III, PL 480 and IMET funds at a $350,000 level for 1982.

d. Total assistance includes IMET funds of $82,000 for 1980, $75,000 for 1981, and $135,000 for 1982.

e. These funds are for the Sahel Development Program, which has its own staff and office and includes expenditures for Senegal River et al.

USAID commissioned a study that confirms the importance of aid. Nadine Horenstein (1979) has estimated that foreign contributions to Sahelian development programs ranged from 63% (Senegal) to 90% (Mali), and her estimates of domestic contributions were relatively optimistic given the decline in basic commodity prices and the continuing rise in imports (see Table 4.5). As the donors recognize, the high foreign contribution provides tremendous leverage over the direction of Sahelian development and the manner in which resources are and can be used.

The report of CILSS and the Club du Sahel on the Official Development Assistance to CILSS member countries from 1975–1978 also shows that the aid is of great magnitude relative to the revenues available to the Sahelian nations, their funds available for investment, and to the per capita income of the region (see Tables 4.6 and 4.7). In all nations, aid is a high percentage of per capita income: the lowest percentage is in Senegal, 12.5%; the highest is in Guinea-Bissau, 116%.

THE FOCUS ON POVERTY

In their Country Development Strategy Statements, AID is now required to provide an analysis of why Sahelians are poor. For the Sahelian nations, explanations rely upon poor resource base, increasing population size, and isolation from roads and markets. There is no discussion, as one might expect, of what "poor" means in the Sahel, whether people there were always "poor," and the relationship of poverty in the Sahel to its place in the world economy. Here are three examples of USAID reasoning:

> Why are the majority of Senegalese poor? This is so primarily because of low resource endowments and rapid population growth which slows per capita growth. Senegalese are not poor because of funda-mental distortions in the way that national income is distributed. Class and caste differences in rural areas are not of primary importance in economic terms. Nor can any systematic corruption be blamed for economic impoverishment. Rather, in the context of Senegal's general economic decline for a combination of reasons, the government's development investments have not significantly touched the poor majority in a way which allows them to productively use those investments [USAID, 1981a: 12].

> The key factor which accounts for Niger's present state of develop-ment and low standard of living is the natural and human resource

TABLE 4.5 Planned Financing and Current Development Plans

	1977 Population (millions)	Rate of Expected Population increase per year	Million $	% Foreign Financing	% Domestic Financing
Chad	4.2	—	—	—	—
Gambia	.5	2.13	153	85	15
Mali	6.0	2.74	1,187	90	10
Mauritania	1.3	2.35	1,130	70.9	29.1
Niger	4.7	2.97	600	75.6	24.4
Senegal	4.6	2.55	1,733	63	37.0
Upper Volta	6.3	2.49	1,660	65	34.6

SOURCE: Horenstein (1979: 10).

TABLE 4.6 General Trends of Official Development Assistance Commitments Received by Sahelian Countries for 1974–78*

	Cape Verde	Chad	Gambia	Mali	Mauritania	Niger	Senegal	Upper Volta	Regional	Total
1974	—	72.5	17.0	125.3	132.8	139.7	141.4	107.4	18.9	754.9
1975	19.5	71.6	12.5	163.3	81.9	121.0	155.3	113.8	78.1	817.0
1976	27.0	115.7	33.3	212.8	234.2	191.7	146.3	120.6	55.3	1,135.8
1977	39.0	86.7	38.8	183.3	136.0	123.1	166.5	151.0	77.7	1,002.2
1978	62.8	182.9	40.8	199.3	143.3	190.6	248.0	223.8	106.3	1,397.9

SOURCE: CILSS and Club du Sahel (1979: 156).
* In millions of U.S. dollars.

TABLE 4.7 Assistance per Inhabitant in Sahelian Nations in 1978

Country	Population (millions)	Total ODA Assistance (in millions of U.S. $)	Per Capita Income 1977 (in U.S. $)	Assistance per Inhabitant (in U.S. $)
Cape Verde	0.3	62.8	180	209
Chad	4.2	182.9	130	44
Gambia	0.5	40.8	220	82
Mali	6.0	199.3	110	33
Mauritania	1.3	143.3	270	110
Niger	4.7	190.6	160	41
Senegal	4.6	248.0	430	54
Upper Volta	6.3	223.8	130	36

base. The soil resource base in this arid land is extremely marginal and subject to rapid deterioration by the incessant misuse and mismanagement resulting from population pressures. Using traditional technology and agriculture practices, this mismanagement has steadily reduced the capacity to produce sufficient foodstuffs to meet the requirements of an expanding population [USAID, 1979b: 12]

Even by LDC standards the Gambian population is among the poorest of the poor. The arid climate, the poverty of the soils, and the lack of mineral resources contribute to the Gambia's low potential for significant change. Climate not only dominates the pattern of agricultural activity but is also the major influence upon the incidence of malaria and other diseases carried by insect vectors as well as a host of debilitating waterborne illnesses. The poverty of virtually all Gambians is, therefore, both a result of factors beyond their control and the cause of their dependence on external donors for marginal means of increasing their standard of living [USAID, 1980: 8–9].

AID insists that the Sahel's requirements for assistance are much greater than its ability to absorb such assistance productively:

In strategy terms, this means that for some time to come large proportions of U.S. assistance to the Sahel will have to go to institution building, technical manpower training and economic infrastructure. This is not to say that the U.S. and other donors should not now be supporting direct-impact programs. The problem is to achieve the proper balance recognizing that there is both a short-run need to alleviate poverty and a longer-term need to remove basic constraints to major broad-based improvements [USAID, 1981c: 70].

It is not hard to see that "proof" of assisting the poor can be easily manipulated where "almost everyone" is poor (Williams, 1981). In addition, any project, transfer of funds, or food assistance, is seen as generosity on the part of the donor and of some assistance to the recipient. Furthermore, much poverty is the fault of the poor countries themselves, the result of mismanagement.

USAID Targets Small Farmers

AID says it is carrying out the CILSS-Club development strategy, but it does so in terms of its own analysis of poverty in the Sahel and its own "mandate to concentrate U.S. assistance on meeting the basic needs of the poor majority" (USAID, 1981c: 47). According to the agency, agriculture programs are seen as part of a broad-based rural development effort and top priority is given to increased small farmers' incomes, equitable distribution of benefits, popular participation and the various relationships between increased production and other basic needs of the rural poor [USAID, 1981c: 47].

It needs to be noted that AID "chooses to interpret the food self-sufficiency goals aiming as long-term food self-sufficiency for the region as a whole" (idem). Self-sufficiency, then, is not national. International stockpiling needs to be undertaken to provide reserves for bad years. Moreover, AID finds no failure of self-sufficiency if a food-deficit country can pay for the food it needs to import.

The focus of AID within the CILSS Club strategy is to increase small farmer productivity.

Since small farmers in the Sahel make up over eighty percent of the population and produce largely food grains, increasing their productivity would achieve increased food production as well as widespread increases in rural incomes. This in turn would provide the basis for improved social services in rural areas. Further, the institution-building and infrastructure-development required to increase small farmer production above the subsistence level would do much to begin the modernization process leading to self-sustaining development [USAID, 1981c: 46].

The problem is clear—increasing productivity of an undefined category that transcends both culture and nation—the small farmers.

Within this larger AID strategy, five objectives are specified:

(1)   Implement agricultural programs using proven technologies that have a moderate potential for the short term (but limited for the long term) and which are to be disseminated through integrated rural development projects (which provide extension, credit, animal traction or other inputs, rural roads, storage facilities, and on-farm trials of new technologies in a balanced package).

(2)   Institution building related to agriculture. Included are institutions for research, extension, policy, monitoring, and evaluating. In particular, organizations are needed to carry out "local, adaptive research on the nature and characteristics of local farming and herding systems, including research in social and economic constraints faced by farmers" (p. 51).

Because experience with traditional extension services has been so unsatisfactory both in the Sahel and elsewhere, AID will experiment with alternate models and approaches to providing extension, including the use of mass communication media, the use of women agents, and the involvement of both farm men and women as cooperating personnel at the village level [p. 53].

The supporting services that require the most urgent attention are agricultural credit, marketing systems, and good grain storage. In addition, AID will provide assistance to governments in planning the agricultural sector.

(3)   Natural resource conservation and energy. "The key goal to be pursued by donors and Sahelians alike is to find solutions to the problem of natural resource degradation during this decade and to begin to reverse the process during the 1990s" (p. 58). Here, AID appears to have moved away from its earlier urgent emphasis upon environmental destruction.

(4)   Infrastructure. The most widespread need here from AID's perspective is roads to transport marketable surpluses of food grains and export crops to markets and to move food from surplus to deficit areas. The other critical need is irrigation. AID would like to assist small- and medium-scale irrigation systems rather than large ones, although AID will participate in river basin feasibility studies.

(5)   Human resources development in the Sahel. Much of AID's claimed emphasis will be training in farm-related technologies and activities, but also nutrition, literacy, and cooperative organization. It is interesting that it is in this section that women's concerns are most visible.

Special care will be taken to assure that all AID projects impact directly and positively upon women. In addition to considering their concerns in the design and implementation of all AID projects, AID will specifically consider how training will involve women, how technology will impact upon women, how women may gain better access to credit, how women may become more productive and how women may better share in the proceeds of higher productivity [pp. 65–66].

There are many additional considerations (for example, health and population) that are included in AID strategy statements, but the essence of the approach to agriculture is contained in the five points.

The Senegal Program

An application of these principles is found in USAID's Senegal program. The USAID and the Government of Senegal engaged in an exercise to plan USAID's coming commitments to Senegal over the next 5 years. The thrust of AID's commitment has been stated by Brown and Magnuson (1980: 1): AID must move away "from the present fixation on the subsistence level peasant and toward an emphasis on greater monetarisation of the rural economy." However, Brown and Magnuson are not arguing for large-scale farming, but rather small, labor-intensive and highly efficient farms. "At the moment, commercial farming for food crops outside of vegetables does not exist in Senegal but it could and should be created. Such a development is required to help the welfare of the poor majority" (1980: 7). The authors later state "we are interested not only in production, but in commercialized production, production that will have an effect on the needs of the country as a whole and not just on an isolated area" (1980: 31). They also argue that AID should select for "investment" those zones or projects that will have the greatest marginal productivity (1980: 24). Thus, aid to promote food self-sufficiency becomes aid to extend commercial farming in favored regions of the country.

USAID's Senegalese strategy meshes with current Senegalese government priorities. Senegal wants to shift away from its total dependence on peanut exports and the importation of rice. Senegal counts upon AID assistance for the commercialization of food crops and river basin development. In a manner reminiscent of Latin America, AID has picked up the challenge and appears willing to redirect Senegalese agriculture through large schemes developing the Gambia and the Senegal river basins, the Institut Senegalais de Recherches Agricoles, the Bakel livestock and grain projects, and others as well.

QUESTIONING THE NEW DIRECTIONS

The Senegal case illustrates the way the New Directions policy could be turned to support a mixture of commercial agriculture and large irrigated projects. The goal of increased food production was never a very restrictive idea even before Reagan became president. On this ground, AID recommendations and projects cover the whole realm of rural development policy. It is argued again and again that money has to go to activities other than food production in order to increase food production or incentives for increasing food production.

Also prior to 1980, the argument of recurrent costs was used against narrowly helping the poor. Who is going to pay for programs once the direct assistance ends? As the CILSS-Club working group observes, "most of the projects have not yet succeeded in establishing viable productive capacity" (CILSS and Club du Sahel, 1980b: 68).

Before the change of administration, there already was great pressure to shift the burdens of cost as rapidly as possible to the Sahelian nations (Derman, 1977). The thrust of such a change is to emphasize commercialization of agriculture, to emphasize agricultural projects that are most likely to generate higher returns, to shift from an emphasis upon rainfed agriculture to irrigated agriculture, and to neglect the more northerly zones in favor of the better watered southern portions of the Sudano-Sahel.

The change in emphasis is even more noticeable in the post-Reagan documents. For example, the budget submission for Upper Volta for fiscal year 1983 gives highest priority to building roads in the eastern development region. The second ranked project is rural health planning and the third is management and technical skills. In the budget submission, AID argues that since AID has gained experience with seed multiplication, food grain research and marketing, livestock, feeder roads, and so on,

> We believe the time has come to begin to weave our assistance in food production related activities into a more coherent whole through an agricultural sector assistance program rather than to continue to attack individual constraints on a project-by-project basis. While promising results have come from many projects, the project approach tends to underemphasize linkages among different aspects of the sector and results are often less than optimal due to constraints and bottlenecks within the sector that are beyond the scope of a specific project [USAID, 1981d: 12].

Note the degree to which AID sees itself as determining agricultural policies for Upper Volta.

Evident is a shift in AID policy (coinciding with Reagan's election) back to the national level and away from a project emphasis, while maintaining the rhetoric of assisting the poor.

> Program beneficiaries will be the rural population whose possibilities for increased food production and income will be enhanced. Immediate beneficiaries will also be those in the Ministry of Rural Development and related agencies who will be provided the technical, financial and physical means to better perform their duties and fulfill their development objectives [USAID, 1981d: 14].

In short, no longer do the poor have to be the "direct beneficiaries" (if they ever did).

Even where projects did reflect the reformed policy thrust, it can still be questioned whether the poor and food production were in fact helped. Detailed field studies are needed to draw firm conclusions, but doubters have a few facts to point to. For example, they might cite the $21 million in assistance to Mali in 1981 of which $5.5 million (26%) is for U.S. and foreign personnel (direct hire and contract) and for housing and office operations; and $5 million (24%) for the Kayes-Nioro Road (USAID Annual Budget Submission FY, 1981). Or, in one of the few case studies that we have, it can be shown that USAID helped deflect a peasant organization from determining its own use of outside assistance, but more importantly, its own patterns of labor organization and crops (Adams, 1977; Derman, 1980; Franke and Chasin, 1980; Weigel, 1981).

There can be no argument, however, that under Reagan, USAID is moving rapidly away from the emphasis of the 1970s. The Reagan administration has adopted a global conflict perspective in which narrow U.S. strategic and economic interests take precedence over all else. The new administrator for USAID M. Peter McPherson (1981: 5) intends to move away from the "project" approach toward assistance at the national levels and larger-scale projects and programs. He would have USAID apply the kind of "tough economic analysis which investment bankers, for instance, conduct before making commitments." While mention is made of the poor majority and women, it is clear that the emphasis is upon the "growth sectors" and private enterprise. Thus, it comes as no surprise to find the Bureau for Private Enterprise has been resurrected and given a budget of $17.9 million and the right to draw an additional $100 million for their projects from AID funds allocated to particular countries. The new head of the Private Enterprise Bureau is Elise Du Pont, who according to the *Food Monitor* (1982, No. 25: 5) has a staff of 50. The budget is potentially larger than most Sahelian assistance programs and the total staff is, relative to West Africa, quite large. It has also been reported that the Africa Bureau of USAID has lost 45 positions or about 20% of its total personnel (Africa Index, 1981).

Assessing the longer-term United States government interest in the Sahel, striking is the lack of clearly defined economic interests. It does not appear that the Sahel figures prominently in transnationals' plans of expanding business: Their interests in the Sahel are weak in comparison to other parts of Africa. Economic interests appear to be located in the mineral area and relatively little in agriculture and livestock (Bennoune, 1978; Bonte, 1975; Higgot, 1980). AID is concerned about larger economic issues as one AID paper, "Macroeconomic Issues in the Sahel," shows:

For most of these countries, the principal export potential lies in cereals and livestock trade with the major West African coastal states. The region also can expect growth in industrial crops (cotton, peanut oil) and off-season produce for European markets. Senegal should continue to capitalize on its excellent ocean fishing resources, and to increase the domestic share in value-added in this sector. Subsoil exploration and development in the Sahel thus far has been minimal, primarily due to logistical constraints. However, in addition to the existing commerical exploitation of uranium in Niger, iron in Mauritania, phosphates in Senegal, and (soon) gold in Mali, it may be expected that other finds will be discovered and developed in the future (hopefully including petroleum) as world shortages make exploration of remote areas and poorer-quality yields more economi-cally justifiable [USAID, 1981c, Annex A: 5].

However, there is widespread acknowledgment that U.S. emphasis upon the Sahel is declining. Informally, I have been told by a few AID personnel that the Sahel is now viewed as hopeless and that it's time to focus elsewhere. This is repeated in the current World Bank view that interventions in the 400–900 mm rainfall zone are only holding operations as the inhabitants seek opportunities outside the area. The Reagan administration has shifted priorities away from the Sahel. The *African Index* (1981) observes that "certain countries and programs favored by the previous administration have lost clout because of socialist policies or lack of strategic significance. Tanzania is a prime example of the first, and the Sahel program of the latter." The "beneficiaries" of these shifts are to be Sudan, Kenya, Somalia, and Zimbabwe.

CONCLUSION

The major documents of 1976 to 1981 show that the familiar intellectual arsenal of modernization is turned on the current problems of increasing food production and helping small farms. The solution is to create the conditions for increasing commercial production of food and for enlarging the commercial role of small farms. In some documents, there is a new appreciation of the force of institutional factors and suspicion of large schemes. But there is no appreciation of the considerable colonial and post-colonial history of structural bias toward export crop production and toward rural class and regional inequalities. Even the new appreciation of the interaction between ecology and production organization is not effectively applied. There is respectful reference to the idea of participation by the supposed beneficiaries, but no concrete methods nor appreciation of the already important history of rural development programs in West Africa.

No significant beginning was made to laying the intellectual basis for a new conception of aid and its goals. When in the 1980s the political atmosphere began to shift from basic needs to market returns, the arguments could be slightly changed to justify abandoning project aid in favor of building roads and strengthening market institutions, and to justify diminishing aid to the Sahel region. Most recently, AID is placing emphasis upon river basin development; schemes are under way in the valleys of the Senegal, Gambia, Casamance, and Niger rivers. Here, again, is a marked shift away from assisting decentralized and small-scale production to reliance upon relatively large, centrally managed projects. The decrease in U.S. contributions to the World Bank, the emphasis upon strategic concerns, the decrease in the effectiveness of CILSS, the economic crisis of the Western nations, and the reanalysis of what needs to be done in Africa by the World Bank lead to major modifications of the original Club of Sahel and CILSS development program. Already visible is the rapid decline of the basic needs approach to rural development. Combined with the enormous financing difficulties posed by recurrent costs, the ideological shift means change away from assisting "the poor," smallholders, and food self-sufficiency and toward an increasing emphasis upon large-scale river basin development.

NOTE

1. In its current usage, the very term "Sahel" is a creation of the agencies that responded to the crisis of 1968–1974. Initially, Sahel referred to a transitional ecological zone between the Sahara to the north and the savannas to the south utilized primarily by pastoralists and culturally, historically, and politically linked to bordering ecological zones. However, agencies and governments now use the term to refer to land within the zone receiving 100 mm to 900 mm of rainfall per year, virtually the whole savannah. Sahel in practice simply refers to the grouping of West African nations that united to seek assistance in a coordinated struggle against drought and its effects. Wilcock (1979) shows

that the percentage of their population falling in the Sahel zone varies from 5% in Upper Volta to 79% in Mauritania.

REFERENCES

ADAMS, A. (1977) Le long voyage des gens du Fleuve. Paris: Maspero. Africa Index (1981) 4, 15.

AMSELLE, J. L. (1981) "Famine, proletarisation et création de nouveaux liens de dépendence au Sahel: les refugies de Mopti et de Lere au Mali." *Politique Africain* I, 1 (January): 5–22.

BENNOUNE, M. (1978) "The political economy of Mauritania: imperialism and class struggle." Review of African Political Economy 12: 31–52.

BONTE, P. (1975) "Conditions et effets de l'implantation d'industries minières en milieu pastoral: l'exemple de la Mauritanie," in Theodore Monod (ed.) Pastoralism in Tropical Africa. London: Oxford Univ. Press.

BROWN, D. and A. MAGNUSON, (1980) Discussion paper on agricultural and rural development strategy for USAID/Senegal in joint planning of U.S. assistance programs in Senegal.

CILSS and Club du Sahel (1980b) "Recurrent costs of development programs in the countries of the Sahel." Working Group on Recurrent Costs.

CILSS and Club du Sahel (1979a) Official Development Assistance to CILSS Member Countries from 1975–1978. Vol. 1.

CILSS and Club du Sahel (1979b) Stratégie et programme de lutte contre la sécheresse et développement dans le Sahel. Paris: OECD.

CILSS and Club du Sahel (1978) "Financing the first generation programme within the overall Sahel development programme." Sahel D (78) 27, November, Vol. II.

Comité Information Sahel (1974) Qui se nourrit de la famine en Afrique? Paris: Maspero.

COPANS, J. [ed.] (1975). Sécheresses et famines du Sahel (2 volumes). Paris: Maspero.

DERMAN, W. (1981) "The Drought in the Sahel reconsidered." Paper presented at conference on Africa in the Eighties, University of Minnesota, Minneapolis.

——— (1980) "Cooperatives, initiative, participation and socio-economic change," in S. P. Reyna (ed.) Sahelian Social Development. Regional Economic Development Services Office, West Africa, USAID, Abidjan.

——— (1977) "Agrarian structures, class formation and development in the Sahel." Unpublished paper.

DOUGLAS, D. (1981) "Famine-proofing the Sahel." Christian Science Monitor 3 (November).

FAURE, H. and J-Y GAC, (1981) "Will the Sahelian drought end in 1985?" Nature 291: 475–478.

Food Monitor (1982) No. 25 (January-February).

FRANKE, R. and B. CHASIN, (1980) Seeds of Famine: Ecological Destruction and the Development Dilemma in the West African Sahel. Montclair, NJ: Allanheld, Osmun.

GLANTZ, M. [ed.] (1976) The Politics of a Natural Disaster. New York: Praeger.

HIGGOTT, R. (1980) "Structural dependence and decolonisation in a West African land-locked state: Niger." Review of African Political Economy 17: 43–59.

HOBEN, A. (1980) "Agricultural decision making in foreign assistance: an anthropological analysis," in P. F. Bartlett (ed.) Agricultural Decision Making: Anthropological Contributions to Rural Development. New York: Academic Press.

HORENSTEIN, N. (1979) "Comparative analysis of national plans and budgets of the Sahelian countries." USAID No. AID/AFR-C-1199, Work Order 20. Washington, DC.

HYDEN, G. (1980) Beyond Ujamaa: Underdevelopment and an Uncaptured Peasantry. Berkeley and Los Angeles: Univ. of California Press.

LOFCHIE, M. (1975) "Political and economic origins of African hunger." J. of Modern African Studies 13: 551–567.

McPHERSON, M. (1981) "The next generation of world development." An address to the UNA-USA Washington Leadership Conference, May 16.

RAYNAUT, C. (1977) "Lessons of a Crisis," in D. Dalby et al. (eds.) Report of the 1973 Symposium on drought in Africa, Vol. II. London: School of Oriental and African Studies.

SHEETS, H. and R. MORRIS, (1974) Disaster in the Desert: Failures of International Relief in the West African Drought. Washington DC: Carnegie Endowment for International Peace.

United States Agency for International Development (1981a) Country development strategy statement FY 83. Senegal.

——— (1981b) Sahel development program: Annual Report to the Congress. SDP. AR 2/81.

——— (1981c) Country development strategy statement FY 83. Sahel regional. Washington, DC.

——— (1981d) Annual budget submission FY 83. Upper Volta.

——— (1981e) Country development strategy statement FY 83. Mali.

——— (1981f) Country development strategy statement FY 83. Gambia.

——— (1980) Country development strategy statement FY 82. Gambia.

——— (1979a) Country development strategy statement FY 1981. Mauritania.

——— (1979b) Country development strategy statement FY 1981. Niger.

——— (1976) Report to the United States Congress. Proposal for a long-term comprehensive development program for the Sahel, Part I: Major findings and programs. Part II: Technical background papers.

USAID & Ministry of Planning and Cooperation, Republic of Senegal (1980) Joint planning of US assistance programs in Senegal, Volume II, Resource papers.

WEIGEL, J. Y. (1980) "Irrigation and the socio-economic system of the Soninke in the Bakel region (Senegal river valley)." Second Workshop on Sahelian Agriculture, Department of Agricultural Economics. Purdue University, May 19–21.

WILCOCK, D. C. (1978) "The political economy of grain marketing and storage in the Sahel." Working Paper No. 24, Department of Agricultural Economics, Michigan State University.

WILLIAMS, G. (1981) "The World Bank and the peasant problem," in J. Heyer et al. (eds) Rural Development in Tropical Africa. New York: St. Martin's Press.

5

CIDA AND AGRICULTURE
IN EAST AND CENTRAL AFRICA

LINDA FREEMAN

One of the central tasks in understanding the initiatives of international and bilateral aid agencies has been to separate rhetoric from reality and implicit agendas from explicit policy. Comprehension has been particularly difficult in the 1970s when agencies like the Canadian International Development Agency (CIDA) absorbed the language of its radical critics and began to adopt strategies that claimed to focus on satisfying basic needs and alleviating absolute poverty. Here CIDA was following the lead of the World Bank that signaled a major change in its approach to development policy in 1973. Both the World Bank and CIDA have placed an increasing emphasis—at least in their official statements—on rural development, particularly food production. They were responding to the long-term implications of the world food crisis in the early 1970s. At that time, food shortages had been severe in many Third World countries as a result of the coincidence of declining world production of food and a cutback in international food aid. In addition, multilateral and bilateral aid agencies have followed and complemented the expansion of Western agribusiness activity in the Third World.

In East and Central Africa, CIDA has become involved directly through its bilateral program in several important projects in the field of food production.[1] This chapter situates the CIDA food projects in the context of evolving strategies of Western donors toward Third

World rural development in the 1970s and 1980s. Secondly, it examines several concrete cases and, in particular, the choices made on technology, the nature of the crop produced, the scale of operations, and the form of ownership. In this way, it is possible to determine the relationship of each project to the agricultural policies of the recipient country, to increases in food production and to the prevailing power structure. There is then a good basis for assessing the extent to which the statements of policy during the 1970s have served an ideological rather than a material role, appearing to address vital issues of development while, in fact, bypassing them.

As the premier multilateral aid agency, the World Bank has been influential in guiding the policies and general philosophy of development within CIDA.[2] Now the emphasis is almost exclusively on economic growth, efficiency and a much greater reliance on the private sector (World Bank, 1981: v, 5). Gone are the 1970s' themes of basic needs and participation. Equity is out. Back are the preoccupations of orthodox Western neoclassical economics—building on the best, creating an open economy and, above all, the "magic of the marketplace."

However, beyond ideology, there are other interests that shape CIDA's program and these are located within the Canadian social formation. The most important are the political interests that have determined the origin and often the destination of Canadian aid (Freeman, 1978, 1980b) and the economic interests that have established the regulations that secure benefits from the programs for Canada (North South Institute, 1977; Jergensen, 1979; Freeman, 1980a; Carty and Smith, 1981). Both the external and internal influences have been important in shaping Canada's aid program in Africa.

CANADIAN ASSISTANCE TO EAST AND CENTRAL AFRICA

Canadian assistance to East and Central Africa grew out of the Special Commonwealth African Assistance Plan that was established in 1960. Since then, the major forms of assistance have changed dramatically. The first emphasis was on technical and educational assistance—sending Canadians to the region and training Africans in Canada. However, by the early 1970s, budget allocations for CIDA began to increase dramatically and regional programs were under pressure to expedite the disbursement of funds. Thus, the second main concentration was on large infrastructural projects that involved heavy capital outlays but less administration. In the early 1970s, disbursements to countries in this region began to double and triple.

However, CIDA was not immune to the critics of this approach. When even the World Bank began to address the problem that the majority of people in the Third World were not benefiting from the growth strategies of the 1960s, it was clearly time for a change. Therefore, in the mid-1970s, CIDA produced an official strategy to guide the agency for the rest of the decade that followed the emphasis set out by the World Bank in this period (Canada, CIDA, 1975). Henceforth, CIDA was going to concentrate on projects that involved food production, rural development, self-reliance, employment, basic needs, "a wide distribution of the benefits of development," an enhancement of the quality of life, and an improved "capacity of all sectors of their populations to participate in national development efforts" (CIDA, 1975: 23). By 1977, CIDA had pledged to spend over a third of its bilateral aid budget on agriculture and rural development schemes for the 1977–1982 period, up from a mere 6.3% in 1974 (Carty and Smith, 1981: 130). In April 1982, Mark MacGuigan, Canada's Secretary of State for External Affairs, stated that, in the next 5 years, agriculture and rural development would account for 45% of CIDA's total aid budget (MacGuigan, 1982: 10).[3]

With this clear definition of priorities, CIDA's emphasis in East and Central Africa was henceforth to be placed on the poorest people in the rural sectors of the poorest countries. Accordingly, CIDA began to expand its assistance to include some of the countries in this category in northeast Africa—Ethiopia, Somalia, and Sudan.

However, when the commitments made by the agency in the latter half of the 1970s are examined, one striking fact emerges. For all the statements of official priorities and promises, CIDA did not change its sectoral concentration. From 1975 to 1979, CIDA's allocations for rural development in its bilateral programs actually declined from 29.5% of the total to 17%, while the sectors of transport, power generation, and power distribution increased from 23.1% to 41.5% (CIDA, 1980a: 20; Carty and Smith, 1981: 134). By 1980–1981, 65% of CIDA's bilateral funds were still committed to the infrastructural sector (CIDA, 1982: 6).

This general pattern at the bilateral level has also been reproduced in the region of East and Central Africa. Throughout the 1970s, CIDA stated in its annual reviews that projects "related to" rural development were receiving a growing share of its budget. What these claims and the bilateral figures represent are a reclassification of many infrastructural projects—electrical power, water supplies, and roads—under the category of rural development. When CIDA was more candid, it admitted that, in Commonwealth Africa as a whole, infrastructure was still receiving the lion's share of the budget—77% at the end of the 1970s—while agriculture got only 5% (CIDA, 1979: 18; CIDA, 1980b: 14). The justification was that infrastructural projects were meeting basic needs in a "more indirect fashion" (CIDA, 1980b: 14). In 1980–1981, the CIDA *Annual Review* again stated that it will double its assistance to food production, distribution, marketing, and storage. It remains to be seen whether the change will come in the 1980s.

A similar faltering in CIDA's intent can be seen with respect to the strategy's commitment to focus on the countries defined as least developed by the United Nations. While there was an immediate jump in aid disbursements to countries in this category from 23% in 1976–1977 to 33% the following year, the proportion has not changed significantly since that date (CIDA, 1979: 59). In fact, CIDA is moving away from this priority. The new Agency Programming Framework for 1982 to 1987 approved by the Cabinet in 1981 has redefined the eligibility of recipient countries for CIDA's assistance. Now the division is between about thirty "core countries" that are allocated three-quarters of the bilateral budget and "non-core countries" that will get the rest. At least one-fifth of CIDA's bilateral budget is to be allocated to middle-income countries "with which Canada wishes to strengthen long-term political and economic ties" (Canadian Council for International Co-operation, 1982: 2). The remainder are lumped together as countries with a 1978 annual per capita income of below $625, with no special mention of the "least developed" category.

In East and Central Africa, the only least-developed country designated a core country has been Tanzania, while three middle-income countries (Kenya, Zambia, and Zimbabwe) are included.[4] Some of the poorest countries in the region—notably Somalia and Ethiopia—receive only minimal assistance mostly in the form of food aid. One CIDA official stated that they have lost out in the decision to concentrate on fewer countries.

Therefore, in both the choice of recipient countries and in the sectoral concentration of its programs, CIDA has tempered or abandoned the central thrust of its 1975–1980 strategy. A major element in this process has been the power of dominant interests within Canada that have worked to ensure that Canadian assistance remains linked to Canadian economic interests. These have been secured by the tying regulations that require that at least 80% of the bilateral program is spent on Canadian goods and services. In addition, there has been an inherent bureaucratic interest in large projects that involve the purchase of Canadian supplies and equipment. Such projects have been easier to administer, have involved fewer risks of public criticism, and can be delivered faster than small rural projects. They have offered the prospect of close co-operation in Canada between the government and the private sector and the opportunity to demonstrate CIDA's operational capability. The result has been that, even when political considerations have directed assistance to poorer countries, these other interests have limited the expansion of CIDA into sectors that would directly serve the poorest people in the rural areas.

As CIDA itself found in the late 1970s when it examined the practicability of the priorities outlined in the strategy, Canada lacks the resources to make a major contribution to comprehensive rural programs. Even in agricultural production projects, Canada does not have a corps of personnel with expertise in tropical agronomy and experience in Third World countries. In addition, tying regulations necessarily mean that Canadian assistance will reproduce the forms of production in the agricultural sector in Canada. These reflect the dominance of agribusiness and large farms using capital-, skill- and energy-intensive technologies. Therefore, in Zimbabwe where such a commercial farming sector already exists, CIDA has not been able yet to find an agricultural production project for its bilateral program.[5]

Not surprisingly, the main form of CIDA's assistance to agriculture in East and Central Africa has been to large-scale mechanized wheat and sorghum farms. CIDA has also provided funds for smaller projects in dairying, livestock, and apiculture. There has been early and extended technical assistance from Canada for African ministries of agriculture and rural development. No doubt, CIDA would claim many large infrastructural projects as rural development—rural roads, water supplies, and electricity. However, the major form of direct assistance has been the large farms involved in crop production and it is to a consideration of these that we shall now turn.

CANADIAN ASSISTANCE TO THE GRAIN SECTOR

Canada's earliest significant involvement in agricultural projects in East and Central Africa was in the field of wheat research and production. As Canada has had extensive experience with dryland wheat farming, this was a natural sector for Canadian expertise. Accordingly, Canada's foreign aid program supported a wheat research project in Kenya in 1965 and, since then, has become involved in a major program of research and production in the wheat sector in Tanzania. Another program of wheat research and testing was also established in Zambia in 1975, but it has not moved past the experimental stage into full-scale production. In 1980, CIDA made a third contribution in this sector by establishing a project to grow sorghum in Sudan. Recently, CIDA has also committed $37.8 million for a project to store maize in Zambia. An earlier crop storage project in Tanzania never got past the feasibility stage. Finally, CIDA's venture into food processing has been confined to the well-known, infamous semiautomatic bakery in Dar es Salaam. This study will focus on the larger projects in wheat production and research and in sorghum farming.

TABLE 5.1 Canadian Assistance to Grain Production and Related Areas: 1965-1982 Allocations*

Wheat research and production	
Tanzania (1968-1982)	44.00
Kenya (1965-1982)	6.75
Zambia (1975-1982)	9.80
Total	60.55
Sorghum production	
Sudan (1980-1982)	15.25
Total	15.25
Storage projects	
Zambia (1982)	37.80
Tanzania (1970s)	.35
Total	38.15
Bakery	
Tanzania (1970s)	1.70
Total	1.70
Total	115.65

SOURCE: Canada, CIDA. Press Releases and interviews.
*in millions of Canadian dollars.

WHEAT RESEARCH IN EAST AND CENTRAL AFRICA[6]

Canada's original involvement in wheat research consisted of technical assistance to the Njoro Research Station, west of Nakuru, Kenya. Until the mid-1970s, Njoro served as the premier institution in the region and, in 1977, fourteen of the fifteen varieties recommended for Tanzania were developed at Njoro or were selected from Njoro breeding materials, varieties, or introductions (Hamilton, 1977: 20). CIDA's project at Njoro centered around the development of wheat strains that were rust free—as rust is a particular problem for wheat grown at high altitudes. Therefore, the original phase of the project was extended from 5 to 10 years as the identification, production, and commercial development of rust-free strains is a continuous process. Also, the crop scientists from the University of Manitoba were training Kenyan plant breeders. In 1975, the Canadians were phased out as local counterparts had been trained and the station was operating smoothly.

However, in 1980, CIDA resumed its involvement in the Njoro Research Station; the original Kenyan counterparts had left and Kenya needed scientists both to fill their places and to train new counterparts. This time, the project has a broader scope. It will train Kenyans as both wheat and rapeseed breeders and will explore the possibility of breeding other oilseeds. An attempt is being made to develop crops for small-scale farms and field tests are conducted with local farmers as well as at the station. Research is also being done on insect control and on a range of agronomic techniques. In this second phase, CIDA's contribution has been extended to include capital assistance for agricultural machinery and spare parts, trucks, and physical support for the station. At present, the Canadians at the station have a highly satisfactory counterpart ratio of almost three local scientists to one Canadian and other Kenyans are doing graduate work in this area in Canada. It is hoped that increasing salaries and status will prevent the outflow of these researchers to the private sector.

Originally, the Njoro research center had been designated to serve the needs of the three partner states of the East African Community. However, in 1976, as a result of difficulties between Kenya and Tanzania over the latter's use of varieties developed in Kenya and paid for by the Kenyan government, some of the most promising wheat varieties from Njoro were not supplied to Tanzania for evaluation under Tanzanian conditions. So far, other external sources such as CIMMYT have not been as useful a source for new varieties. These developments have encouraged Tanzania to create its own independent research capabilities and these have been supported by CIDA.

In fact, the Tanzanian wheat research project had been launched earlier in 1970 to strengthen Tanzanian capabilities in testing the varieties developed in the more basic research program at Njoro. CIDA's research project in Tanzania was designed to work closely with its wheat production schemes. Therefore, Canadian and Tanzanian researchers have not only been developing and testing varieties of wheat but also have been testing soil conditions and agronomic practices (soil and crop management). In recent years, they have also been testing rapeseed, other oilseeds, and barley.

By 1980, the research had achieved exciting results with the farms producing up to 25 bushels an acre—equivalent to average yields in Saskatchewan. The key to this improvement has been increased moisture conservation through improved tillage practices and the development of a new variety of wheat, Trophy. Currently, CIDA is involved in establishing a new research station near Arusha and therefore will likely continue to assist this project well into the 1980s to see that the new station is running smoothly.

The Zambian wheat project has not been as successful. Originally, a Canadian team went to Zambia in 1975 to initiate a rainfed wheat development program which was to begin with research and experimental testing and then was to proceed to large-scale production. The project was designed to include a significant training component—recruiting individual Zambians from the National Resources Development College or the University of Zambia to work with Canadian farmers for several years. Then they were to work under supervision on farms made available to them through concessional loans from the Zambian government. Ultimately, they were meant to train other Zambians. The objective of the project was not only to restore Zambian food self-sufficiency but also to balance the expatriate-owned grain farms with an increased indigenous capability.

At first, the CIDA project was administered by the Saskatchewan Wheat Pool with one counterpart Zambian in liaison with the Zambian Ministry of Rural Development. In a second phase, from 1979 on, AGDEVCO, a crown corporation of the Saskatchewan government, took over the management of the project. Under their aegis, Canadians have gone to Zambia to do research and to run the farms where the varieties were tested. Others have trained Zambians in the care and maintenance of farm machinery. In addition to this technical assistance, CIDA has supplied agricultural machinery and equipment, farm vehicles, and farm buildings. Ultimately, CIDA is prepared to provide local infrastructure including roads, water supplies, electricity, and even schools and health services for Zambians involved in the scheme. Its total commitment to 1982 for the project has been almost $10 million and the Zambian contribution about $2 million.

Originally, the project began growing and testing varieties of wheat mostly in Southern Province but also with smaller test plots running toward the north. After disappointing results in the first two seasons in the south, the project was moved to the Mbala region in Northern Province, a higher, cooler location. At this point, the Zambian government assembled and cleared 1,600 acres for planting. The project began to experiment with production on a large scale with an intensive application of fertilizers and use of machinery and with small scale production on peasant holdings. In the latter category, 25 to 30 farmers were induced to plant about an acre of their two to three acre farms in wheat with seed and some fertilizer provided by extension officers. Experiments are continuing with a variety of farm sizes and the project has expanded to grow maize and other crops.

By 1982, the project had not proceeded beyond the experimental stage into full-scale production as originally conceived. So far, the results have not justified the cost of production, although there is some hope that triticale (a hybrid of wheat and rye developed by the University of Manitoba) will be more promising. Although the first yields from a small plot in the north were high—at 30 bushels an acre—since then, yields have either been low or erratic. The very acid soil in the Mbala area requires heavy lime applications, twice that in Canada. At a cost in the late 1970s of $60 an acre for fertilizer alone, total production costs were exceeding the international market price for wheat. Secondly, the wheat was attacked by unidentified plant diseases. Although a Saskatchewan plant pathologist was brought into the project, there was some concern that a long-term breeding project might be necessary to develop resistant varieties. As a result of these problems, CIDA abandoned the wheat scheme in Mbala in 1983, but it is continuing research in rainfed wheat production in other areas.

FOOD PRODUCTION: WHEAT AND SORGHUM

After research, a second major component of CIDA's involvement has been its support for food production on large state wheat farms in north-central Tanzania and on a sorghum farm in central Sudan. In both cases, CIDA has funded Canadian technical and capital assistance—Canadian personnel, agricultural machinery, and farm vehicles. While the project in Sudan only began production in 1982, the Tanzanian wheat farms have been in production for most of the 1970s. By the end of the decade, they were considered to be one of CIDA's most successful programs in the agricultural sector. A recent CIDA *Annual Review* even went so far as to suggest that the "Tanzanians thank God—and Canadians" for the wheat project! (CIDA, 1982: 20)

The Tanzania project has gone through two distinct stages: for the first period from 1970 to 1975, the project did not attract much attention from either donor or recipient. However, after a severe food shortage in Tanzania in 1974-1975, CIDA increased its commitment to the project dramatically and plans were made to extend total farm acreage from 7,300 acres in 1976 to about 70,000 acres in the 1980s. Also, financial support for the project now amounts to $44 million with more likely to be added after 1984. Each 10,000 acre farm has one Canadian adviser and one Canadian mechanic. CIDA is also funding the construction of a central maintenance depot that will receive and check new equipment, store and distribute spare parts, and perform maintenance operations.

For its part, the Tanzanian government has covered the costs for the development of new farms, hiring and keeping trainees and counterparts, operating expenses, the provision of water, and buildings on the farms. The Tanzanian government has also provided some of the financing for farm machinery and equipment. In fact, one CIDA official estimated that the local contribution had exceeded the value of CIDA's commitment.

In 1980, CIDA began a second major dryland farming project in Sudan on a 10,000 acre state farm at Sim Sim near Gedaref, southeast of Khartoum. Originally, CIDA had supported a private Canadian company, Interimco, that was farming on another farm at Agadi. The results of its first few years were used as a pilot study for the Canadians who were to farm at Sim Sim. With the appointment of Walter Burns (for 6 years the Director of the Tanzania wheat project) as the first leader at Sim Sim, the project began with the advantage of his long practical experience in African agriculture. Planting began at Sim Sim in 1982 and the Canadian team was able to get almost 4,000 acres under cultivation for the first trials.

The project is to conduct research into how to produce good yields of sorghum (and, possibly, sesame) economically and, if successful, to demonstrate the applicability of the improved methods to local farmers. The Canadian team will be attempting to overcome the difficult problem of weed control and to establish good agronomic and production management practices. Ultimately, the farm is intended to serve as a model for large mechanized schemes. At a later stage, the project may conduct research on the optimum farm size and on a variety of schemes—including cooperative use of agricultural machinery and forms of sharecropping—whereby tenant farmers pay for inputs supplied by private corporations with a portion of their crop. The Sudanese government is paying for only a few of the local costs of the operation, primarily salaries. Another source of local currency financing has been the earnings from the sale of Canadian wheat that has been sent to Sudan in the form of food aid.

AN ASSESSMENT

Generally, the issues that rise out of these wheat and sorghum projects lie in their overall conception—the larger sociopolitical context of both donor and recipient—rather than in their execution. While there have been problems and frustrations, these projects are not the stuff of newspaper horror stories about waste and mismanagement. At most, there is an indication of political patronage in the Sudanese project. Canadian involvement in dryland farming in Sudan had been pioneered by Interimco, and its president had established close relations with senior officials of the Sudanese government. After four seasons (from 1978 to 1981), the company had also developed considerable practical experience and was instrumental in promoting CIDA's venture. However, even though Interimco was the lowest bidder on the Sim Sim project (according to its president) and was eminently qualified to undertake its management, the contract went instead to Agrodev, a company without comparable experience in this sector and country. The contract decision was taken at the Cabinet level in Canada and reflected the presence as Vice-President of Agrodev of Paul Gérin-Lajoie, a francophone Liberal and former president of CIDA. The importance of francophone connections to the Liberal government in Canada is well known and was clearly being demonstrated again in this case. While Agrodev hired many of the same people that Interimco had suggested on its application, the project has started under a comparative handicap.[7]

Generally, though, this sort of practice is exceptional. During the 1970s, CIDA developed considerable sophistication in designing and operating its agricultural production projects. Technically, the Tanzanian wheat project has been a success with imaginative components built in—especially the early related research and production projects, the attention to developing counterparts, the provision of proper maintenance for agricultural machinery, and the emphasis on ensuring a regular supply of spare parts. The later years of the project have successfully addressed some of the earlier problems with counterparts and with waste and misuse of agricultural machinery and equipment. Similarly in the Njoro wheat research project in Kenya, the second phase paid increased attention to building a permanent corps of local crop scientists.

The Zambian case is different, and CIDA recognizes that the project is in trouble. There are clear signs of difficulty in the changes in Canadian management of the project, the search for an appropriate location and the failure to achieve cost efficient production of rainfed wheat. With the failure to get the necessary yields, Zambian counterparts have been difficult to attract and keep. Also, Canadian farmers who were involved in the management of experimental plots suggest that 6-month contracts are far too short for maximum effectiveness (Gleave, 1977: 13).

The aim of all the projects has been to develop an indigenous capacity to become more self-sufficient in food production. Tanzania, Sudan, and Kenya are all overwhelmingly agricultural countries experiencing very rapid urban growth. They require increases in food production that will more than match their large population growth rates.[8] If successful, these projects will save recipient countries foreign exchange on food imports and will reduce dependence on foreign donors for food aid. The research in Kenya is seminal for the region. The wheat farms in Tanzania now supply about one-quarter of the country's needs and, ultimately, they will provide about one-half. Also, the state farms reversed the drop in production that accompanied the nationalization of expatriate wheat farmers. So far, domestic costs of production of the wheat on the CIDA-assisted state farms have been comparable to import costs (Hamilton, 1977: 43). In Sudan, increased food production is crucial for local consumption, for foreign exchange from exports, and, above all, for political stability. Initial yields from the first year's planting have been three times those being realized elsewhere in clay plains in Sudan by farmers using traditional methods. Finally, Zambia hopes to overcome the drop in food production that followed independence, the departure of many European farmers and the failure of its agricultural policies. With a rapid growth in its urban population, Zambia's need for food has increased and, in the 1970s, shortages led to the highly embarrassing situation of having to import food from its enemies in white Southern Africa. Therefore, there were strong political motivations for the development of the wheat project with Canadian assistance. Moreover, the fluctuations in Zambia's copper revenues in the 1970s and its decreasing capacity to afford imports have brought home, as never before, the importance of food self-sufficiency.

For Canada, there is an element of altruism in helping other countries develop an indigenous capacity to grow wheat. Canada is a major world exporter of wheat and has a direct and explicit interest in Third World markets for its wheat exports (Williams and Young, 1981: 341). Therefore, one Canadian Cabinet Minister is reported to have opposed such projects as harmful to the Canadian interest (Carty and Smith, 1981: 126). However, any lost benefits to Canada are tempered by the new markets for Canadian agricultural machinery, other inputs and consultancies that the projects have opened up. Now that home markets are saturated, North American agricultural machinery companies are looking for markets in the Third World. This was the motivation for Interimco, a company promoting sales of Canadian agricultural machinery, to get involved in Sudan. International Harvester, the supplier for the Tanzanian project, built up its sales outside North America from less than one-fifth of its total in 1968 to almost one-third in 1975 (Lappé and Collins, 1977: 151). John Deere, the supplier for the Zambian project, increased its sales overseas in the period from 16% to 23% and Canada's own Massey-Ferguson, the supplier for the Sudanese project, now makes 70% of its sales outside North America.[9] Also, CIDA seems anxious to offer contracts to private agricultural consulting firms rather than to rely on Agriculture Canada to manage its projects.

For the recipient countries, the issues raised by these projects center around the methods of production, the structure of ownership, and the nature of the product—especially wheat. In particular, large-scale, capital intensive, high technology projects in Third World countries—and Tanzania and Sudan are in the category of least developed countries—are criticized (Tandon, 1978; Johnston, 1979; Wallace, 1981) for their burden on scarce foreign exchange and their level of technology. They build in future dependencies on imports of inputs—agricultural machinery, transport vehicles, spare parts, fuel, agricultural chemicals for weed and pest control, management, technology, maintenance skills and extension services—which, while available in Canada, are very scarce in these countries. Moreover, they offer few benefits to the poorest people in the rural sectors. Let us turn to a full consideration of each of these issues.

Shortages of foreign exchange are now critical for all the recipient countries mentioned in this study. While CIDA's assistance is in the form of grants for least developed countries, there will be problems when CIDA terminates its involvement. Building in imported inputs for part of the nation's food supply is exceedingly dangerous unless conditions are to change dramatically.

In August 1981, Tanzania's foreign reserves had fallen to $1.4 million (U.S.) or barely *two days* import cover (Globe and Mail, 1981). Arrears in payments to foreign suppliers exceeded $400 million and delays in payment stretched back 24 months. For the wheat farms, Tanzania has already had to search for other donors for tractors when replacements were needed for some of the early farms. CIDA does not provide assistance for fuel supplies, which are now desperately short even in Dar es Salaam. How long the farms will continue to receive sufficient fuel when national supplies are so low remains to be seen. While CIDA has supplied a spare parts program for all its projects in Tanzania, there are still shortages and delays. These can be crucial, as can be witnessed by the fact that in 1981, CIDA had to fly in three spare tires for machinery needed to bring in the harvest. The point is that all these components are needed to ensure that planting and harvesting are completed rapidly. The results of the project are dependent on correct timing. Given Tanzania's extreme vulnerability, such a sophisticated project is predicated on a number of increasingly problematic factors. Should any element not be in its proper place at its proper time, the project as a whole could founder.

Sudan's foreign exchange situation has also become increasingly desperate in recent years. With one of the largest debts in Africa ($7 billion), increasing balance of payments deficits ($700 million in 1980-1981) and declining production of its main export crop, cotton, the Numeiry regime has been forced to turn to the International Monetary Fund (IMF) regularly for support (Pomonti, 1982; Globe and Mail, 1982; Connell, 1982). In return for a $220 million credit from the IMF in late 1981, Numeiry has been required to undertake strict austerity measures, withdrawing subsidies on fuel and staple foods, devaluing the Sudanese pound, and reviewing all major development projects (Africa News, 1982: 5). With rising prices for sugar, gasoline, and other consumer goods, the result has been political instability; riots and demonstrations have shaken the country.

Sudan's plight has caused some observers (Johnston, 1979) to question its growing reliance on mechanized agriculture. By 1979, the shortages of spare parts, lubricants, and fuels had reached "epidemic proportions"—exacerbated by the general shortage of foreign exchange. Tractor costs had doubled over the past five years and the price of gasoline had more than doubled in the past twelve months (Johnston, 1979: 16).[10] These factors led Robert Johnston to conclude that,

> Given the high capital cost and import content of farm machinery and petroleum products as well as the inadequacies of Sudan's transportation infrastructure, it is becoming evident that the cost of mechanized agricultural production may, in fact, be excessive [Johnston, 1979: 16].

Rising import costs and shortages of foreign exchange have already affected Canada's involvement in Sudan. Interimco shut down its farm operations in 1982 in the face of oil costs of $350/barrel at the farm and the uncertain supply of oil and other inputs. CIDA has included funds for fuel in the Sim Sim project, but will probably have to rebudget as costs are escalating rapidly. At the moment, CIDA is contemplating adding another $9 million to the $12 million already committed to the project. Also, in 1982, CIDA provided $3 million for general balance of payments support to Sudan, although the money is tied to Canadian goods and is intended for the purchase of agricultural equipment.

Zambia's situation is equally bad—at least until the price of copper recovers. The world copper market has been depressed since 1975 and cobalt prices fell in 1981. The result is that the country's main source of foreign exchange has disappeared with the mines occasionally operating at a deficit. In 1981, the Zambian government was forced to borrow heavily—$150 million from the Euromarkets, $200 million from an American bank consortium, and a 3-year $946 million loan from the IMF (Africa News, 1981: 6). As with Sudan, the Zambian government has had to agree to a number of economic policy changes, including tax increases, cuts in subsidies to state enterprises and agricultural marketing boards, and a doubling in the price for the main food staple, maize. Observers predict continuing political instability as a result of these measures. Despite these constraints, the CIDA wheat project in Zambia—if it ever moves forward to the production stage—is definitely intended to be in the mold of the Tanzanian and Sudanese farms and thus highly dependent on imported inputs.

In all cases, CIDA officials and Canadians involved in these projects anticipate that, eventually, revenues from farm produce will be sufficient to secure the necessary allocation of foreign exchange for imported inputs. Needless to say, this will involve strong political support in each recipient country as there are many competing claims for what little foreign exchange there is. Should the farms not secure the allocations necessary for their survival once CIDA's assistance is withdrawn, they will have to search for other donors or contemplate a series of "white elephants." At best, then, CIDA's projects are likely to involve continued dependence on foreign assistance for a considerable length of time.

The second major issue after the shortage of foreign exchange is the question of the appropriateness of the technology for the recipient countries. In this form of "enclave" agriculture, only a few highly trained Africans will be the recipients of the technology that is being diffused. Approximately, 140 to 175 Tanzanians are permanent staff on the wheat farms and 20 to 25 more are involved in research. Another 35 to 50 are training in Canada each year in mechanics or farm management and another 5 to 10 in crop science. In Kenya, there are about 25 local people at the station and 14 doing graduate work in Canada. Each of the 6 full-time Canadians in Sudan will have 2 full-time counterparts and there will be about 8 others hired occasionally. In Zambia, there are about 20 to 30 Zambians serving as counterparts for the 6 to 8 Canadians and funds are available for up to 10 counterpart trainees to study each year in Canada. In a very rough calculation using the maximum numbers above, this works out to about 350 skilled or semiskilled jobs for Africans in programs for which CIDA has contributed $75.8 million or about $217,000 a person. If the local contribution is added, the figure would be significantly higher. There are, of course, more Africans hired as casual laborers in each of the projects.

Not only are these projects capital intensive, but they are also very skill intensive. Some seasoned participants in the projects have found that attracting, developing, and keeping competent local personnel are the most serious problems the projects face. Despite the attention paid to counterpart training, there has been at least a 50% failure rate in incorporating Tanzanian trainees on the wheat farms.[11] Generally, as in all of these projects, local personnel have not had much background in operating and maintaining machinery and equipment. Even in Sudan with its greater experience in mechanized farming, there is a dearth of skilled and semiskilled labor—the technicians, agricultural engineers, extension workers, mechanics, tractor and machine operators to support the country's drive for mechanization (Johnston, 1979: 24).

Moreover, once such people are trained, they are difficult to keep, especially if they are able to take advantage of opportunities in the private sector or lucrative contracts in the Middle East. One Sudanese working at Sim Sim was able to set up a private mechanics shop with the expertise gained from (and the equipment pilfered from) the CIDA project.

Given the original choice by the recipient country to opt for rapid production of food surpluses, the package of capital, skill, and energy intensive technology followed. In addition, once the crop and site locations were chosen, CIDA officials argued that mechanization was absolutely crucial for the success of both the Sudanese and Tanzanian projects. In both cases, heavy soils would have made cultivation by hand or by small mechanized equipment difficult, time consuming, and generally inefficient. In Tanzania, haste was needed to plant the crop rapidly after the rains, to harvest the crop, and to transport it safely to market before the next rainy season. CIDA goes so far as to attribute the increased crop yields in Tanzania to improved agronomic practices made possible by machines.

Also, the alternative of labor intensive production with animals was never feasible in the areas chosen for the two CIDA projects. In Tanzania, the lack of water ruled out a concentration of people or animals. Even without this problem, the area is thinly populated and would have needed major resettlement to promote labor intensive production of wheat. While there is a long history of labor migration in Sudan since the colonial cotton schemes were created, the Sim Sim farm is located in a region that has long been devoted to mechanized farming with little employment of migrant labor.

Moreover, as noted at the outset, given the demise of the small farm in Canada, the sort of assistance that CIDA is prepared to offer is large-scale, mechanized forms of production. Therefore, even when small farmers are included nominally in these CIDA projects, the Canadians are not particularly interested in working with them. A CIDA official attached to the Kenya wheat research project noted that there were popular pressures for research that would be useful for small farmers. However, he argued that such a focus would take more effort and time and was unrelated to Canadian expertise. Similarly, one observer of the Zambian wheat project felt that the Canadians were more interested in determining the economic viability of large-scale production of wheat than on developing smallholder production, even when initial trials with smallholders had resulted in a respectable production of ten to twelve bushels an acre.

Another set of questions revolves around the choice of wheat in three of these projects. In most East and Central African countries, the majority of rural people eat other staples—primarily maize, sorghum, cassava, millet, bananas, and plantain. Wheat is a product that has been associated with urbanization and with a white settler population. In Kenya, the Njoro research station was established in the early part of the century by Lord Delamere and wheat served the tastes of expatriates and urban Africans. The taste for bread was introduced in Zambia in the 1920s with the influx of white colonists that followed the development of the copper industry. It developed later in Tanzania, again for expatriates and tourists. From expatriates, the taste for bread spread to the African population in the cities and towns, stimulated in part by food aid in the form of wheat (Canada is a major donor).

Therefore, although CIDA's projects have been touted as its support for rural development, their product is actually intended to help African governments achieve food security in the urban areas. In this way, CIDA is serving the urban bias of the recipient countries' development strategies rather than the poorest rural dwellers focused on by CIDA's aid strategy. It is also doubtful whether bread reaches the poorest urban dwellers. Bread is more expensive than maize or cassava, a large consideration for workers whose purchasing power is declining, not to mention the even poorer unemployed. In Tanzania, one critic went so far as to term bread "a luxury" in the context of Tanzanian needs and poverty (Kakosa, 1972). By contrast, the sorghum project in Sudan is related much more closely to the food requirements of the majority of the people.

Not only is consumption of wheat confined to a minority, but also, as we have seen, wheat production has been undertaken by a small corps of highly trained Africans and not by peasant farmers. The few large wheat farms in Tanzania have been easier to administer and control than a plethora of smaller farms would have been, particularly given the conflictual nature of relations between the Tanzanian state and the peasantry. Indeed, the state farms in Tanzania have served as an alternative to dependence on the peasant sector and have thus helped to strengthen an already dominant bureaucratic class (Freeman, 1982).

A final set of issues revolves around the ideological preconceptions that condition CIDA's relationship to these projects—particularly a critical view of state ownership and a highly reductionist, technology-centered view of the problems of development.

So far, CIDA has been operating on state farms or in association with government research programs. Yet, ironically, there is a marked preference within CIDA for assisting the private sector—particularly the large African farmers—rather than the state sector. Both CIDA officials and Canadians involved in these projects are imbued with an unquestioning belief in the appropriateness of liberal capitalism for African countries. They are opposed to direct involvement by the state in agriculture, and several senior officials, including Walter Burns, the former director of the Tanzanian wheat project, have been openly critical of Tanzania's socialist policies. Even though Tanzanian state wheat farms have been relatively successful, one CIDA official felt that the government should turn them over to the private sector. Certainly the conception of CIDA's projects in both Zambia and Sudan has been to support the development of a class of large private farmers, albeit through state programs. In Zambia, CIDA's contribution has been to support the government's attempt to replace European commercial farmers with Zambians, while in Sudan, the government is in the process of turning state farms over to the private sector.

The approach of Canadians involved in these projects has been ideological in a second way—in the conviction that the primary problem to be overcome is a technical problem of developing the indigenous capacity and methods to improve food production. Taken together with the underlying belief in the superiority of capitalist institutions and ideology, these attitudes form a capsule that has insulated Canadian aid personnel from many of the political, social, and ecological issues in the African environment. As just one example of the perils of ignoring the wider context in which CIDA projects operate and glibly relying on the large private farmer in agriculture, let us turn to a brief examination of some of the effects of mechanized sorghum farming in Sudan.

PRIVATE MECHANIZED FARMING IN SUDAN

With the assistance of the World Bank and the IDA, the Sudanese government set up the Mechanized Farming Corporation (MFC) in 1968 to oversee the development of mechanized agriculture in Sudan. The MFC leases large blocks of land (500 to 1,500 feddans)[12] for a nominal fee to Sudanese individuals with sufficient capital to develop the farms. Loans are offered to help them clear the land, purchase tractors, and undertake seasonal operations.

These schemes have brought a great deal of land into production with accompanying increases in total agricultural output. Yet, mechanization has failed to deliver the promised level of surplus; yields have been disappointing (Johnston, 1979: 19). At the same time, great inequities have arisen within Sudan as a result of the government's approach. The effect of state allotment and credit regulations has been to restrict land distribution to a very narrow and relatively wealthy stratum of absentee landlords—primarily urban merchants and, to a lesser extent, civil servants and civil and military pensioners (O'Brien, forthcoming: 20–23). This class has made lucrative profits—ranging in some areas from a conservative estimate of 100% on annual investment (including depreciation) in good years to 50% in bad years (O'Brien, forthcoming: 26; 1981: 25). Yet, seasonal wage rates for the Sudanese hired in these schemes have been below the legislated minimum wage, and returns to labor have been very low (Johnston, 1979: 20).

Moreover, the government's concentration of its development expenditures on mechanized farming has led to the neglect of the traditional agricultural sector that employs the majority of Sudanese people (Johnston, 1979: 12–13). Therefore, while a small class of urban landlords has profited immensely from these schemes, the majority of Sudan's rural population has continued to farm unassisted in the traditional way. In addition, the development of mechanized farming has contributed to the marginalization of the pastoral nomads who constitute one-quarter of Sudan's total population (O'Brien, 1981: 21). As in Tanzania, the overcrowding and deterioration of grazing land and the blocking of traditional migration routes have left nomadic peoples desperate and, at times, violent (O'Brien, forthcoming: 16–19; Johnston, 1979: 21).[13]

Besides their social costs, observers (Johnston, 1979: 21; O'Brien, forthcoming, 10–26; O'Brien, 1981: 25) have pointed to the ecological damage that has accompanied the schemes. Studies show that, under present conditions, it has been more profitable (particularly in bad years) for private farmers to ignore government requirements regarding sound agricultural practices—particularly crop rotation and fallowing. Instead, participants in mechanized farming schemes have adopted what Jay O'Brien has called "agricultural strip mining techniques." The practice is to farm a block of land intensively for 5 to 7 years until yields have decreased, and then to move on to another block leased from the government, with the profits from the depleted farm serving as proof of their qualifications as "progressive" farmers. Those who follow rotation guidelines would do little better than break even in a poor year. Also, as the demand for these profitable ventures outstrips the supply, large tracts are farmed outside the regulated areas without regard to environmental considerations.[14]

The government's failure to check this process of environmental degradation is related to its fragile political hold on the country. Given the opposition from the Islamic right, the Communist left, and the relatively underdeveloped southern and western regions of the country, the Numeiry regime has used mechanized schemes to consolidate and extend internal support (Johnston, 1979: 27–31). Not surprisingly, "consideration of balanced growth, income distribution and the actual performance of the technology concerned are purely secondary" (Johnston, 1979: 31). Given the present economic crisis in Sudan and its chronic political instability, the regime is in no position to alienate supporters. Moreover, should conditions change and the government feel secure enough to deal with some of the social and ecological abuses (as suggested by an ILO report in 1975), the result would likely be capital flight from the countryside for investment in other more profitable spheres of the economy (O'Brien, forthcoming: 26, 28). As it is, one study shows that fully 89% of private profits from one rural area were invested in the urban areas, leaving only 11% for the rural sector, a minimal spinoff for rural development (O'Brien, forthcoming: 27). Yet, it is precisely this class of merchants, civil servants, and army officers that CIDA's sorghum project is ultimately to benefit.

CONCLUSION

Quite clearly, there are profound political, social, economic, and ecological implications in the kind of technology adopted and the sector in which it is employed in recipient countries. Most CIDA officials who support rainfed mechanized agriculture for the private sector in East and Central Africa either ignore these nontechnical features or assume that a class of agricultural entrepreneurs will act as a catalyst for wider economic growth, with productive spinoffs in the rural economy. Ultimately, they retain a faith in the much discredited trickle-down theory that holds that everyone will benefit from agricultural modernization.

As the case of mechanized farming in Sudan has shown, nontechnical features are an important part of the process of technical change. To focus on the advantages that modern technology is expected to bring—the payoff in productivity and economic growth—is both to miss a second level of issues and to beg a lot of questions. Specifically, these deal with the distribution of income and power, with who bears the costs and who receives the benefits. They also open to question the belief that all will benefit from economic growth in the long run.

Whether they choose to recognize it or not, donors like CIDA are involved in a process whereby the expansion of mechanized agriculture has also facilitated the consolidation of power by certain classes over others—generally bureaucrats and/or private merchants over the majority of the population. Moreover, the assumption that the activities of this class will have a ripple effect on the rest of the rural economy is more an article of faith than of reality. The irony that emerges from this study is that, even when official policies countenance Canadian assistance to the agricultural sector in service of rural development and equity, the programs, in fact, offer limited benefits for all but a few Africans and most of these are part of the dominant classes in the urban sector. The choices made in determining these projects illustrate the structures of power and the major interests in social formations in Canada and in these four recipient African countries.

On the recipient side, the choice of the option presented by this Western model of import substitution agriculture provides a telling comment about the major forces within each of these social formations. The governing classes have expressed their preference for large schemes that are comparatively easy to administer and control, and that offer the possibility for an even greater extension of their influence. Alternatively, they are attempting to build support in the rural areas by developing a class of large private farmers. In addition, the adoption of these projects demonstrates, once again, the irresistible attraction of the latest Western models of development for African bureaucracies, a predisposition that makes them receptive to Western development "experts," consultants, and salesmen of agricultural machinery.

On the Canadian side, official bilateral assistance is intended to lay the basis for further commercial exports of agricultural inputs. So long as the dominant forces within Canada ensure that Canadian assistance is tied to the provision of Canadian goods and services, Canada will not be in any position to make a major contribution to small-scale farmers or to technology that they can use. So much for the rhetorical commitment to the poor and the small farmers.

Canada's assistance is not unlike that promoted by proponents of the Green Revolution. Given the literature on the negative side effects of those supposedly technically neutral projects (Cleaver, 1972; Griffin, 1974; George, 1976; Galli, 1978), it is open to question whether CIDA's assistance will not be destructive in the long term too. As long as CIDA is able to manage its projects as if they were in Canada—with special care given to the provision of supplementary spare parts, maintenance, fuel costs, import privileges, and skilled personnel—they should at least be able to sustain these projects. Of course, should the necessary infrastructure falter in the near future, the projects would rapidly break down. Therefore, as a contribution to the problem of food shortages in Africa, CIDA's projects are not only limited in terms of the benefits they offer to the African majorities in each of the recipient countries, but also are highly vulnerable to change in a region that is economically depressed and politically volatile.

NOTES

1. These are government-to-government projects and the study will not include other assistance that CIDA provides through special programs—its Non Governmental Organization division, its Institutional Co-operation and Development Services division, and its Voluntary Agricultural Development Aid. About one-third to one-half of CIDA's assistance to multilateral programs (which constitutes about 40% of CIDA's total budget) also goes to the food and agricultural sector. (CIDA, 1981: 4)

2. See, for example, the statement of CIDA's Acting President, Margaret Catley-Carlson, in Canada, House of Commons, Special Committee on North-South Relations (1980), *Minutes of Proceedings and Evidence*, 19 (October 28): 52.

3. See also (Canada, CIDA 1981) for a statement that assisting developing countries to become self-reliant in food production is a CIDA priority for the 1980s.

4. These are the categories used by the World Bank (1981: 143)

5. However, CIDA is supporting a CUSO (Canadian University Service Overseas) project in Zimbabwe which involves training people in farming techniques.

6. Unless otherwise specified, the material in this chapter is derived from interviews with CIDA officials, Canadians participating in these projects, or Canadian observers.

7. In November 1982, Interimco was awarded a $3 million contract to supply disc harrows, spare parts, and maintenance for the project.

8. In the 1970s, Tanzanian and Kenyan populations grew at an average annual rate of 3.4% and Sudan's by 2.6% (World Bank, 1981: 176).

9. Massey-Ferguson supplies no less than 60% of the Sudan's market for tractors (Johnston, 1979: 36).

10. A black market had developed, with diesel fuel and gasoline selling for five to ten times the official price (Johnston, 1979: 25).

11. This figure was given by Eugene Whelan, Canada's Minister of Agriculture, in a speech to the symposium "Food for All," Ottawa, 16 October 1981.

12. One feddan equals 1.039 acres.

13. The farm at Sim Sim is providing a strip through which nomads may pass.

14. Overall, desertification is advancing south in Sudan at an estimated rate of ten kilometers each year (O'Brien, 1981: 26).

REFERENCES

Africa News (1982) "Sudan—economic, regional tensions explode." January 18: 5–6.
—— (1981) "Zambia-IMF loan, maize crop give breathing space." June 8: 6–7.
Canada, CIDA (1982) "Canadians in the Third World—CIDA's year in review 1980/ 1981." February.
—— (1981) "CIDA's contribution to food self-reliance in developing countries." September.
—— (1980a) Annual Review 1980—Memorandum of Canada to the Development Assistance Committee of the OECD.
—— (1980b) Canada and Development Cooperation—Annual Report 1979/1980.
—— (1979) Canada and Development Cooperation—Annual Report 1978/1979.
—— (1976) Rural Development and Renewable Resources—Sectoral Guidelines 1.
—— (1975) Canada—Strategy for International Development Co-Operation 1975–1980.
Canadian Council for International Cooperation [CCIC] (1982) Excerpts from a CIDA paper on the Agency Programming Framework (APF).
CARTY R. and V. SMITH (1981) Perpetuating Poverty—The Political Economy of Canadian Foreign Aid. Toronto: Between the Lines.
CLAUSEN, A. (1981) "Address to the Board of Governors." September 29.
CLEAVER, H. (1972) "The contradictions of the green revolution." American Economic Review 62, 2: 177–186.
CONNELL, D. (1982) "Protests shake Sudanese regime." The Globe and Mail (Toronto) January 12: 13.
FREEMAN, L. (1982) "CIDA, wheat and rural development in Tanzania." Canadian Journal of African Studies 16, 3.
—— (1980a) "The political economy of Canada's foreign aid programme." Paper presented at the annual meeting of the Canadian Political Science Association, Montreal, June.
—— (1980b) "Canada and Africa in the 1970s." International Journal 35, 4: 794–820.
—— (1978) "The nature of Canadian interests in black southern Africa." Unpublished Ph.D. dissertation, University of Toronto.
GALLI, R. (1978) "Rural development as social control: international agencies and class struggle in the Colombian countryside." Latin American Perspectives, 5, 4: 71–89.
GEORGE, S. (1976) How the Other Half Dies—The Real Reasons for World Hunger. Harmondsworth: Penguin.
GILMARTIN, W. et al. (1981) "Economic memorandum on Tanzania—Eastern Africa country programs 1." World Bank report 3086-TA, January 23.
GLEAVE, A. (1977) "The Canadian rural community in international development." Unpublished manuscript.
The Globe and Mail [Toronto] (1982) "Students clash with police in Khartoum demonstration" January 7: 2.
—— (1981) "Tanzania's economic crisis grows." August 10: B–4.
GRIFFIN, K. (1974) The Political Economy of Agrarian Change: An Essay on the Green Revolution. Cambridge, Mass: Harvard Univ. Press.
HAMILTON, F. et al. (1977) "Report of the wheat sector study team (Tanzania 1977)." Unpublished study for CIDA, November.

JOHNSTON, R. (1979) "The politics of mechanization in Sudanese agriculture." Paper presented at the annual meeting of the Canadian Association of African Studies, Winnipeg.

JORGENSEN, J. (1979) "The Canadian response to Third World needs." Unpublished manuscript.

KAKOSA, N. (1972) "Aid—What aid?" The Nationalist (Dar es Salaam), January 31: 4.

LAPPÉ, F. and J. COLLINS (1977) Food First—Beyond the Myth of Scarcity. Boston: Houghton Mifflin.

MacGUIGAN, M. (1982) "Canada and global food issues." Notes for an address to the Canada Grains Council, Winnipeg, April 6.

McNAMARA, R. (1973) "Address to the Board of Governors." September 24.

North South Institute (1977) North South Encounter—The Third World and Canadian Performance. Ottawa: North South Institute.

O'BRIEN, J. (1981) "Sudan: an Arab breadbasket?" Middle East Research and Information Project (MERIP) Reports 99 (September): 20–26.

——— (forthcoming) "The political economy of capitalist agriculture in the central rainlands of Sudan." Unpublished manuscript.

POMONTI, J. (1982) "Sudan—regional instability and internal tension." Le Monde (Manchester Guardian Weekly) February 14: 12.

TANDON, Y. (1978) "The food question in East Africa—a partial case study of Tanzania." Africa Q. 17, 4: 5–45.

WALLACE, T. (1981) "The challenge of food: Nigeria's approach to agriculture." Canadian J. of African Studies 15, 2: 239–241.

WILLIAMS, D. and R. YOUNG (1981) "Canadian food aid: surpluses and hunger." Int. J. 36, 2: 335–352.

World Bank (1981) Accelerated Development in Sub-Saharan Africa (the Berg Report). Washington DC: Author.

NATIONAL AND LOCAL CONTEXTS

6

PEASANTS AND CAPITAL
IN UPPER VOLTA

MYRIAM GERVAIS

Long afflicted
with climatic uncertainties, the Sahel underwent a period of intense
drought at the beginning of the 1970s. Largely through efforts of
international aid organizations, world opinion became aware of the
consequences of the drought and equated them with endemic famine.
For perhaps the first time, the Sahel became an object of international
concern.

This chapter will not take up the question of the drought as a cause
of the present social problems in the Sahel. Instead, it will recall the
general conclusion of most work done on this question; the drought
cannot be seen as an object of research in itself because the most
frequently identified effects of this disaster were observable well before
the period of the drought (Copans, 1975; Comité d'Information Sahel,
1975; Deriennic, 1977; Meillassoux, 1974).

To understand the situation of peasants in the Sahel in all its
complexity in the period following the drought and the massive
deployment of international aid in the region, it is necessary to consider
the particular conditions of production and of reproduction in rural
societies. Contrary to the assumptions of two influential approaches,
the subsistence economy has not been kept apart from the capitalist
market (FAO, 1976), nor has it been totally destroyed by capitalism
(Amin, 1972). It has undergone profound transformations and altera-

tions imposed by the dynamic of capital. Since the colonial era began, capital has tried to exploit these populations as much as possible, turning to its own profit the productive and reproductive capacities of this type of economy. In the following discussion, the emphasis will be upon identifying the current consequences and repercussions for the rural population in Upper Volta of integration with the capitalist economy.

THE INTEGRATION OF UPPER VOLTA PEASANTS IN THE CAPITALIST ECONOMY

Before taking up the contemporary era, it is necessary to trace the historical phases of peasant integration into the capitalist system in Upper Volta. This account helps to answer the following questions: what interest did capital have in integrating these subsistence economies into the capitalist circuits? How and how deeply were the subsistence economies inserted into the world capitalist economy? And why were they not completely integrated into it?

The Colonial Pattern

At first, maximal exploitation of a commandeered labor force was an adequate solution for building roads and railroads to drain the wealth of the Sahel towards the metropole. But after 1945, the extraction of raw materials and cash crops required the suppression of forced labor and the stabilization of the rural populations (Magasa, 1978: 130-131).

Thus, instead of basing itself on a destructive, short-term exploitation of local populations, the colonial administration and the interests that it served facilitated the penetration of mercantile ties in Upper Volta. They gave priority to two forms of exploitation: market agriculture (cotton), and seasonal labor migration to the farms of Ivory Coast. The existence from this time of an embryonic money economy does not mean the destruction of the subsistence economy. In fact, as stated by Claude Meillassoux (1975), it was profitable for capital to keep domestic economies for two reasons: (1) the labor of an individual is the social product of the entire community; therefore to exploit it is also to exploit the whole family group to which the individual belongs; and (2) the domestic community produces surplus labor that represents for capital a potentially extractable surplus. According to Meillassoux (1975: 166):

Surplus labour equals the period of "free time", that is the difference between (1) the labour-time needed to produce subsistence goods and means of production for subsistence goods and (2) the total period over which the product is consumed, normally the solar year.

The preservation of the social structures that insure the conditions of production and reproduction within these communities proved vital to the maintenance of the surplus labor that capital wished to claim for itself. Colonial policy sought on the one hand to maintain the subsistence cultivation necessary to sustain the domestic community and on the other hand to instigate production of cash crops for the market using the surplus labor of domestic communities. Seasonal migratory labor is another way colonialism exhibits the same surplus labor; male peasant producers go to neighboring regions or countries to work for cash earnings during the slack season in their home area.

Both market agriculture and seasonal labor migration altered the organization of production (new division of labor between men and women, increase of work time, and the loss of a substantial part of production power); often the capacity for reproduction in the domestic societies was weakened or compromised (diminution of stocks of foods products, for example).

The Postcolonial Pattern Before the Drought

Until the drought of 1972–1973, the postcolonial state continued to exploit and transform rural society in much the same way as the colonial state had. The fundamental orientation of the state apparatus from 1960 to 1972 tended to promote the development of export crops and their commercialization, thus maintaining continuity with the colonial economic pattern in the Sahel. The various governments that followed one another in Upper Volta during this period all gave to agriculture the task of producing an investable surplus that could be channeled into the industrial sector. Giving this function to agriculture meant promoting crops that could be taxed in some way. The emphasis placed on cultivation of cotton by the new leaders was not the result of chance, but was rather the result of circumstances originating in the colonial economy.

The Compagnie Française pour le Développement des Fibres Textiles (CFDT) began to implement cotton production in Upper Volta in 1950. The CFDT was formed in 1946 with French government subsidies to develop cotton production to supply the French textile industry. The company was given (and still has) the task of organizing production and marketing. It has gradually come under the control of French private capital. Currently, the CFDT has a monopoly on the sale of inputs to farmers and on the processing and marketing of their harvests. It operates according to the terms of a cooperation agreement with the Upper Volta government that requires it to adopt the producer prices and other cost values fixed by the government. The government's "organismes de développement" (ORD) act as purchasing agents for the CFDT and in return receive a commission.

Through the CFDT, the infrastructure necessary for cotton expansion—management, technical review, improved seed supply, and marketing network—were in place in the 1950s. According to the predictions made at the time, this one product was to provide the principal source of foreign exchange. In fact, the production of cotton increased tenfold during the decade 1960–1970, going from a little less than 3,000 tons in 1961 to more than 30,000 tons in 1969. It accounted for about 20% of official exports from 1967 to 1972 (World Bank, 1975; CILSS et Club du Sahel, 1977). But this rise in production is not the result of a love for growing cotton on the part of peasants. It is rather the direct result of the policy of agricultural development that the authorities chose to impose on rural society, most often by subtle socioeconomic constraints (which will be discussed below). The policy centered primarily on cotton and caused stagnation and indeed decline in food production, thus creating the conditions necessary to make of any drought a catastrophic famine. The failure to recognize this reality leads a number of experts to misconstrue the problem of the Sahel famine as a problem strictly of drought.

In fact, the regression in food production preceded the drought. The quantities of millet, maize, and sorghum harvested in 1972–1973 were respectively 22%, 9%, and 7% lower than they had been in 1967–1968 (an average production year for the 1963–1970 period). Over the same period from 1967–1968 to 1972–1973, the production of cotton rose regularly and steeply by 88% (Banque Mondiale, 1975). Although it is difficult to assess the magnitude of production for each crop, the figures do reveal accurately the general growth of export crops over food crops. The farmers thus tend to "invade" the best soils of the country.

Several factors help to account for this regression in the subsistence sector: climatic as well as ecological and demographic factors (migrations into the Ivory Coast), and so on. The government's pricing and marketing policy was also a contributing factor.

Several different agencies market food crops: state enterprises, licensed or unlicensed merchants, and sometimes the producers themselves. The very low official producer price is indicative only; the real price can vary. Since cotton marketing is controlled by the monopsony of the CFDT, the official price is also the real price. The greater ease of marketing cotton and the certainty of its selling price encouraged peasants to look to it for their money income. Logically, a decline in food crops and a rise in cotton production ought to follow, as was shown to be the case.

There are other reasons for the decline of food production that are linked, directly or indirectly, to the priority given by the government to cash crops. The government has centered its action in the agricultural sector on a policy of inducements to grow cotton. Subsidies provided for technical inputs, the number and size of projects devoted to the development of cotton, and the close supervision supplied by the CFDT are examples of this policy. At the same time, there is a definite incompatibility between the work schedules of cotton and the food products and a problem in dividing times between them:

> The grower who is not able to increase his worktime—since the same tasks of seeding, weeding and harvesting must be performed during the same period between June-July and October-November—must choose and every time he chooses to limit his millet fields [Dériennic, 1977: 1983].

The first preoccupation of the producers, however, remains food production for their consumption. The average farm rarely exceeds 5 hectares in area and the proportion of the cultivated area devoted to millet and to sorghum rarely falls below 70% (CILSS et Club du Sahel, 1977: 2). These figures have had to be modified by changes occuring after 1972 (for example, the creation of the Authority of the Volta Valley), but they still furnish a close approximation to reality.

Until the end of the 1960s, the promotion of the agricultural sector was thus based on increasing export crops in order to increase the inflow of foreign exchange thought necessary for the development of other sectors of economic activity. The stagnation of food crops was already noticeable in 1966 in Upper Volta, but it was not until the drought and its social consequences that the planners of development (the government, international aid organizations such as the FAO and the World Bank) reoriented the development strategy.

The Post-Drought Strategy

The new strategy was one of integrated programs of rural development. It claimed to be a response to the preoccupation with food self-sufficiency and with improving the lot of the "poor peasants" which was becoming more and more evident in the 1970s.[1]

The elaboration and implementation of this strategy coincided with a substantial increase in international aid in the several countries of the Sahel. In Upper Volta, the UNDP (1976: 4) estimated external aid had increased from some FCFA 10,000 million in 1971 to FCFA 29,000 million in 1975. An analysis of the initial forecasts for the financing of the 1972–1976 plan shows Upper Volta's resources contributing 19.3%, and external aid contributing 61.8% (Haute-Volta, 1975). Moreover, the list of donors, until then limited to a few traditional sources, begins to diversify, and there is a strong presence of the World Bank group in financing integrated development projects. In the framework of the 1977–1981 5-year plan the International Development Association, the soft-loan affiliate of the World Bank, funded two huge cotton projects: FCFA 1,950 million of a total investment of FCFA 4,630 million for the West-Volta project; 8 million out of a total of 10.2 million for the Bougouriba Valley projects (CILSS, 1977; Haute-Volta, 1977).

The substantial contribution of the World Bank in these agricultural projects demonstrates its new attitude toward agriculture. Before the 1970s, it neglected this sector in Africa in favor of industrial activity. The presence of the World Bank in Sahel agriculture is an example of the shift toward the new strategy promoted by its experts. Briefly, this strategy seeks to raise peasant incomes, inducing them to produce more, thereby stimulating the economy as a whole.

Concretely, in Upper Volta this strategy has four principal themes:

(1)   Regional planning that redefines agricultural production zones in terms of crop specialization and concentration, seeking an optimal allocation of production. Several projects are supposed to promote food production, but only as a complement to cash crops.

(2)   Modernization of cultivation techniques through use of technical inputs (fertilizers, selected seeds, irrigation, etc.).

(3)   Development of marketing channels for food crops, leading peasants to sell more of their production. The aim is to create an internal market for grains and a source for reserve stocks, thus insuring a better supply to the cities as well as diminishing the risk of a repetition of the situation that prevailed after the Sahel drought.

(4) Reform of the policy of agricultural credit and guarantee of adequate producer prices.

In other words, this policy seeks to improve production through a deeper integration of the peasants of Upper Volta in the capitalist economy. Globally, the new strategy seeks to standardize and to rationalize agricultural production destined for both the domestic and the international markets. There is also an emphasis on the complementarity between agriculture and the incipient industrial sector, agriculture supplying raw materials for industry (cotton textiles, sugar refining, fruit processing).

The example of the project Aménagement des Vallées des Volta (AVV) illustrates that the remodeled strategy transforms social relations of production in rural society and increases dependence of peasants on the market and on the classes that dominate the market.

THE TRANSFORMATION OF SOCIAL RELATIONS OF PRODUCTION IN THE PEASANT WORLD

Within the framework of the optimal reallocation of Upper Volta's resources, each region has been given a precise productive goal based upon an evaluation of its agricultural and pastoral potential. The AVV is a project that operates within this perspective because it seeks to reclaim and to develop river basins judged to be particularly fertile. Since the land was considered sparsely populated, the project took on the task of settling and administering people from overpopulated zones (in particular those of the Mossi plateau where population density and soil exhaustion have apparently reached a critical threshold). However, before undertaking the resettlement, the project had to come to grips with a health constraint: onchocerciasis (river blindness) was widespread in this area.

The project was thus begun in 1974 by a large campaign to eradicate this disease. The first phase of the project was undertaken at great cost under the direction of the World Health Organisation, but without giving any conclusive results.

To facilitate the administration of this territory, the Upper Volta government created in September 1974 the Volta Valley Development Authority (l'Autorité des Aménagements des Vallées des Volta), an industrial and commercial public corporation endowed with a measure of financial autonomy. This parastatal body is overseen by the Minister of Rural Development, and is "charged with studying, promoting, coordinating, implementing or supervising the implementation of all the operations necessary to the economic and social development of the planning zone" (AAVV, 1977: 2).

Land and Settlement

To allow the execution of this project, the state appropriated by decree the land concerned, an area representing 7.5% of the total national territory (PNUD, 1976: 2). This territory had been regarded vacant because it was thinly populated when compared to the rest of Upper Volta. There were certainly villages within its boundaries, especially in the Bougouriba valley, and certain villages that bordered on the AVV territory had customary rights over parts of the land decreed to fall under AVV control. This decree marked a new stage in the modification of land rights taking place in Upper Volta: the state appropriated land without regard to the ancestral usage rights of the local population.

The development of hitherto uncultivated lands is projected for the valleys of the Red, White, and Black Volta Rivers, over a period of 25 years. The plan estimates that out of 450,000 hectares reclaimed, 263,000 are arable. But to the present, the operation has concentrated above all along the valleys of the White Volta, from Ghana to Ouagadougou, and in the valley of the Red Volta, close to Ghana in the vicinity of Manga. A total of 50,000 families are to be settled, 18,000 on rain-fed farms and 32,000 on irrigated lands (CILSS, équipe des Terres Neuves, 1977: 1; AAVV, 1977).

Since 1975, a certain number of families have been moved onto these "frontier lands" and it is possible to draw certain conclusions about the organization of production and reproduction specific to this project: weak direct investments of capital in production; direct interventions of capital in the organization of production; augmentation of productivity; the existence of nonclassical capital-labor relations in the process of production and of reproduction.[2]

The AVV agrees to furnish the infrastructure for the villages (roads, water, schools, dispensaries) in exchange for the adoption by the peasants of modern farming techniques and of the cash crops the AVV recommends (AAVV, 1977: 3). Direct investment was limited to the infrastructure and to field preparation for the first year of settlement.

Controlling Production for Profit

Capital exercises control over production—by imposing the choice of crop and the schedule of the agricultural operations—even though work relations are not mediated by wage payments. Moreover, the CFDT has a monopoly on the buying of cotton, the present cash crop. The peasants are under strict supervision, and cannot sell their harvest to private dealers who offer better prices than the CFDT.

Farm credit is another mechanism for controlling production and it insures for capital the self-financing of the means of production. Short-term credit permits the purchase of fertilizers, seeds, insecticides, and so on (AAVV, 1979: 9). These loans have to be reimbursed each year after the harvest. Conditions described for other peasant regions are observable in this project as well: indebtedness, poor yields per hectare, low official prices, thus the incapacity fully to repay loans, and the following year's increase in area planted in order to try to meet the deadlines set by the lenders—that is the AVV. Farm credit is thus a means to insure that the peasants do not abandon cash crop cultivation. In addition, those peasants who cannot reimburse the AVV within the time period it sets are expelled from the project. The AVV is able to do this because the land belongs by decree to the state, and the means of production (cattle, carts, etc.) stay in the hands of the project. Consequently, the means of production finance themselves and capital can reduce its investment in production to a minimum, all the time keeping firm control of that production.

The capital-labor relationship is articulated around the sale of produce through a marketing monopoly. The profit from such a project is based not only upon weak investment in production, but upon the substantial contribution made by the work of peasant men and women, and upon the noncontribution of capital to the reproduction of their labor power. This last characteristic is one of the most important sources of the process of accumulation in Upper Volta.

Within the framework of this project, the nuclear family constitutes the basis of the social organization of production and of reproduction. In fact, the AVV prefers to accept only those settlers who make up a family in the strict sense of the term (a man, a woman, and children). The role of the woman is profoundly modified, for this transformation of the social organization undercuts her economic independence and increases her work load in the process of production and reproduction.

Formerly, and in other regions, women owned a piece of land on which they could grow the ingredients needed to prepare meals and other products of which they controlled the production and the sale. In addition, they were able to participate in other commercial activities (such as selling dolo, fried yams, tomato paste, etc.) on market days in their own villages or in nearby ones.

But in the case of the AVV project, the women have lost their piece of land and no longer have the free time for other commercial occupations. Consequently, they are completely dependent upon their husbands. The overloaded farming schedule and the intensification of work time allotted to the crops controlled by the AVV demand the constant participation of all members of the family (Conti, 1979: 88). In addition, the women see their role in the process of reproduction altered by an increase in the time devoted to domestic jobs (going for water, pounding millet, fetching firewood, etc.). "In the original village they would have had a mill for crushing the millet. Since they still lack this facility in AVV villages the women have to devote two additional hours of their time to this work" (Conti, 1977: 88).

The AVV project illustrates the application of the rural components of the new strategy and reveals just how far it reaches. The strategy definitely seeks to rationalize production, to make it more efficient (to increase its productivity) without calling into question the pattern of exploitation of the rural population. In spite of the fact that there has been some modification of the production process in the agricultural sector, the immediate organization of work remains the sole responsibility of the peasants. The peasants continue to look after the process of reproduction and the social security functions (the maintenance of subsistence production remains with this group). Since the subsistence production that guarantees the immediate and long-term reproduction of the work force is undertaken directly by the peasants, the policy of low purchase prices for cash crop permits a double exploitation of the peasants.

THE PROCESS OF PEASANT DIFFERENTIATION

In this discussion, we have so far presented peasant communities as homogeneous, nonstratified. This position ought to be qualified, a task that would require a microeconomic analysis that has not yet been done thoroughly, and certainly not for the contemporary period. We can, however, give certain indications about the process of peasant differentiation.

Modern Peasants

In the first place, the penetration of the capitalist mode of production and the monetization of the economy have strongly contributed to the fragmentation of families (rural exodus, migrations, development projects such as the AVV) in the communities of origin. The appearance of nuclear families within the subsistence economy has caused, among other things, a fall in production due to the loss of some family labor. The process favors those family units that are the least deprived of young producers and those with access to land and capital. Notables, traders, and functionaries who have turned to farming often are the ones the experts identify as "modern peasants," that is to say, those peasants whose output is satisfactory, who have the spirit of initiative, and who have a positive view of technological progress.

The notables and traditional chiefs who kept some real power through colonization or who acquired it thanks to the support of the colonial administration and maintained it since independence, have been able to profit from their position. Some have appropriated communal lands to themselves; others have been able to have more and more land cultivated for their personal benefit by members of the community operating under customary relations (Kohler, 1971: 231). Their integration does not come from the fact that they are harder workers than other peasants, but only from their ability to profit from a situation that was favorable to them. Certain traditional traders who have been able to increase their wealth by following a policy of usurious loans have thereby acquired large farming estates and become successful farmers.

Another element of differentiation appears to be increasing in importance in Upper Volta: that of the functionaries, the educated elite who invest part of their high salaries in agriculture. Often, this is a case of functionaries who use their familial plots, or new ones given them by the traditional headman, to cultivate cash crops on an area that is large when compared with that of other peasants. Moreover, they are able to come back often with enough capital to buy, not only seed and fertilizer, but machinery as well (e.g., diesel pumps), which increases their returns to land.

For the production of cotton, the wealthier farmers draw a significant advantage from the subsidy of technical inputs such as fertilizer. In fact, the subsidizer price of fertilizer stayed around FCFA 35/kg during the decade 1960–1970, although its real cost was from FCFA 100 to FCFA 105/kg. (CILSS et Club du Sahel, 1977: 16). These subsidies are taken from the "special productivity fund" made up of the profits earned on the sale of cotton. For the producers as a whole, the subsidies in principle have no effect on earnings; the reduced costs of production are balanced by a reduction in the producer price. But there is redistributive logic to the subsidy; it is paid by all cotton producers while it benefits only those who use the inputs. This works as a subsidy for modernization paid from the poor cotton producers who use none of these inputs to the better-off peasants who do use them.

Differentiation by wealth and techniques of production creates new conditions for the appropriation and ownership of land and for the recruitment of labor. One of the tendencies observable to differing degrees according to the region is the breakdown of the communitary mode of production and its replacement by property owners who employ wage workers. But this breakdown is only at an early stage and nowhere constitutes the main tendency among the peasant population in Upper Volta.

Following from differentiation, the main trend is the polarization of peasant communities and an increase in the income gap between peasants: the increasing impoverishment of the majority of peasants while the "modern peasants" seem to succeed and get wealthier.

Mechanisms of Impoverishment

This first appearance of polarization among the farming population in Upper Volta contributes to a rise in the level of cash-crop production by the use of new cultivating techniques and new inputs. The new technology has the effect of lowering the average cost for the well-to-do-peasants, which consequently puts downward pressure on the price paid for the crop. Since the poorer peasants have an unchanging yield, prices that fluctuate downward imply a lower return to their labor time.

The poorer peasants produce in order to obtain a certain amount of cash. They are thus induced to produce more of the cash crop, to spend more of their work time on cash crops to keep their monetary income stable. This is an absolutely impoverishing dynamic in the sense that the work time of peasants is worth less and less and the subsistence base is eventually threatened.

In Upper Volta, the peasants who are undergoing a devaluation of their labor time constitute the large majority of agricultural producers. Why and how such a phenomenon can be maintained and perpetuated deserves an explanation. On this point, Jannik Boesen (1979: 157) has something relevant to say:

[T]he peasant is not "liberated" from his means of production, the land; on the contrary he is tied to it, as in most cases there is no way he can secure the simple reproduction of his family labour by selling its labour power . . . the very persistence of the peasantry is conditioned, and forced upon it, by its own ability to produce commodities and exchange them *below* their value (under capitalist conditions of production) in order to obtain items necessary for simple reproduction.

This ability in turn depends upon the maintenance of a significant self-provisioning capacity.

In the light of the capacity of peasants to produce cash crops while exchanging them below their value, and the necessity they face of maintaining a subsistence base, we can explain the refusal of the peasants to cultivate cotton at the time of the drought and the stagnation of cotton production during the 1970s. With the drought, millet and sorghum granaries were emptied. The peasants judged it essential to build up a stock of grain. This was a vital necessity according to the logic of peasant production, and it induced the peasants to increase the acreage planted to food grain at the expense of cotton. In addition, in response to grain scarcity, the price of millet and sorghum rose and unofficial markets sprang up. Peasants began to treat millet and sorghum as cash crops selling surplus production for cash income. Once the stocks of grain were restored and market conditions returned to normal, the peasants went back to their production of cotton, which explains the resumption of cotton production in Upper Volta since 1977.[3]

CONCLUSION

We have seen that the initiation of a process of peasant differentiation alongside the maintenance of a subsistence economy are not, finally, contradictory elements in the agricultural policy planned for Upper Volta by the state, large financial institutions, and organizations of international aid. The existence of these two phenomena ought to be seen rather as the reflection of a tendency to broaden the extraction of the surplus created in the agricultural sector in Upper Volta, which was becoming insufficient.

This understanding raises the following question: Has the strategy of capital in the agricultural sector in the 1970s been a success or not from its own logic? In an earlier phase, capital used to speculate on the goods produced by the subsistence economy, by taking out a substantial profit by means of capitalist trading networks. But the production on which the whole process was based seemed so unpredictable that a new strategy was intended to match the survival of a structure of production that baffled capital by giving peasants the capacity to resist strongly at moments they judged to be critical (e.g., the drought in the Sahel). In this perspective, the rethinking of the capitalist strategy of intervention in the agricultural sector becomes understandable: the goal is a more developed integration of the peasants into the monetary economy. The planners hope to make the peasants "susceptible" to the objectives of cash-crop production, in order to increase surplus extraction from their participation into the market.

From the standpoint of the intervening organizations, this strategy has achieved a certain degree of success. The peasants tended to produce more salable goods when the price payed to the producer dropped (a drop due in part to the increased productivity of the "modern" peasants), in order to maintain the daily reproduction of their labor power. I believe that such a strategy can perpetuate itself as long as the peasants manage to combine subsistence production and commercial production in a way that maintains the simple reproduction of the family group.

Nonetheless, the peasants still have a certain margin of autonomy with respect to this strategy of cash-crop promotion. This degree of autonomy or this form of resistance comes from the control the peasants still have over their food production. For them, growing millet remains an alternative solution, in the context of a strategy that has not devoted enough attention to subsistence agriculture.

NOTES

1. For the World Bank, poor peasants in the Sahel were those with little land, very low yields, using few if any technical inputs, and rarely specializing.

2. The theoretical concepts that underlie this presentation of the AVV project are largely inspired by the analysis and the observations made by Anna Conti (1979) in her study of the effects of these large development projects on the condition of women in Upper Volta.

3. During a recent stay in Mali, I again became aware of the importance of buying and selling networks in motivating peasants to grow cash crops. When the marketing agency opened a maize "window" alongside its cotton "window" in the South Mali project, there followed a rise in the land areas planted to maize and a fall in that planted to cotton.

REFERENCES

AMIN, S. (1972) "Le modèle théorique d'accumulation et de développement dans le monde contemporain." Tiers-Monde, Tome XIII, no. 52.

Autorité des Aménagements des Vallées des Volta [AAVV] (1977) La mise en valeur des zones onchocerquiennes en Haute-Volta (Principes et Méthodes, premiers résultats). Ministère du Plan, Ouagadougou, mai 1977.

Banque Mondiale [World Bank] (1975) Situation économique et perspective de développement de la Haute-Volta. Washington, DC: Author.

BOESEN, J. (1979) "On peasantry and the 'modes of production debate.'" Rev. of African Political Economy 15–16 (May-December).

CILSS, Equipe des cultures sèches, Haute-Volta (1977) Rapport de synthèse. Préliminaire, mars 1977.

CILSS et Club du Sahel (1977) Commercialisation, politique des prix et stockage des céréales au Sahel. Sous la direction d'Elliot Berg. août.

Comité D'information Sahel (1975) Qui se nourrit de la famine en Afrique. Paris: Maspéro.

CONTI, A. (1979) "Capitalist organisation of production through non-capitalist relations: women's role in a pilot resettlement in Upper Volta." Rev. of African Pol. Economy 15–16 (May-December).

COPANS, J. [ed.] (1975) Sécheresses et Famines au Sahel, Tome 1 et 2. Paris: Maspéro.

DERIENNIC, H. (1975) Domination en Afrique Noire: paysans et éleveurs sous le joug. Paris: L'Harmattan.

FAO (1976) Etude prospective pour le développement agricole des pays de la zone sahélienne 1975–1990, vols. I et II. Author, mars.

GERVAIS, M. (1981) Les transformations des rapports sociaux de production dans la région sahélienne. Mémoire de maîtrise, no. 678, Université du Québec à Montréal.

Haute-Volta (1977) IIIe Plan de Développement Economique et Social 1977–1981. Ministère du Plan et de la Coopération, République de la Haute-Volta.

——— (1975) "Le plan quinquennal de 1972–1976 de la Haute-Volta." Les Plans de développement des pays de l'Afrique Noire. Paris: Ediafric.

KOHLER, J-M. (1971) Activités agricoles et changements sociaux dans l'Ouest-Mossi. ORSTOM, mémoire 46.

MAGASA, A. (1978) Papa-commandant a jeté un grand filet devant nous, les exploités des rives du Niger 1902–1962. Paris: Maspéro.

MEILLASSOUX, C. (1975) Femmes, greniers et capitaux. Paris: Maspéro.

——— (1974) "The Sahel famine." Rev. of African Political Economy 1.

PNUD [UNDP] (1976) Assistance demandée au PNUD par le gouvernement de la Haute-Volta pour la période 1977–1981. January.

7

INSIDE THE MIRACLE
Cotton in the Ivory Coast

BONNIE K. CAMPBELL

The Ivory Coast is most often presented as a success story of continued growth based on commercial agriculture. The dominant pattern has been the expansion in the forest zone of export crops, mainly coffee, cocoa, timber, and palm oil, drawing on the labor of surrounding Sahelian countries, notably Upper Volta and Mali.[1]

The vulnerability of the extensive pattern of export-oriented growth and the regional imbalances that it is recognized to have caused explain the interest in the introduction of crops that would permit diversification. A recent much talked about "success" in this regard is cotton production in the central and northern savannah region. The extension of this crop is presented as a significant effort to redress regional imbalances and to integrate agriculture and industry.

A new selected variety of cotton was introduced in the 1960s; in 1980, it was cultivated by over 90,000 peasant producers and was responsible for the monetary revenue of approximately 900,000 people in areas of the Ivory Coast where there is frequently no alternative cash crop.[2]

This chapter analyzes the techniques used to introduce and extend production, laying emphasis upon the heavy demands they impose on total family labor for cash as well as food crops. It investigates the socioeconomic consequences of these techniques on productive relations, and raises questions concerning to whose advantage and with what social and political implications the extension of cotton production has taken place in the Ivory Coast. The recent introduction in the 1970s of more intensive techniques of cotton production suggests the eventual emergence of a pattern of enlarged reproduction in the place of the past extensive colonial pattern. The project coincides with a period in which European sources of capital appear to be increasingly replaced by North American sources, notably with the involvement of the World Bank in debt financing.[3] The new efforts to raise productivity have internal as well as transnational ramifications. They imply new patterns in the distribution of resources and in rural differentiation, changes that may provoke modifications in the existing distribution of power.

The very centralized control that the government has maintained over the organization of the production and marketing of cotton, and the nature of the new productive techniques introduced, are key factors in explaining the new lines of class formation that are beginning to emerge in the rural sector. If in the short term the emergence of a group of wealthier producers will serve to stabilize production and consolidate centralized control over the rural areas, in the longer term it will accentuate contradictions within the cotton growing areas and between these regions and other areas of the country. In this sense, the study of cotton production in the Ivory Coast is also the study of the evolving nature of the state and its relations to foreign capital and, above all, to new social groups that emerge in the process of rural differentiation.

THE INTRODUCTION OF COMMERCIALIZED COTTON PRODUCTION IN THE IVORY COAST 1960–1970

Before the beginning of French colonialism in this area of West Africa, women interplanted traditional Mono cotton with food crops and spun it into yarn, which men then wove into cloth. During the colonial period, metropolitan textile imports supplied the Ivorian market, and local cotton production, essentially because of the shorter staple of the local variety, remained of secondary importance. Other colonial producers of longer staples and better quality fibres, such as Chad, supplied the metropolitan industry.

The changes in Ivorian cotton production that began during the transition to independence provide a useful illustration of the meaning and consequences of the process of decolonization.

The abolition of forced labor and the introduction of more intensive techniques of production made possible through the support of French overseas "aid," were accompanied by a redefinition of French overseas economic interests. In the Ivory Coast, the Code des Investissements of 1959 encouraged investment in new productive activity. It opened the possibility of creating local textile production to replace European imports, but improvements would first have to be made in the cotton grown locally. To supply the raw material needs of the factories that the French textile interests planned to install in the Ivory Coast, a massive program for the introduction of Allen cotton, an improved variety, was begun in 1960.

In agriculture as in industry, the new policies required the intervention not only of the metropolitan power, but increasingly of the newly created state. French textile interests had recommended the creation of publicly supported specialized agencies to further colonial cotton production. As a result, the French government established in 1946 a textile fiber research institute, Institut de Recherches des Cotons et Textiles (IRCT), and in 1949 it created an agricultural extension and cotton production company, Compagnie Française pour le Développement des Fibres Textiles (CFDT). Finally, in 1955 it set up colonial marketing boards or Caisses de Stabilisation. In supporting, during the process of political decolonization, a new cotton and textile industry in the Ivory Coast and other colonies, the French textile interests and the French government were not just favoring a reorientation of the colonial economy. Instead, they were ensuring that the colonial economic orientation would be carried to a higher level of integration and endure under the conditions of political independence.[4] The analysis of postindependence Ivorian public policies concerning the production and marketing of cotton illustrates well that the intervention of the newly created Ivory Coast state served to perpetuate and to deepen rather than to weaken the control that metropolitan interests exercised over all aspects of the organization of production.

THE INTRODUCTION AND ORGANIZATION OF PRODUCTION OF INDUSTRIAL COTTON

The Ivory Coast government gave several social and economic justifications for the introduction in 1960 of an industrial and marketable cotton crop into the northern part of the country. The peasant producers would benefit from integration into the monetized national economy (I.C. Ministry of Agriculture, 1969: Vol. 2, 74). The national economy would benefit from a reduction in the regional disparities that existed between northern and southern parts of the country. Monetary revenue in the north was considered to be about one third of that of the south (Atemengue, 1966: 21).

A third objective also appears to have been fundamental to the decision: supplying the textile industry with locally produced raw material. The value of imported textile products increased 36% in 1960–1961 and was to increase another 45% in 1964–1965 to a value exceeding FCFA 5 million in 1965 (I.C. Ministry of Finance, Economic Affairs and the Plan, 1968: 98). There appeared to be ample economic justification for introducing the cultivation of a variety of cotton suitable for cloth manufacture in the nascent local industry.

All aspects of the introduction, production, and marketing of the improved variety, Allen 333, were to be the responsibility of CFDT. The company had control over the choice of land, the distribution of seeds and fertilizers, and the supervision of all aspects of cultivating, collecting, purchasing, ginning, transporting, stocking, and marketing the new crop. Allen cotton was to be introduced among smallholding peasant producers on plots ranging in size from 0.25 ha. to 1.00 ha. and averaging 0.76 ha. It was to be cultivated under very strict technical supervision and according to a detailed agricultural timetable. The technical requirements included straight row cultivation, repeated weeding, the use of fertilizers, and antiparasitic treatments. The intense methods of cultivation were to produce a long and fine fiber and an average yield of 900 kilograms of seed cotton per hectare. Through the introduction of higher yielding varieties (e.g., Allen 444–2) and improvements in pest control, the average yield reached approximately 1,000 kilograms per hectare by 1973–74 (see Table 7.1). The improved variety of cotton has a ginning yield of about 40% lint or fiber.

The Financing of Cotton Production

The French government institutionalized subsidies for the extension of cotton production in French West Africa in the postwar period with the allocation of funds from its Fonds d'Investissement pour le Développement Economique et Social (FIDES) to the activities of the Office du Niger between 1947 and 1957. The source of financing remained the same when IRCT and CFDT decided to introduce Allen cotton into the Ivory Coast in 1959–1960. The cost of the program until 1966 was supported by the Fonds d'Aide et de Coopération (FAC), which replaced FIDES in 1958. Further metropolitan funds were subsequently made available in the form of loans from the Caisse Centrale de Coopération Economique (CCCE) and from the French

TABLE 7.1 Allen Cotton Production Statistics 1960–61 to 1970–71

Season	Acreage (Ha.)	Production (seed) (T)	Yield (Kg/Ha)	Production (fibre) (T)	Ginning Yield
1960–61	137	69	501	—	—
1961–62	272	240	885	—	—
1962–63	1278	765	600	290	38.00
1963–64	2518	2051	815	746	36.40
1964–65	6408	5527	863	3224	40.30
1965–66	11768	9125	775	3631	39.80
1966–67	23810	22047	925	8689	39.50
1967–68	38968	32284	828	13281	39.27
1968–69	48139	41739	867	16799	40.24
1969–70	33345	32320	970	13175	40.17
1970–71	35867	29316	817	11653	39.72

SOURCE: Compagnie Française pour le Développement des Fibres Textiles, Côte d'Ivoire (1972), Annexe au Rapport Annuel, 1970–1971: 1.

capital market. From 1966, the cost of agricultural extension programs for cotton began increasingly to be assumed by the Ivory Coast and financed by the Budget Spécial d'Investissement et d'Equipment (BSIE).[5] In this manner, activities initiated externally became activities of the Ivory Coast state (see Table 7.2).

In 1970–1971, the plan was for agricultural extension costs for cotton production to be shared for a period of three years by the Ivory Coast and the European Development Fund. The EDF program together with loans from the European Investment Bank were to total FCFA 1,788,498,000. The aim was to boost cotton output to 80,000 tons seed cotton (about 32,000 tons lint) on 85,000 hectares. The Ivory Coast was to bear an increasing portion of costs with each successive year. According to the 1971–1975 Five Year Economic Plan, the Ivorian government anticipated that considerable increases in the output of locally grown cotton would be required to supply industrial needs of lint cotton that were expected to increase from 4,400 tons in 1970 to 33,000 tons in 1980.

Before the end of the 1960s, it had become evident that these estimates would have to be revised. From the peak 42,000 tons seed cotton obtained in 1968–1969 on which future proposals were based, output decreased to 32,000 tons in 1970 and still further to 29,000 tons in 1971. The explanation for these decreases given by the CFDT and government officials, blaming climate and other "unaccountable"

TABLE 7.2 The Financing of Ivorian Allen Cotton Production*

Year	Production Source	(Recurrent expenditure) Amount	Investment Source	Amount
1960	FAC			
1961	FAC			
1962	FAC	60		
1963	FAC	70		
1964	French loan (FAC, CCCE)	200	Private investment (Escarré Company)	230
1965	FAC	200	Loan (CCCE), (Bouaké factory)	(not known)
1966	BSIE	250		
1967	CCCE	300	Subsidy (FAC) Loan (CCCE), (Boundiali factory)	200
1968	CCCE	340	Loan (CCCE), (Mankono factory)	200
1969	BSIE	334	Private investment (Escarré)	130
1970–71	EDF 66% I.C. 33% BSIE	439	Loan BEI (ginning and stocking) Banque européenne d'investissement	65
1971–72	EDF 60% I.C. 40% BSIE	495		
1972–73	EDF 50% I.C. 50% BSIE	490	Loan BEI	465

SOURCE: Interview with CFDT Bouaké, February 1972.
* Figures in million FCFA.

factors, appears neither complete nor very convincing. As will be shown, the temporary stabilization of output at approximately 35,000 tons seed cotton reached by the Ivory Coast by 1970, was in fact a reflection of a complex set of factors that stem above all from the manner in which the production of Allen cotton was introduced and organized.

The instrument through which the new state intervened in local cotton production was the Caisse de Stabilisation. The involvement of the Caisse, however, both in the financing of production and in supporting prices, in no way altered the organization of production, a matter that until 1973 remained entirely in the hands of the established French company, the CFDT. On October 1st of that year, the CFDT in the Ivory Coast became a semipublic transnational company in which the Ivorian government held 55% of shares and the CFDT 45%. However, in view of the fact that the CFDT has retained official control over all aspects of technical expertise and over the sale of Ivorian cotton on the world market (a critical aspect of its financing), it will be argued in what follows that state participation has in no fundamental way altered the orientation of the productive activities of the new CIDT, Compagnie Ivoirienne pour le Développement des Textiles.

The involvement of the Ivorian Caisse made the CFDT the agent of the Ivory Coast government, in spite of the CFDT's affiliation to metropolitan industrial and international banking interests. In the 1970s, the CFDT was linked to the Banque d'Indochine by the Banque de Paris et des Pays-Bas, which had important interests in the French textile industry (Agache-Willot and Prouvost). Because every aspect of the marketing and production that the Caisse helped to subsidize reflected above all the commercial considerations of the single company responsible, in its intervention into cotton production the Caisse might more correctly have been considered the "agent" of the CFDT.

The Marketing of Cotton Production

As of 1964, the Caisse assumed responsibility for guaranteeing the price of cotton as the colonial body, the Caisse Inter-Etats de Bobo-Dioulasso, had previously done. The transfer of responsibility to a local institution was to legitimize the unmodified continuation of the existing organization of production and marketing of Ivorian cotton.

As in the case of coffee and cocoa, the Ivorian Caisse operates as a price supporter and stabilizer to both producer and purchaser of cotton. The Caisse's role in the marketing of cotton is very much limited, however, by the existing structures of production and distribution. There is in fact only one seller of cotton, the CFDT (now the CIDT), the company responsible for both production and marketing (I.C. Caisse de Stabilisation, 1970: 35). There is, moreover, only one Abidjan buyer for Ivorian cotton exports, the CFDT (I.C. Caisse de Stabilisation, 1970: 36). The Caisse's stabilizing and price supporting operations are consequently intimately linked with the activities of the CFDT/CIDT.

Supported cotton prices are fixed yearly and based on a price to the producer for raw cotton at the local buying point to which is added a series of expenses incurred by the CFDT/CIDT in collecting and processing the cotton and delivering it to Abidjan. If the world price of cotton (f.o.b.) is above that set at the beginning of the marketing period, the CFDT/CIDT pays a rebate to the Caisse. If the world price is below that assumed in the calculations, the Caisse pays a rebate to the CFDT/CIDT.

The price guaranteed to the CFDT/CIDT by the Caisse is based on the price guaranteed to the peasant producer plus the declared costs of the CFDT/CIDT for its own operations such as transport and ginning. The high cost of the overall monopolistic organization of production was never questioned. The measures introduced by the government to reduce costs have tended, as will be seen, to pass costs on to those who are least organized and least capable of bearing them—the peasant producers.

Resistance in the 1960s to Growing Cotton

For peasants accustomed to growing Mono cotton, Allen cotton in 1960 posed several difficulties. Most important was that it required a much greater supply of labor. It is estimated (I.C. Ministry of the Plan, 1968: 4) that Allen cotton required approximately three times as many days of labor per hectare as the former variety: 150 days per hectare for Allen as against 40 days per hectare for Mono. The government employed various methods, both economic and political, to mobilize the necessary labor. The political methods differed at times only in degree from the forced labor policies the colonial administration had used to meet its export quotas.

Furthermore, while Mono could be planted simultaneously with food crops, the CFDT/CIDT recommended intensive cultivation of Allen cotton in single crop fields. Where the conditions existed for the producers to apply the intensive techniques—where they could purchase fertilizer and equipment and supply the large labor requirements—the yields of the commercial variety of cotton would be far superior to those of the traditional variety and the returns to a day's labor would double from FCFA 100 to FCFA 200.[6] The crucial point about the introduction of Allen cotton, however, is that it was imposed in precisely those areas of the Ivory Coast where the necessary conditions *did not exist*. Research shows that the cultivation and harvesting of Allen cotton competed for labor with subsistence crops and otherwise disrupted production activity. The research reveals that calculations of returns to labor without regard to the whole pattern of labor use, simplify beyond the point of usefulness.

Studies carried out in three cotton growing areas—the Malinké Kadadougou Sofo area in the Odiéné region of northwestern Ivory Coast; the Sénoufo (Tagban) area in northern Ivory Coast, and the Agni area of Moronou in eastern Ivory Coast (Institut d'Ethno-sociologie, 1970, 1971, 1972), reveal many of the socioeconomic consequences of the introduction of Allen cotton in the 1960s. They include the risk of poor returns from cotton, the absence of improvement in the techniques and productivity of subsistence crops, the disruption of the agricultural timetable, sacrifice of food crops, the emergence of parallel trading circuits for cash crops, the lack of incentive for production in traditional exchange circuits, and finally the use of coercion by the authorities, as in colonial times, to confront peasant resistance to cotton production.

As coercion alone obviously did not represent a lasting solution to the problem, the government resorted in addition to the price mechanism. By increasing the price for Allen cotton, and as of 1969–1970, for sorted over unsorted Allen cotton, the government hoped to draw labor away from other requirements to the production of a high quality industrial crop. To this end, officially guaranteed producer price for Allen cotton that was FCFA 30 per kilogram in 1960 was raised to FCFA 33.50 in 1964. The price of sorted cotton was raised in 1969 to FCFA 35 (while unsorted was held at FCFA 33.50), and in 1970 to FCFA 40 (while unsorted dropped to FCFA 30). But whether coercion or prices were the mechanism to spread cotton production, one crucial fact remained: peasant producers exercised no control over the introduction of the new crop. Their only power against its disruptive effects was the power of refusal.

Studies of areas where resistance to growing cotton has been especially strong and where cotton growing has had particularly severe implications for traditional agriculture reveal consequences of the CFDT's cotton program that are less evident but nonetheless present in other areas of the country. These case studies help explain why after an extensive 10-year campaign, cotton production in many areas remained "unstable" and marginal to other crops. Between 1968–1969 and 1970, the national acreage planted shrunk from 48,000 hectares to 33,000 hectares, and output dropped from 42,000 to 32,000 tons. When it is realized (1) that at the end of the 1960s, in regions such as Korhogo the majority of cultivators supervised by the CFDT spent a minimum amount of time on cotton, (2) that only residual acreage not essential to food crops was made available for cotton, and (3) that returns were neither immediate nor very certain, then the official view that "climatological" and other "unaccountable" factors explain the decreases in cotton output appear particularly unsatisfactory. Rather, it is in the manner in which cotton production and marketing was organized that a good part of the explanation for the decreases lies.

NEW FORMS OF STATE INTERVENTION IN THE 1970s AND THEIR RESULTS

The drop in output and the decrease in planting reflected the response of peasant producers to the contradictions of attempts to intensify labor without any significant development of productive forces in peasant agriculture. The disappointing results were to lead to a new effort in the 1970s. While output was indeed raised, the breakthrough to expanded reproduction at the end of the 1970s was very modest. Yet the impact on productive relations was significant and merits close attention.

Big Gain in Output, Small Gain in Productivity

As of 1971, new projects were adopted and new measures taken to overcome certain obstacles to increased production of cotton, but they made no fundamental change in the system first implemented. Officially, reforms included price increases and subsidies to producers, the intensification of the means of production through the introduction of animal traction and motorized farming, and an initial attempt to better integrate cotton into the agricultural system. In order to generate and redistribute the new resources that these measures implied, two conditions were necessary: (1) the Ivorian state had to intervene more closely into cotton production, and (2) new sources of financing had to be found. To gain new sources of funding, the state has entered new alliances with foreign capital. An initial experimental "Project de diversification et de modernisation" called "Opération Riz-Coton" began in 1972. It was financed jointly by the European Development Fund and the Ivory Coast government; the EDF contribution was to be FCFA 1,310 million (including a loan of CFA 305 million) and the Ivorian counterpart was FCFA 650 million. An extension to this project that covered the period 1972–1976 brought an additional FCFA 230 million from the EDF and FCFA 510 million from the Ivorian state's BSIE. The project proposed to introduce light animal-drawn implements in the north and center-west regions, to undertake an experimental project of partial mechanization on farming "blocs," and to better integrate cotton and food crops.

The "Opération Riz-Coton" reflects changes in government policies toward rural development, notably toward land reorganization. The scattered strips that the population cultivated were to be consolidated into "blocs." While agricultural policy-makers justified the measure as a way to facilitate supplying the rural population with social amenities, the consolidation also had the affect of stabilizing production (Raven-hill, 1978: 63).

Furthermore, although the new techniques continued to be based on family holdings, they called for an increase in the size of family plots to between 2 and 5 hectares. The far-reaching implications of such changes—the growing dependence of producers on inputs and conditions of production that they do not control and the growing social differentiation that these techniques brought about—will be discussed in the final section of this chapter.

Under the highly centralized control of the cotton extension company, even the question of the distribution of land is subordinated to the objectives of the cotton programs. Land may be reallocated to new producers where those who possess it by traditional right are not considered apt for participation in new cotton extension programs (I.C. Ministry of Agriculture, CIDT, and Institut d'Ethno-sociologie, 1977: 100). If owners of the selected land refuse to turn it over voluntarily, it is confiscated without compensation (pp. 124–125).

While increases in the output of cotton were obtained over the period of "Opération Riz-Coton", from 48,528 T. in 1971–1972 to 59,939 T. in 1974–1975, it was officially recognized that the project was only partially successful:

> However, certain objectives have only been partially achieved, notably those concerning foodcrops where production has not kept pace with that of cotton. There has not been any real crop integration, as initiatives to modernize production have centred essentially on cotton [I.C. Ministry of Agriculture, 1979: 4].

Nevertheless, the success of this project in terms of its principal objective—increasing cotton output—was to lead to its generalization to all cotton-growing areas with what was called the "Five-Year Development Project for the Cotton Regions" extending from

1975–1976 to 1979–1980. The object of this project was to increase the production of cotton and food crops through improved farming techniques, wider use of fertilizers and insecticides, better rural extension services, and, in certain areas, the selective introduction of ox-drawn cultivation. Cotton growing areas were to be increased by 23,000 hectares and food crop areas by 62,000 hectares. The financing of this project was to be as follows: the Ivory Coast BSIE FCFA 1,499 million, IBRD FCFA 7,500 million and the CCCE FCFA 1,046 million for a total of FCFA 10,045 million.

The fact that the World Bank loaned $31 million to the project is significant. While this reflects a more general tendency concerning Ivorian debt financing, it suggests as well new sources of influence over the orientation of Ivorian rural development. As with all IBRD loans, the agreement set out a series of conditions that must be "satisfactory to the Bank" concerning the selection qualifications and the experience of engineering consultants; the selection of contractors; the timing of the implementation of the ox-cultivation program; the construction of wells; the criteria of distribution of subsidies; and the level of subsidies to participating cultivators; and so forth. Moreover, by the end of the decade as the country's economic difficulties became all the more apparent, the negotiations with the bank appeared to force the Ivorian government to exercise tighter control over such critical matters as pricing and subsidy policies.

During the latter half of the 1970s, however, in order to increase cotton output, the policies of the Ivorian government appear to have depended above all on price changes and subsidies to producers. In view of the relatively disappointing output of unginned cotton in 1974–75 and 1975–1976, around 60,000 T. a level only 36% higher than in 1968–1969, the government decided to introduce new price increases in 1976–1977, as it had in 1974–1975 (see Table 7.3). In 1974, to reactivate cotton production, the producer price had been raised by 56% to FCFA 70 per kilo for unginned cotton, while subsidies were provided to farmers for adopting animal traction and mechanized land clearing.

The lack of response of peasant producers to these incentives is interpreted by International Monetary Fund experts as being due at least in part to the more competitive returns from other crops— especially rice (IMF, 1975: 8). The fact that the price of first quality paddy was increased 132% in March 1974, from FCFA 28 per kg. to FCFA 65 per kg., while the price of cotton rose only 56% supports this interpretation. This increase had been decided by the government in order to counteract rapid increases in rice imports between 1968 and

1974. Moreover, in view of the much lighter labor requirements of rice cultivation, as the Five Year Plan 1976–1980 recognized, rice production was two times as profitable as that of cotton. Consequently, in spite of the increase in cotton producer prices between 1973–1974 and 1974–1975, cotton output barely increased (58,465 T. in 1973–1974 and 58,939 T. in 1974–1975).

In order to increase production, new emphasis was placed by government on policies that were bound to increase rural differentiation: subsidies were used to promote fertilizers and insecticides and, as of 1975, attempts were made to extend ox-drawn and mechanized plowing. As of 1977–1978, fertilizers were subsidised by the government. In 1979–1980, subsidies for seeds, fertilizers, and insecticides were valued at FCFA 6,000 million. The quantity of fertilizers used in the Ivory Coast in the cultivation of cotton is the highest in West Africa, one third more than in Mali and Chad and three times as high as in Senegal (Bulletin de l'Afrique Noire, 1980: 20089).

On the other hand, the attempts to replace the hand hoe have had limited impact. As may be seen from Table 3, by 1979–1980, ox-drawn equipment was used on 21,558 ha. or 17.5% of the 122,983 ha. of cotton, while mechanized equipment was used on only 8530 ha. Overall, 75.5% of cotton production remained manual. Finally, an additional increase raised producer prices to FCFA 80 and FCFA 70 for first and second quality cotton as of 1976–1977.

The large increase in output to more than 100,000 T. in 1978–1979 has been accomplished by almost doubling the area under cultivation in three years, from 64,767 ha. in 1977–1978 to 122,983 ha. in 1979–1980. Output per hectare has ceased to increase since it began to exceed 1 ton per hectare in 1973–1974. It has remained relatively stable since that time.

The new conditions of production that have been imposed on producers have inevitably made them more dependent on market forces. Selected seed varieties require massive use of fertilizers and insecticides, products whose world prices are subject to rapid increases over which producers have no control whatsoever. According to the World Bank, the price of fertilizer used in cotton production in the Ivory Coast doubled between 1972 and 1975 (Tuinder den, 1978: 413). As long as fertilizers were subsidized by the government, the vulnerability of the producer was scarcely apparent. However, in view of the increasing economic difficulties of the Ivorian state and the need to reduce the production costs of cotton, on the advice of the World Bank the Ivorian government decided to begin reducing cotton fertilizer

TABLE 7.3 The Development of Allen Cotton Production in the Ivory Coast 1971–72 to 1979–80

	—	—	1 888	1 989	2 141	2 074	2 361	2 749	2 623
Number of villages under extension services	—	—	1 888	1 989	2 141	2 074	2 361	2 749	2 623
Number of plots	61 866	66 621	68 353	69 203	78 656	71 373	90 416	93 943	97 897
Number of pairs of oxen	126	367	741	1 335	3 263	5 791	7 712	9 773	11 625
Surfaces ha.									
Manual cultivation	49 126	52 915	54 261	54 040	57 576	50 921	68 399	83 257	92 895
Animal-drawn cultivation	320	795	1 589	2 740	5 583	10 853	14 817	17 428	21 558
Mechanized cultivation	1 954	2 785	2 338	1 976	2 316	2 993	4 333	6 569	8 530
Total	51 400	56 495	58 188	58 756	65 475	64 767	87 549	107 254	122 983

Productivity of Seed Cotton (kg./ha.)									
Manual cultivation	—	945	1 014	1 024	988	1 196	1 206	1 075	1 173
Animal-drawn cultivation	—	1 031	1 110	1 083	1 104	1 062	1 142	1 185	1 315
Mechanized cultivation	—	700	727	818	854	1 009	806	720	647
Total	944	935	1 005	1 020	994	1 164	1 176	1 071	1 161
Producer price FCFA/kg. (1st and 2nd quality)	40/30	40/30	45/35	70/60	70/60	80/70	80/70	80/70	80/70
Fertilizer used (tons)	7 324	10 468	10 682	12 237	15 192	16 140	21 324	26 135	28 165
Output of seed cotton (T.)	48 528	52 798	58 465	59 939	65 038	75 413	102 929	114 886	142 975
Ginning coefficient %	40,85	40,39	39,57	39,99	40,22	40,68	40,16	40,56	41,26
Output of cotton fiber (T.)	19 743	21 356	23 138	23 931	26 245	30 733	41 406	46 7709	59 010

SOURCE: I.C. Ministry of Agriculture (1980: 126).

subsidies as of 1981–1982 and in a few years to eliminate them completely. In order to meet increasing production costs, producers will have to increase output. In the absence of more significant improvements in productivity, rising costs will inevitably favor producers who can mobilize the labor necessary to expand production.

The impact on the rural sector of the introduction of these new conditions of production will be examined in the final section of this chapter. First, however, the question of the transfer of resources between cotton growing areas and other sectors of the economy will be addressed.

Who Subsidizes Whom?

The empirical evaluation of the costs and consequences of the cotton program on the collectivity as a whole is difficult because the data available are incomplete and reflect the divergent objectives that the program is supposed to fulfill. One view claims that, although high quality cotton has been supplied to the local industry by the cotton program, it has been extremely costly to the government and to other producers, notably in the forest area (I.C. Ministry of the Economy, of Finance and the Plan and Ministry of Commerce, 1978: 12). A contrasting argument holds that the surplus revenues generated by the cotton program have in fact approximately equalled the cost of the government subsidies that have been necessary to extend production (I.C. Ministry of the Economy, of Finance and the Plan, 1980: Vol. I, 167).

Although it is true that producer prices doubled over the period 1972–1973 to 1980–1981, certain internal costs set exclusively by the CIDT increased far more rapidly over the same period. Ginning and financial charges for ginning in 1980–1981 increased 267% as compared to the 1972–1973 charge. For banking interest the increase was 446%; for handling and storage, 353%; and for transit costs and port taxes, 297%.

Documents of the Ministère d'Etat Chargé de la Réforme des Sociétés d'Etat reveal the arbitrary way in which certain items in the cotton budget are established (I.C. Ministry of State in Charge of the Reform of Public Corporations, 1980a: 2; 1980b).

The declared costs of the CIDT are particularly important as it is on them and the world price of cotton that the stabilization operation of the Caisse is based. The actual sale of Ivorian cotton (together with cotton from Mali and Upper Volta) on the world market is not the responsibility of the Caisse, but remains under the control of the French company, the CFDT, through its representative in Abidjan. This arrangement significantly limits the control of the Caisse over the returns from sales.

Finally, Ivorian cotton is sold officially to local industrialists at international prices minus transport costs saved. In fact, since 1973–1974, the government has subsidized local industry at the rate of FCFA 75 per kilogram of cotton. The annual subsidy over the period of operation has been increased steeply from FCFA 366 million in 1974–1975 to FCFA 1,268 million in 1978–1979. Since this subsidy can in no way be considered an aspect of the productive costs of cotton, it is difficult to see how its inclusion in the cotton accounts is justified.

Government sources present an overall picture of systematic subsidy to the cotton operations reflected in a continuing negative balance in the cotton account of the Caisse. For example, according to the former Minister of Agriculture, Abdoulaye Sawadogo, the cotton account registered an annual deficit of approximately FCFA 500 million until 1973, and cotton producers were subsidized through the surpluses from coffee, cocoa, and palm oil (Sawadogo, 1977: 137). Significantly, this interpretation does not accord with the figures of the 1974 study undertaken by a World Bank mission, which suggest that, while there was a deficit 1964–1965 through 1966–1967, the cotton account remained positive from 1967–1968 through to 1972–1973, to produce a total surplus of FCFA 1,586 million (IBRD 1974). Nor does it find support in the IMF study, which quotes the Caisse as its source and which confirms a positive cotton account from 1972–1973 through 1974–1975, with a deficit beginning in 1975–1976 (IMF, 1975: 65). Even Ivorian Ministry of Agriculture sources suggest a surplus in 1973, and 1974, a deficit in 1975, a surplus in 1976 and a deficit again in 1977–1978–1979 (I.C. Ministry of Agriculture, 1979: 21). Various other Ivorian sources confirm that the cotton account of the Caisse has been negative since 1977–1978 through 1980–1981. The official explanation remains the same: subsidies to producers, in view of the social character of cotton production.

There can be no doubt that the gradual doubling of prices to producers over the period 1969–1970 to 1979–1980, and the distribution of subsidized fertilizers as of 1977–1978 has substantially increased costs to the government. However, the fact that the operating costs of the CIDT have also been increasing, and at a faster rate than have price increases to producers, suggests that the deficit subsidizes the CIDT more than it does the producer. Moreover, whereas the subsidization of fertilizers has been presented as a measure of national solidarity towards the poorer northern regions, nothing is said concerning the subsidy to industry (mentioned above) begun in 1973–1974 and charged to the cotton account of the Caisse.

The quantitative evaluation of the transfer of surplus that results from the activities of the CIDT and of the Caisse, clearly reveals the continuation of a pattern of highly centralized control by the CIDT. This is reflected in the nature of its accounts, in its silent subsidy to industry and in its capacity to transfer increasing costs to peasant producers.

THE IMPACT ON PRODUCTIVE RELATIONS IN THE RURAL SECTOR

During the 1970s, the social, economic, and political consequences of the extension of cotton production were considerable. The greatly increased and rationalized central control over the production process was accompanied by the neglect and decline of food crops, a loss of food autonomy, more work for women, and new lines of social differentiation.

In this section, as throughout the chapter, our focus is on the policies and hence the logic of accumulation of the CFDT/CIDT as reinforced by the Ivory Coast state. Consequently, the analysis of the impact of these policies on changes in the rural sector will be undertaken solely in terms of this external logic, rather than in terms of specific qualities of the rural communities concerned. It is important to underline the limitations of this perspective: it attempts to understand changes in the rural sector, and the evolution of social relations of production only in terms of *labor relations*. It does not attempt the much more global analysis that would be necessary to identify the central and active role of ideological, social, and political factors in rural change.

The expansion of cotton production in the 1970s has been the result of a rapid, nearly four-fold, increase in land area cultivated. The increase from 35,868 ha. in 1970–1971 to 122,983 ha. in 1979–1980 was accompanied by an increase in output from 29,316 tons in 1970–1971 to 142,975 in 1979–1980. The rapid extension of the area devoted to cotton has in fact had severe ecological consequences, notably in the destruction of much forest (Ravenhill, 1978: 63–64). In more densely populated areas of the north, the pressure on the land resulting from the extensions of cotton production, has resulted in less frequent and shorter fallow periods for land, a change that may lead to soil exhaustion. Shortage of land has also been recognized as a cause of rural migration out of the area (I.C. Ministry of Agriculture, 1981b: 137).

Very much less attention has been paid to the fact that in order to achieve this output, tremendous increases in labor time had to be forthcoming. The following presentation will show (1) how techniques have increased labor requirements; (2) how these new requirements have been met; and (3) how meeting the increased labor requirements has affected social relations of production.

Increased Labor Requirements

As noted above, as compared to the former traditional Mono cotton that was intercropped and cultivated by women, the introduction of Allen cotton at the beginning of the 1960s increased labor requirements per hectare and brought important changes in the organization of family labor.

The introduction of new techniques of cotton cultivation in the 1970s such as ox-drawn or mechanized plowing, further increased labor requirements. The 1974 preliminary study of the cotton program by the IBRD describes these changes in terms of "increasing productive family employment opportunities," from a range of 260 to 320 worker days per year to about 465 worker days, a rise of 60%. In the perspective of the report, which follows most conventional analysis in assuming high rural unemployment, the additional labor would be rewarded by increasing productivity which would

> also about triple the return per manday from about CFAF 220 (US $0.90) to between CFAF 525 and CFAC 625 (US $2.20). These returns to family labor compare favourably with the prevailing wage rate in the project area of CFAF 200 [IBRD, 1974: 24].

Since at the time there was little alternative source of money income in the project area, the report (p. 24) reasons that "these benefits would provide farmers a strong incentive to participate in the project." There is, however, no detailed discussion in the study of the ways in which such increases in labor are to be met.

Although labor requirements vary with regional characteristics and most significantly with techniques (whether manual, animal traction, or mechanized), certain considerations remain constant. The first is that in cotton production, labor requirements are particularly heavy for certain operations and especially exacting for operations that must be performed in a short amount of time. In evaluating labor requirements, cotton production may be described on the basis of nine operations: clearing, burning, ridging, sowing, transplanting, spreading fertilizers, weeding, applying insecticide, and harvesting. It is particularly significant to see how new techniques release time from or add time to such operations.

It is estimated by one study that the average yearly labor requirement for cotton production in 1978 (when 76% of the cotton land was cultivated manually) was approximately 200 days per hectare (Ravenhill, 1978: 73). The most exacting operation is that of harvesting. One study undertaken in northern Ivory Coast in 1977 estimated that harvesting one hectare of cotton required 320 hours (Savignac, 1979: 33). Harvesting represents approximately 40% of labor time devoted to this crop. As production is extended, the labor required for this operation will obviously increase proportionately, accentuating the already extreme unevenness of distribution of labor demand across the season. The rigid timetable imposed by the CIDT in the collection of cotton has increased the number of laborers required for certain operations more than proportionately to output. And some of the new techniques introduced have the same effect (Ravenhill, 1978: 73).

Meeting the New Labor Requirements

The increased labor requirements have had numerous important implications. For it is access to abundant and readily available labor, whether family or salaried, which determines which peasant producers can adopt the new techniques (I.C. Ministry of Agriculture, CIDT, Institut d'Ethno-sociologie, 1977: 85).

Increasing the Labor Time of Women

When cotton became a cash crop, managing its production became the exclusive privilege of men. However, increases in output have significantly increased the labor time of women. Not only has the extension of the crop increased labor required at the time of the harvest, it has given women new and supplementary tasks, such as the uprooting of old cotton plants during the months of January, February or March (Savignac, 1979: 26):

> The new techniques which have been adopted at present by the Sénoufo peasants bring improvements to only certain types of heavy tasks accomplished by men. Nothing so far has been done to lessen

simultaneously jobs such as weeding, transplanting, or domestic tasks which are accomplished by women (Savignac, 1979: 36).

Women have less time to produce goods that in the past provided them with a small personal revenue (such as making "karité" butter or tobacco powder). These changes suggest diminishing autonomy of women and their increasing subordination to and dependence on men.

Implications for Collective Labor Services

In the past, when labor requirements were heaviest, such as at the harvest, a group of planters formed an informal "association" to undertake the task collectively. The harvest would be done by all for each individual producer, providing each member with the benefit of numerous helpers to harvest his crop. This traditional reciprocal labor arrangement on a collective basis works well if labor needs are roughly equal for all heads of concessions.

However, the introduction of more intensive techniques and the resulting uneven extension of land holdings, make it impossible for all planters to benefit equally from the principle of mutual help. Consequently, when a producer needs extra labor to harvest his cotton, increasingly he must hire wage labor by the day, a solution which brings important changes in the meaning and practice of collective help (Savignac, 1979: 25).

Similar results follow the introduction of animal-drawn plowing. Because only a very few producers have the equipment, plowing services are rented out. Not only does the new technique contribute to growing social differentiation, a point to which we shall return, but it implies redefinition of social relations of production.

> The soil gradually loses its foremost significance as the provider of food and takes on a mercantile value as the means by which to produce cash crops. . . . As a result, the traditional notion of labor is challenged, as are the values on which rest the organisation of society (initiation, dependance on the aged . . .) [Savignac, 1979: 30].

Drawing Labor Away from Other Crops —Notably, Food Crops

In the 1970s, improved and intensified techniques have been applied almost exclusively to cotton and have ignored food crops, creating a hierarchy of products, differences in productivity, conflicts in the agricultural timetables, and competition between crops for labor time.

This is true whether cotton projects involved animal traction or mechanization. The study of the Wan area of northern Ivory Coast (Ravenhill, 1978: 78), that of the Sénoufo region of Odoro undertaken in 1977, and the study by Xavier Le Roy undertaken in the Boundiali area referred to by Savignac (1977: 28), all substantiate this conflict. It becomes all the more evident with the continuing intensification of techniques, notably the creation of "blocs culturaux" for the purpose of mechanization. The study undertaken in the Mankono area identified the conflict between the traditional food crop, yams, and cotton:

> It is in April and May that peasants normally cultivate yams. However, these are precisely the same months during which peasants are called upon by the CIDT to weed the consolidated cotton plots [IC Ministry of Agriculture, CIDT, Institut d'Ethno-sociologie, 1977: 90].

One of the most serious consequences of labor constraints is the shrinking of time devoted to weeding food crops, which often leads to a drop in their output. The study of the Bagoué region notes that in 1975 weeding of cotton was two and a half times more frequent than weeding of food crops. The same source concluded that if more time was not devoted to weeding food crops their output would inevitably drop (Peltre-Wurtz and Steck, 1979: 404).

In the study undertaken in the Bagoué region on the impact of the introduction of animal traction, it was noted in 1975 that the area in cotton increased to the detriment of food crops. Whereas cotton increased per peasant from an average of 0.40 hectares in 1974 to 0.54 in 1975, traditional food crops decreased from 0.74 ha. in 1974 to 0.54 ha. in 1975, and purchases of corn and rice increased in 1977 and 1978 (Peltre-Wurtz and Steck, 1979: 404). In the study undertaken in 1977 in the Sénoufo area of Odoro, the conflictual choice between food crops and cotton was recognized by peasant producers themselves:

> We cannot stop producing cotton because we need the money; but we cannot produce less food because we need to eat [Savignac, 1977: 26].

Since the 1970s, policies have, at least officially, emphasized the integration of cotton and rice production. The viability of rice production was underlined in the 1976–1980 Development Plan. When the plan was written, the producer price of cotton was FCFA 69 per kg. and the return to labor for manual cultivation was only FCFA 300 per day, whereas during the same period, the producer price of rice permitted a return to labor twice as high (I.C. Ministry of the Plan, 1977: Vol. II: 251).

The study of the Bagoué region noted that in 1978 irrigated rice could be nearly as profitable a cash crop as cotton and bring a return of FCFA 500 per day to labor, as opposed to FCFA 600 for cotton, if in both cases fertilizers were supplied free of charge (Peltre-Wurtz and Steck, 1979: 406). However, in practice, there were several difficulties that prevented rice from becoming an alternative to cotton. The first was the fact that the market for rice had not been developed in the Bagoué region. Second, and more fundamentally, it appears that given the present organization of techniques of cultivation labor demands are so heavy that they cannot be met. Cotton producers are unable to field enough family labor to do all the necessary work and they lack the cash resources to employ wage labor. It is the labor situation that is the principal reason for the decrease in the area devoted to irrigated rice according to the Bagoué study (Peltre-Wurtz and Steck, 1979: 399). Official reports that in the past denied the fact that the decrease in food crops might be attributable to the very rapid expansion of cotton, have come to recognize the possibility of competition between rice and cotton as a source of monetary revenue (I.C. Ministry of Agriculture, 1981b: 102). The same report notes that rice production has decreased since 1975 (I.C. Ministry of Agriculture, 1981b: 101).

The third aspect influencing the decision of peasant producers is the fluctuation of purchase prices to producers for the various cash crops on which they depend for their monetary revenue. In spite of the decreasing output and resulting costly increases in rice imports — rice imports increased from 1,636 tons in 1975 to 242,441 tons in 1980 (I.C. Ministry of Agriculture, 1980b: 66) — the Ivorian government decided in 1980 to *lower* the producer price of rice at collection centers from FCFA 70 per kilo to FCFA 50 per kilo (I.C. Ministry of Agriculture, 1980b: 63). The decrease and the dissolution of the Soderiz in 1977 are recognized officially as the reasons for the substitution of cotton for rice as a source of monetary revenue (I.C. Ministry of Agriculture, 1981b: 140).[7]

It would be difficult to establish on the basis of available information to what extent the conversion from one crop to another was a projected and well-defined objective. We can only note that the result of pricing policy over this period is the growing dependence of the rural areas such as those described, on market relations not only for the sale of cotton, but also for the purchase of foodstuffs.

The constraints on labor time in cotton-producing areas that have forced a redefinition of productive relations in the family unit, at the village level and between regions, are in fact a reflection of the hardening of the conditions of production imposed by the logic of accumulation of the local textile industry.

More Pressures on Producers

Although it is not possible to enter into the details of this process here, the initial, very protected, and costly import-substitution phase of Ivorian industrialization has resulted in an industrial structure that depends on continued protection and subsidization. Unable to compete in international markets (such as those of the EEC), unable to export to neighboring countries where similar subsidiaries of the same parent companies also have surplus capacity, and unable to compete on the local market (which explains the very high proportion of contraband textiles evaluated officially at FCFA 9 billion in 1980), local industry is no longer able to expand. Consequently, it will not be in a position to absorb increasing quantities of locally grown cotton. Already in 1980, of the 59,000 tons of ginned cotton, 41,000 tons were exported and only 8,000 tons or 30% were used by local industry. Much less emphasis is being placed on future increases in cotton production. On the contrary, official documents speak of a leveling off of production and greater emphasis on the reduction of the costs of production:

> The objective of stabilising production should be achieved simultaneously with the partial assumption of the cost of inputs by the peasant, and the doing away with the subsidy paid by the CIDT. The subsidy should be replaced by a bonus on the productivity per supervised hectare, which would apply on output over and beyond the present average output of 1.13 tons per hectare [I.C. Ministry of State in Charge of the Reform of Public Corporations, 1980b: 2].

As long as there remain alternatives that permit producers to opt out and produce alternate crops, the subordination of producers to a single market price is to some extent mitigated. Also, under more flexible circumstances, producers may prefer not to enter into new schemes. This remained a possibility at the time of the Mankono project when certain villages refused to be integrated into the Guma (Groupement d'Utilisation du Matériel Agricole) mechanization program. Because some of the producers integrated into the motorized consolidated plots decided to withdraw, wariness developed and in some regions, notably in the Faraba area, villages refused en masse to be involved in an eventual project of the same sort which was intended for their area.[8] However, there appears to be a combination of factors including pressures created by land and labor constraints that will increasingly limit the options for most producers and accentuate the patterns of rural differentiation that are already becoming apparent.

In this regard the study of Bagoué in the 1970s showed that having extra family labor for cotton production reinforced the economic position of heads of families: they received four-fifths of the cotton revenue. It does not appear, however, that these producers will form the basis of a new socially and economically dominant rural group. For one thing, the heads of large families do not invest in sufficiently profitable areas to become independent of their family labor. For another, their relation to family labor and their capacity to extract labor services is necessarily unstable and dependent on marriage and other fluctuating family relations; it does not have the predictability and control of strictly defined wage relations in which labor is seen as a commodity. It is more likely that these heads of families will lose some of their power while other younger families will become more economically powerful on the basis of new productive relations.

Rural extension programs in cotton growing areas have as a basic and recurrent principle: "To train young peasants and especially selected cultivators in order that they may become individual agents— dynamic elements—at the village level and in the training centres created in each zone" (I.C. Ministry of Agriculture, 1981d: 5). The criteria on which the new group of modern cotton producers are to be selected include their ability to assume the increasing proportion of production costs that is being transferred to producers, such as the cost of fertilizers. To this end, their capacity to increase output, to hire wage labor, to mechanize, and to meet credit requirements is assessed (I.C. Ministry of Agriculture, 1979: 22).

The orientation of future credit policies and principles determining the distribution of credit in the rural sector merit special attention:

> Increases in credit will be linked to increases in agricultural revenue, and in particular to monetary revenue which permits the reimbursement of loans. Credit operations will be applied, therefore, to production programmes which increase the monetary revenue of planters and for the encouragement of crops which are assured market outlets and high prices [I.C. Ministry of Agriculture, 1981c: 15].

While perfectly in keeping with profitable credit operations, for at least two reasons the above orientation will reinforce rather than redefine existing inequalities in the cotton growing areas. First, credit policies are oriented to the more privileged groups of producers as the criterion for obtaining credit is the capacity to reimburse it. Second, given the present lack of sales outlets for food crops, it is not to those crops but to cash crop activities that credit will be made available, in spite of the urgent need that credit serve as well for improving cultivation techniques of food crops.

The gradual emergence in the northern savannah and central cotton growing areas of a new wealthier group of producers using intensified techniques and requiring larger and larger quantities of hired labor is not in doubt. New techniques of production such as ox-drawn and mechanized plowing will gradually raise labor productivity. Consequently, a new pattern of labor relations, stabilized through the emergence of wealthier producers, will permit a greater proportion of production costs to be assumed by the rural sector.

While those responsible for agricultural policies may have to accommodate certain demands of the wealthier group of producers, their emergence has not resulted from or implied a redefinition of the past orientation of agricultural change. On the contrary, the very existence of this wealthier group and their reinforcement depends on the continuation of a particular organization of production—one with increasingly centralized techniques of production and marketing—over which the wealthier group of producers itself has no control. However, if in the short term the emergence of a group of wealthier producers stabilizes relations of production and increases the value of surplus created, the conditions and techniques of production introduced to this end will accentuate social differences and contradictions both within the cotton growing areas themselves and between these areas and other sectors of the economy.

NOTES

1. In 1980, the Ivory Coast had a population of 8.3 million of which approximately 2.5 million were non-Ivorian. With a land area of 322,000 square kilometers, population density averages 25.8 people per square kilometer. In 1979, coffee and cocoa exports continued to represent 58% of the total value of Ivorian exports (I.C. Ministry of Agriculture, 1980b: 171), and these two crops assured the livelihood of approximately 400,000 peasant producers.

2. A less frequently emphasized aspect of the cotton variety selected by the Institut de Recherches des Cotons et Textiles for European industrial purposes is the fact that the length of the staple developed could not be used by traditional weavers (Cinétique, 1972: 13).

3. The $150 million IBRD loan announced December 1, 1981 for a program of structural readjustment of the Ivorian economy brought World Bank total lending to the country to $906 million (Fraternité Matin, 1981: December 2).

4. A detailed discussion of the development of cotton production in the Ivory Coast is provided in Chapter VII, "Post Colonial Change in Agriculture. Cotton Production in the Ivory Coast, 1960-1970" (Campbell, 1974: 244–302).

5. To the above costs must be added approximately FCFA 30 million per year for the agricultural extension work of IRCT. It is significant that in spite of the extensive public support extended to the CFDT since 1960 and particularly since 1966, when research on this period was conducted in 1972, it was impossible to find complete accounts for the outlays in favor of cotton production in any of the Ivorian ministries concerned. Certain estimates are available from the CFDT, but these are neither consistent nor complete.

6. The figures presented here correspond with subsequent estimates that suggest a daily monetary return of FCFA 215 for the family cultivation of 1.1 tons/ha. of Allen cotton (I.C. Ministry of the Plan, 1970: 166).

7. For an analysis of the contradictory objectives pursued by SODERIZ and the reasons for its dissolution in 1977, see Dozon (1979: 37–58).

8. One must interpret the attitudes of peasants towards "blocs motorisés" with care because the same study suggests that 61.92% of those interviewed said they wanted such a scheme because they thought it would overcome labor shortages in plowing and planting operations (I.C. Ministry of Agriculture, CIDT, Institut d'Ethno-sociologie, 1977: 118).

REFERENCES

ATEMENGUE, J. (1966) "Des avantages concrets tirés de la coopération franco-africaine." Les Cahiers de l'Afrique, Etudes et Documents, Vol. II., Paris.

Bulletin de l'Afrique Noire (1980) March 19, No. 1041: 20089.

Caisse de Stabilisation et de Soutien des Prix Agricoles, Information Service (1970) "Quinze années bien remplies au service du pays." Abidjan, Guy Delaporte, Chef du Service des Produits de Marchés Tropicaux et méditerannéens.

CAMPBELL, B. (1974) "The social, political and economic consequences of French private investment in the Ivory Coast 1960-1970." Unpublished Ph.D. dissertation, University of Sussex.

Cinéthique (1972) "Enquête pour un film contre l'impérialisme français: l'impérialisme français au Tchad." 4e trimestre, No. 15, Paris.

Compagnie française pour le Développement des Fibres Textiles, Côte d'Ivoire (1972) Annexe au Rapport annuel 1970-1971.

DESVEAUX, E. (1978) "Goripla, Kouatta: une étude comparative de deux villages en pays Wan, Côte d'Ivoire." Unpublished dissertation, Institut de Géographie, Université de Paris, VIII, Vincennes.

DOZON, J.-P. (1979) "Impasses et contradictions d'une société de développement: l'exemple de l'opération 'riziculture irriguée' en Côte d'Ivoire," Cahiers *ORSTOM* Série Sciences Humaines, Vol. XVI, nos. 1 and 2: 37-58.

Fraternité Matin (1981) December 2, Abidjan.

Institut d'Ethno-sociologie (1970, 1971, 1972) Opinions et attitudes des paysans et ouvriers ivoiriens face au développement. University of Abidjan.

IBRD (1974) Appraisal of Cotton Areas Rural Development Project, Ivory Coast, Report No. 606, I.V.C., December 30, Washington, DC.

——— (1970) Economic Growth and Prospects of the Ivory Coast, Agricultural Development, Vol. 2., July 24, Washington, DC.

IMF (1975) Ivory Coast: Recent Economic Developments. April 15.

I.C. Ministry of Agriculture (1981a) Compagnie ivoirienne pour le Développement des Textiles. Rapport Annuel d'Activités, Campagne 1979–1980, Abidjan.

——— (1981b) Projet de Développement Agricole Intégré de la Région Nord, Bilan Diagnostic. Bureau d'Etudes Techniques des Projets Agricoles, January, Abidjan.

——— (1981c) Note d'orientation pour l'identification des projets de développement intégré du Nord et Nord Ouest. February, Bouaké.

——— (1981d) Organisation et Gestion du Développement, Commission 2, Mission d'Identification, Projet Nord et Nord Ouest, March 12, Bouaké.

——— (1980a) Compagnie ivoirienne pour le Développement des Textiles, Rapport Annuel d'Activités, Campagne 1978-1979, Abidjan.

——— (1980b) Statistiques agricoles. Direction des Statistiques Rurales et des Enquêtes agricoles, Abidjan.

——— (1979) Préparation du bilan agricole des 20 années d'indépendance. Direction de la Planification, de la Budgétisation et du Contrôle de gestion, June, Abidjan.

——— (1969) Développement de la production cotonnière en Côte d'Ivoire, Vols. 1 and 2, January, Abidjan.

——— CIDT and Institut d'Ethno-sociologie (1977) Attitudes et comportement d'un groupe de paysans de la région de Mankono face à la mécanisation de l'agriculture. Exemple de Guma, Abidjan.

I.C. Ministry of the Economy, of Finance and the Plan and Ministry of Commerce (1980). L'industrialisation des Régions en Côte d'Ivoire, Direction Générale de l'Economie. Direction du Développement Régional, 2 Vols., May, Abidjan.

——— (1978) Memorandum Textile pour la Communauté Economique Européenne. December, Abidjan.

I.C. Ministry of Finance, Economic Affairs and the Plan (1968) Supplément Trimestriel au Bulletin Mensuel de Statistiques, Etudes et Rapports. Direction de la Statistique, 10 Vol. No. 1, Abidjan.

I.C. Ministry of the Plan (1977) Plan Quinquennal de Développement économique, social et culturel 1976-1980, 3 Vols., Abidjan.

——— (1970) Deuxième Esquisse du Plan Quinquennal de Développement 1971–1975, June, Abidjan.

——— (1968) Travaux Préparatoires au Plan 1971-1975. Objectifs de Production Agricole, Le Coton, Report no. 63, January, Abidjan.

I.C. Ministry of State in Charge of the Reform of Public Corporations (1980a) Structures des prix des produits cotonniers. April, Abidjan.

——— (1980b) Rapport du Groupe de Travail " Bilan Financier." Commission ad hoc chargée des problèmes de structure de la CIDT Abidjan.

————— (1980c) Rapport du Groupe de Travail "Bilan Financier," Commission ad hoc chargée des problèmes de structures de la CIDT, June 12, Abidjan.

PELTRE-WURTZ, J. and B. STECK (1979). Influence d'une société de développement sur le milieu paysan. Coton et culture attelée dans la région de la Bagoué (Nord Côte d'Ivoire). ORSTOM and CIDT, Abidjan.

RAVENHILL, P. (1978) L'économie d'auto-subsistance Wan face au développement cotonnier. Institut d'Ethno-sociologie, Université d'Abidjan, Ministère de l'Agriculture and CIDT.

Société d'Etudes pour le Développement économique et social (1965) Région de Korhogo, Study prepared for the Ivorian Ministry of Finance, Economic Affairs and the Plan. Rapport de Synthèse.

SAVIGNAC, C. (1979) "Approche des conditions de travail en agriculture dans le nord de la Côte d'Ivoire" Cahiers ivoiriens de recherche économique et sociale 22, September, Abidjan.

SAWADOGO, A. (1977) L'Agriculture en Côte d'Ivoire. Paris: Presses Universitaires de France.

8

STATE AND AGRARIAN TRANSFORMATION IN NIGERIA

MICHAEL WATTS and ROBERT SHENTON

The dimensions of the current crisis of agricultural production in Nigeria are depressingly well documented. Once a major agricultural goods exporter, Nigeria has now become an importer of such commodities on a grand scale. Of Nigeria's former agricultural exports, groundnuts, palm oil, and rubber have more or less disappeared completely, while exports of cocoa and palm kernels have fallen dramatically (Table 8.1). At the same time, real food output per capita has probably fallen by 1.5% per annum (1970–1978). Simultaneously, food imports have grown dramatically (Table 8.2). While in 1965 Nigeria's food import bill amounted to N 46.4 million, by 1978 it stood at N 790 million. In 1980 alone, the federal government spent N 1.5 billion on imported cereals, which constituted roughly 15% of the gross calorie supply of the nation. According to the recent "green revolution" strategy published by the federal government (1980), the continuation of current trends will result in a staggering 5.2 million ton food deficit by the year 1985. In order to close this gap, the domestic food sector would have required an equally astonishing 11% per annum growth rate between 1981 and 1985.

How is this dismal state of affairs to be comprehended? Is it simply a reflection of Nigeria's rapidly growing petroleum revenues? Although it is clear that the specific factors of Nigeria's agrarian dilemma are

TABLE 8.1 Agricultural Exports 1972-1977

Commodity	('000 tons)							
	1972	1973	1974	1975	1976	1977	1978	1979
Groundnuts, decorticat- ed	106	199	30	—	—	8	—	—
Cocoa, raw	228	211	180	202	231	165	205	125
Palm kernels	212	137	185	173	257	169	63	72
Palm oil	2	—	—	—	—	—	—	—
Cotton, raw	1	8	—	—	—	9	8	25
Rubber	41	49	59	57	39	18	29	—

SOURCE: Quarterly Economic Review of Nigeria (1981).

TABLE 8.2 Food Imports 1970–1977

Year	Total Food Imports (N millions)	% of Total	Wheat Quantity[a]	Wheat Value[b]	Rice Quantity	Rice Value	Barley Quantity	Barley Value	Maize Quantity[c]	Maize Value	Fish Quantity	Fish Value	Meat Quantity	Meat Value
1964–1966	46.4	8.8	55.6	7.6	1.2	0.2	no	data	no	data	34.3	14.3	0.5	0.3
1970	57.7	7.6	258.7	15.4	1.7	0.1	no	data	no	data	6.6	2.9		
1972	95.1	9.6	296.7	22.0	5.8	1.0	no	data	no	data	20.8	5.3		
1974	154.8	8.9	318.3	50.7	4.8	1.4	9.7	0.009	20,171	0.6	14.7	7.4	0.4	0.3
1977	790.3	10.9	720.0	96.0	413.0	155.0	94.9	0.04	2,440	3.4	100.0	71.0	23.0	21.6

SOURCE: Forrest (1981) Federal Office of Statistics.

a. In '000's of metric tons.
b. N million.
c. In '000's of Kg's.

inextricably linked to the rapid growth of the oil economy, it would be specious to assign to it *the* central place in any analytical schema. Perhaps the most important reason for doing so lies in the recognition that Nigeria is not alone in its difficulties (World Bank, 1981a). Not only have agrarian troubles beset Nigeria, but severe crises also confront Ghana, Sudan, Tanzania, and Uganda; that is to say, for the losers as well as the beneficiaries of the oil price hikes of the 1970s. All are now in great difficulties regarding their export production and all have become less and less able to adequately feed their populations. In relation to the genesis of a crisis in agricultural production, then, the presence or absence of oil revenues cannot be attributed a causal significance. In order to understand the origins and evolution of Nigeria's agricultural malaise, we must begin our search elsewhere.

CAPITALISM AND AGRICULTURE

Historically, the relationship between capitalism and agriculture has been both pivotal and contradictory. Thus, while it is certainly true that the transformation of the conditions and relations of agricultural production in Western Europe were of determinant importance in the genesis of capitalism, it is equally true that the highly differentiated and incomplete nature of this transformation—even in the North American heartland of "advanced capitalism"—has been an important obstacle to the expanded reproduction of capital.

The essence of this obstacle has been the failure to fully "industrialize" agriculture. As Mann and Dickenson (1978) have convincingly argued, in agricultural endeavours, production is intimately linked to natural forces over which capital's control has so far been limited; indeed, the duration needed to produce a commodity is greatly in excess of the time that labor is actively engaged in its production. Moreover, for similar reasons, the turnover time of capital in agriculture tends to be greater than in industrial production proper. The result is that average costs of production are likely to be higher than in industry and the average rate of profit lower. Yet, because of the existence of private property in land—itself a prerequisite for the process of primitive accumulation—landlords, in the absence of competition, would be virtually guaranteed that a portion of the surplus value created in industry would be appropriated by them in the form of groundrent by virtue of their monopoly position.

This transfer of surplus value could occur in two ways. First, food, the most crucial wage good, was likely to be highly priced, resulting in turn in a possible increase in the portion of the working day needed for labor to reproduce itself. Second, raw materials for various industrial processes produced by the agricultural sector were likely to be highly priced as well, resulting in a possible increase in the constant capital necessary for the production of industrial commodities.

In reality, both of these obstacles were met by British industrial capitalism and both partially overcome by the breaking of the "natural" monopoly of landed property and the consequent lowering of ground-rent. This was done through the expansion of the sources of production to include areas of the world in which the process of the commoditization of land and/or labor was either incomplete or in which it had hardly begun.

Although this process already had in part begun as one aspect of the primary accumulation of capital itself (principally with sugar and later cotton which were exported to England from hitherto unbroken lands) the development of capital's control of grain, however, remained blocked until the abolition of the corn laws in the 1840s. The aftermath of the abolition witnessed the expansion of the sources of grain supplies and in so doing broke the back of English landlordism. The result for capital as a whole was a shift in the dominant form of the extraction of surplus value.

ABSOLUTE AND RELATIVE SURPLUS VALUE AND THE MAKING OF THE COLONIAL STATE IN NIGERIA

The period immediately following the abolition of the corn laws in England also saw a change in the characteristic mode of capitalist exploitation from a regime based upon the extraction of absolute surplus value to one dominated by the extraction of relative surplus value. While this change has often been seen as the result of the increased productivity of the wage goods sector, equally important was the opening up of new, unmonopolized and only partially commoditized sources of food and raw materials.

Although this change in the dominant form of capitalist accumulation was of decisive importance for capital, it did not happen automatically as the unfolding of some immutable law. Rather, it resulted from the competition among industrial capitalists, between industrial capitalists and landlords, and between capitalists as a group and the working class. The political complexities of this process need not detain us here. It suffices to say that working class pressures both for a higher level of subsistence *and* for a shorter working day, in conjunction with the intensified competition among industrial capitalists, were of decisive importance in expanding the sources of food and raw materials supplies.

The abolition of the slave trade and of slavery itself in Britain's colonies was part and parcel of this process. Like their landlord counterparts in Britain, the plantation owners of the West Indies came to enjoy a monopoly position in the marketing of one agricultural commodity—in this case, sugar. The abolition of the slave trade was largely an attack on this monopoly. Cheaper sources of supply were potentially available but largely forbidden. The attack on slavery and slavetrading was the counterpart of the attack on landlordism at home.

For what was eventually to become Nigeria, both the attack on slavery and the rise of *relative surplus value* as the dominant form of surplus extraction were especially significant. For, while abolition gradually deprived African coastal middlemen of what had hitherto been their most profitable and marketable commodity—slaves—the rise of *relative surplus value* as the dominant form of appropriation offered them an expanding market for the sale of foodstuffs and raw materials. This change heralded the arrival of capitalism as an historic force which was not only to begin to penetrate the very essence of the rural economy but also was to bring Nigeria itself into existence.

The acquisition of Nigeria as a British colony was for British capitalism as a whole a reluctant endeavor. As had been well recognized throughout the nineteenth century, the conquest and administration of colonies was an expensive proposition. Thus, it was only when British capitalism was faced with the foreclosure of real and potential supply areas of raw materials and wage goods that action was taken.

Colonial parsimony reflected the reality that the expenses of conquest and administration in relation to political demands in Africa, represented in part a deduction from capitalist profits as a whole. The attitude of the Imperial state was in turn reflected in the basic tenet of Imperial rule in Nigeria. The expenses of conquest and administration were to be minimized, and hence there were to be no changes in the indigenous society that might lead to expensive colonial wars and civil disobedience. In particular, this trajectory in conjunction with the historic local dominance of merchants' capital was to operate in such a manner as to block the direct intervention of industrial capital in agricultural production (Shenton, 1984). The main barrier to such interventions was colonial laws which barred the alienation of land to non-indigenes and which also limited the development of legally recognized private property in land of indigenes as well. Thus, the bases of smallholding agricultural production in Nigeria were established. The continued existence of smallholding production was at one level functional for the colonial state. Smallholder production required no dramatic or expensive changes in social or political organization. Moreover, smallholder production could be taxed through indirect means by duties on imports and exports and with the exception of Northern Nigeria until 1914, such indirect levies became the overwhelming source of colonial state finance. As a result, there was virtually no direct intervention in agricultural production per se (Forrest, 1981).

By the 1920s, the contradictions inherent in this situation had already become clear, especially during the boom and bust following World War I. The primary contradiction centered around the fact that while the financial existence of the colonial state depended almost entirely on the production of agricultural commodities, neither the mandarins of the colonial state nor British merchants exercised any direct control over the means, conditions, or relations of such production. The principal axis of colonial political economy was that of labor control; the measure of peasant autonomy conferred by indirect rule simply meant that, from the state perspective, commodities did not always appear in the right place, in the right amount, at the right time.

THE FISCAL CRISIS OF THE COLONIAL STATE AND THE ORIGINS OF DEVELOPMENT

The global capitalist crisis of the Great Depression exposed the contradictory position of the colonial state. As primary goods prices fell, so the fiscal basis of the state was eroded. Yet, the state lacked any instrument, aside from the crude use of high levels of direct taxation in the north, to intervene directly in production. The concentration, centralization, and real subsumption of merchant by industrial capital associated with the depression further heightened the crisis by lowering prices still further. Reeling from the erosion of state revenue, colonial officials initially feared that smallholder producers would cease production altogether.

By this point, however, European manufacturers had become so imbedded in the circuit of simple household reproduction that, rather than withdraw, smallholders actually *increased* their output to compensate for the fall in prices. The response to the crisis was not to be withdrawal but political opposition.

The primary source of this opposition initially arose from the ranks of indigenous merchant capitalists who had been first subsumed and then increasingly squeezed by the process of the concentration and centralization of European merchant capital. Initially, it arose in opposition to European capital per se. But, as the crisis intensified, indigenous merchant capitalists were joined by smallholding producers, low-level indigenous members of the colonial bureaucracy, and elements of the numerically small but critically placed Nigerian working class who were also bearing the burden of the depression. The result was that the opposition took on an explicitly political tone. The fiscal crisis of the colonial state thus became a legitimation crisis as well.

The initial response of the colonial state reflected its preoccupation with matters fiscal. Cooperatives and mixed farming were promoted as a means of reducing the costs of smallholder production and marketing, though with little practical success. The subsequent and more crucial response of the state reflected the political dimension of the crisis.

The most important element in this secondary response was the direct intervention of the state into the marketing of export crops as an attempt to control the effects of capitalist competition on the direct producer. The establishment of state marketing boards and the regulation of European capital reflected the seriousness of the crisis of the 1930s. However, the fact that the major response to the crisis occurred in the sphere of exchange and not production reflected once again the contradictory nature of a state whose ruling class held no direct control over the means or conditions of production.

THE POLITICAL ECONOMY OF NATIONALISM

The central effect of World War II was to heighten both state intervention and nationalist militancy. State intervention in marketing added a new and increasingly indispensable source of revenue in the form of marketing board surpluses. Given the lack of the development of the means of production, control of state revenue itself came to be seen by the coalition of indigenous civil servants and merchant capitalists that comprised the leadership of the nationalist movement as the major prize of independence. However, this petit bourgeois alliance fractured along the lines which broadly reflected Nigeria's highly regionalized economy. Because this fracturing of the Nigerian aspirant ruling class was crucial to the unfolding of Nigeria's political economy in the years leading up to and following independence, it is now

Michael Watts and Robert Shenton 181

necessary to address what has come to be called "tribalism" or more politely if no less inaccurately "ethnic conflict."

Although it is impossible to deny the existence of precapitalist or precolonial cultural, religious, and linguistic identification on the part of Nigeria's peoples, it is also impossible to use the existence of such self-identification as the central explanation for the specific manner in which regionalism or "tribalism" has characterized the Nigerian polity. Rather, it is crucial to understand the manner in which these various multifaceted identifications, have been heightened if not produced in the evolution of the Nigerian state or indeed created where they did not already exist. The preeminent role of such conflict in Nigeria, then, is neither odd nor incomprehensible and indeed can best be understood in the context of a more general understanding of the penetration of capital into Nigeria and the consequent unfolding of the contradictions of that penetration.

Central to this rough and jagged process of penetration and contradiction had been its unevenness in both time and space. As has been outlined above, what is today Nigeria first entered world capitalism as a purveyor of slaves in the period of the primary accumulation of capital. But capitalism first confronted the rural economy of Nigeria in the crucial period from the mid-nineteenth century on—the period of the transition from absolute to relative surplus value as the dominant form of capitalist accumulation— through the purchase of agricultural commodities. Beginning in the southern region of Nigeria in the 1850s with the export of palm produce, the production of agricultural commodities for export was to spread over and come to dominate the political economy of Nigeria.

The history of the spread of export crop cultivation is intimately linked with the development of capitalism itself. Palm oil was first exported in the latter half of the nineteenth century as a raw material for the production of candles, soap and industrial lubricants in the wake of a contracting market for slaves. Initially, real prices were high but later dropped off as both new areas of supply, in particular Malaya and Sumatra, came into production and as palm oil substitutes, most importantly Australian tallow and petroleum, were developed.

This process reached fruition in the capitalist crisis of the late nineteenth century when prices fell off dramatically. The results of this crisis were manifold. First, as European and African merchant capitalists struggled to maintain their profit margins the economic crisis was transformed into a political one with merchants on all sides using martial means to protect their commercial hegemony. The result was that the British state was forced to intervene to safeguard the position of its merchants against both African and other European trade interests. It did so in piecemeal fashion, but eventually it formally declared a protectorate over the southern portion of the country that contained the palm oil producing regions. Second, in the face of falling prices at the end of the nineteenth century, some African merchants in and around the port of Lagos in the southwest promoted the production of cocoa, which realized higher prices than palm oil, as a means of maintaining their profit margins. Initially, prices were high for cocoa as well. Later, however, competition from other producing regions was to increase the supply and lower the price for this commodity. Third, as the process of state intervention expanded to protect extant spheres of commercial endeavor, production was extended to new areas of commercial interest. Such a frontier was what came to be the northern region of Nigeria. In this case, export crop production, rather than arising spontaneously had to be promoted through transport, taxation, and monetary policy in order to provide the fiscal wherewithal of the colonial state. This need for export crop production as a source of state revenue dovetailed neatly with technical developments of European capitalism. In particular the hydrogenation of vegetable oils for the production of margarine—the cheap butter substitute for the European working classes—created a ready market for oil pressed from groundnuts that were to become the main agricultural export from the north from 1913 on. Once again, initial prices were high and once again as substitutes and new sources of supply were added to the world market, the returns to Nigerian producers began to deteriorate.

If the particular crop that each region exported—palm produce in the southeast, cocoa in the southwest, and groundnuts in the north—was different, the fundamental unit of crop production—the household—and the results of a commitment to export crop production, were basically the same. In each instance high prices—and in the north high prices in combination with the pressure of direct taxation—were the lure that enticed rural producers to cultivate commodities for the world market. In each case, the level of development of the means of production in agriculture remained stagnant. Yet in each case as well, as prices of export produce fell, the long-term response of rural dwellers was to increase their output for the world market. The logic of this so-called perverse reaction can only be understood within the context of the reproduction of rural society itself.

Given the stagnation of the level of development of the means of production in agriculture, the increase in export crop production happened as a result of an increase in the *absolute surplus product* of rural labor. Such an increase could be achieved in a number of ways. Time spent resting could be reduced, household food production could be cut in favor of food purchases—a switch could be made to foods which required less time and labor to produce or prepare—or migrant labor power (which was largely reproduced elsewhere) could be imported into the export crop zone at below the cost of its reproduction. In addition to these means and others, areas that had hitherto not been involved in export crop production were projected into the market. The result in each case in terms of export crop output would be the same: an increase in output without a commensurate development in the means of production; in other words, commercial expansion could and did go hand in hand with a stagnation in productivity.

In the initial period of high prices, export crop production expanded and as a consequence imported manufactures as well as domestically produced ones, and in some cases food produced elsewhere in Nigeria, became important elements in the simple reproduction of domestic labor. As prices fell, however, although it was possible to dispense with some of these new commodities, the general trend was to attempt to maintain the newly defined standard of social reproduction through devoting more time to export production. Thus, even during the hard times of the Great Depression and World War II when prices dropped to a fraction of their former levels, export crop production continued to increase. However, such an increase was clearly based in turn upon the continued existence of noncommoditized or only partially commoditized labor and goods for the reproduction of labor and as such it was the result of a process that could not go on forever. Moreover, as a result of the expansion of the export crop economy, an ever larger number of individuals left the countryside to find work in urban areas. This process of rural-urban migration arose in a number of ways. First, those such as merchant middlemen, brokers, and so on, who had benefited from the expansion of export corp production left agriculture to become teachers, civil servants, or full-time men of commerce. And second, those who were members of households that were no longer able to reproduce themselves were pushed to seek employment in urban areas. The effect of this exodus was to increase the demand for food which in turn accelerated the commoditization of rural society. Commoditization gradually eliminated the sources of noncommoditized or partially commoditized labor; items of necessary consumption conversely demanded an increase of export crop production that fed the cycle of commoditization. This vectoring of forces resulted in a decreasing rate of increase, a stabilization, and ultimately a collapse of each of the regional export crop economies.

Yet if the trajectory of each export crop economy was similar, the location of each on that trajectory differed considerably by the early 1950s. This difference was to be of decisive political importance in the emergence of the regional conflicts that characterized Nigerian politics in the immediate pre- and post-independence period.

Coeval with the direct entry of the colonial state into the marketing of export crops that resulted from the crisis of the 1930s, there emerged a new philosophy of colonial rule, also rooted in the crisis. This new philosophy had two principal aspects. First, the state was to take a more active role in agricultural production. And second, to enable this increase to take place in an atmosphere of political quiescence, an increase in the level of social welfare of colonial peoples was attempted. This new philosophy was given substance in the Colonial Development and Welfare Acts of 1940 and 1945 and for Nigeria in the first Nigerian 10-year development plan.

In order to transform this philosophy into concrete action, however, a restructuring of the colonial state was necessary. For, while a half-century of colonial rule had produced a mass of clerks and traders, it had not created a structure to match or manage a social transformation on the scale envisioned by the architects of colonial welfarism. As a result, then, it was necessary to find both Nigerians and institutions in Nigeria that could serve the role of *interlocuteur valable*. The manner in which this was achieved is of decisive importance.

The attempted political transformation was initiated at the bottom of the administrative apparatus and then proceeded to the apex. The result was that a class of administrative cadres was created whose first allegiance was to a particular section of Nigeria rather than to Nigeria as a whole. The creation of a functional, locally financed but nationally subsidized administrative apparatus was seen by the British as the first set of building blocks in the creation of a set of regional bureaucracies that would be the instrument of their postwar designs. However, as the nationalist agitation of the 1950s increased, and as a hard pressed postwar Britain was forced by American pressure and economic crises to begin to see colonies as both a political and economic liability, the administrative instruments created for the implementation of the 10-year plan came to fulfill the new agenda of decolonization.

Once in motion, the pace of decolonization increased as the nationalist petit bourgeoisie squabbled for the spoils of independence. Under increasing pressure, the British rather than being able to create their own *interlocuteurs valables* had to take these where they could be found. In the north, where nationalist fervor was weak, these were to be had in the old instruments of indirect rule. In the south, however, where indirect rule had never effectively functioned, the British were forced to accept the formerly reviled leaders of the nationalist movement in this role.

The 1954 Richards constitution, related constitutional reform, and concomitant fiscal arrangements all impelled the process of the fractionalization of the Nigerian polity. These fiscal arrangements vastly augmented the financial autonomy of the regions through a major overhaul of the entire revenue allocating system. Revenue appropriated primarily from the export crop sector through import and export duties, produce purchase taxes, and marketing board trading surpluses was allocated to the regions on the basis of both derivation and need. The autonomy of the regions was augmented as well; they were given the responsibility for education, health, agriculture, industrial development, and secondary roads.

The financial basis for this reorganization was the new marketing boards. The old groundnut, cocoa, and palm produce marketing boards became the nuclei of the new Northern, Western, and Eastern Region Marketing Boards respectively. As a result, the marketing agency for each commodity became associated with a region in both a financial and a political sense (Helleiner, 1966).

The effect of this regionalization and of a revenue allocation system based on derivation and need was to enhance the fragmentation of Nigeria's aspiring nationalist bourgeoisie along ethnic, religious, and geographical lines. The stark regionalization of the economic base of the state not only differentially tied each of the subeconomies to the world market, that is, based on the world price for its particular export, but also pitted each region against the others in the revenue allocation scramble. Since each region contained a numerically dominant ethnic and/or religious, and/or linguistic group, the regionalization of the economy came increasingly to be perceived along these lines as members of the aspiring nationalist bourgeoisie attempted to mobilize regional forces on the basis of ethnic, religious, and/or linguistic identification.

Regionalization was greatly intensified by the changes in the world market for Nigerian export produce. The postwar marketing boards accumulated huge surpluses until the mid 1950s; extremely favorable prices followed World War II and the Korean war while export volume rose rapidly, standing in 1952 at four times its 1945 level. Moreover, since import prices lagged behind the buoyant export sector, the terms of trade turned sharply in Nigeria's favor. This era of prosperity, however, was not to last. In fact, 1954, the critical year in the process of regionalization, was to be the zenith of the postwar boom (Table 8.3). From 1954 on to the outbreak of the civil war in 1967, export prices either stagnated or declined. Net barter terms of trade declined as well. As a result Nigeria's foreign exchange reserves plummetted from £260 million in 1955 to less than £70 million in 1964 (Onitiri, 1971).

In the context of this deterioration in the terms of trade, the pressure for higher wages among workers and for the greater provision of social services increased. In addition, the importation of capital goods for the industrialization programs initiated in the 1950s and the burden of debt servicing increased with the result that the balance of payments in visible and invisible accounts moved into deficit and external assets declined. Each of the regions, and the Nigerian state at large, were thrown into a second fiscal crisis.

If this fiscal crisis represented the disintegration of the regional economies, it nevertheless was experienced differently by each. Its effect was greatest in the southeast where a combination of high and increasing population densities and 1964 real prices lower than those of the depression, had made an increase in the export of palm produce impossible. The north, dependent on groundnuts, fared somewhat better while the west, which relied on cocoa, found itself in increasingly dire straits.

Nor could the regions easily resort to other sources of state income. In the north where direct taxation had been effective but politically unpopular, it had been allowed to decline in real terms during the postwar boom. In the east and west where it had never been effectively

TABLE 8.3 Real Producer Price Index for Export Commodities (1960 = 100)

	Cocoa	Palm Oil	Palm Kernel	Groundnuts
1952–53	129	140	143	100
1959–60	97	108	100	100
1960–61	100	100	100	100
1961–62	53	97	97	82
1962–63	60	67	69	81
1963–64	62	70	72	81
1964–65	66	69	76	82
1965–66	31	69	76	78

SOURCE: Helleiner (1966), Williams (1980).

implemented, the politicians of nationalism saw its institution as a politically difficult and ultimately impossible task. Thus the politicians of nationalism who had called for vastly increased health and education expenditures as a means of garnering political support now found themselves faced with the prospect of instituting new or unpopular taxes in order to finance their electoral promises. In the context of regionalism, the fiscal crisis of the state was transformed into a national political crisis.

The ability of rural producers to continue to increase their output of export produce hinged on the existence of a reservoir of noncommoditized or partially commoditized labor and goods for the reproduction of labor. By the 1960s, both that reservoir and the ability to increase exports were evaporating. This process was aggravated by the fall in the terms of trade and intensified by marketing board appropriations that withheld potential revenue from the producer. Furthermore, the effects of this process were differentially experienced; the palm produce and cocoa economies of the east and west respectively were hit the hardest.

In this context, the importance of the allocation of funds by the federal government loomed progressively larger, especially as expanding petroleum exports became a new source of revenue. Control over the federal state, then, became the avowed goal of each aspiring regional bourgeoisie; the prize was control of federal revenue allocation and the struggle was legitimized by mobilizing political forces based on ethnic, religious, and linguistic identification. In the face of rising costs of rural production and an increasingly volatile urban poor, the question of the provision of cheap food assumed a strategic significance. Faced with rising class conflict, the politicians of nationalism sought only too successfully to channel class anger along the conduits of language, religion, and place of origin. The result, of course, was the collapse of the First Republic, the secession of the east, and the ensuing civil war that commenced in 1967.

THE CIVIL WAR, OIL, RECONSTRUCTION, AND THE ORIGINS OF NIGERIA'S AGRARIAN CRISIS

The state crisis that had generated the civil war was in turn intensified by the war itself. Federal defense/security spending increased by almost 800% over a 2-year period while planned economic growth ground to a halt. The necessities of war finance required massive cuts in social services, increases in import duties, and substantial internal borrowing (£ 468.9 million by 1970). The war profoundly dislocated agricultural production and transport. In the war's aftermath, the export volume of Nigeria's three major exports— cocoa, palm oil, and groundnuts—fell by 20%, 40%, and 50% respectively (Wells, 1974). Moreover, a series of drought years that affected the entire Sudano-Sahelian zone and that culminated in the infamous 1972-1974 famine exacted their toll from the Nigerian economy. It is estimated that the lives of some 12 million individuals were at risk in Nigeria at the height of the famine, with the cost of state relief—ineffectual as it was—exceeding $100 million and food imports (including concessional sales) topping one million tons.

Yet, ironically, given its central role in the genesis of the civil war, the rapid growth of oil revenue enabled the Nigerian economy to emerge from the war on a financially, if not structurally, sound footing. While in 1961 oil production stood at 46,000 b/d and had grown to 420,000 b/d just prior to the collapse of the First Republic, by 1973 oil production increased to 2.06 million b/d. Simultaneously, the Nigerian government's share of this rapidly growing production increased as well—from 35% after 1973 to 55% in 1977 to 60% in 1979. By late 1979, the Nigerian National Petroleum Company held title to 1.7 million b/d of oil produced in joint ventures with foreign oil companies, making it one of the world's largest sellers. Moreover, the successful OPEC initiative of 1973, which brought about a massive increase in the price of crude oil, improved Nigeria's terms of trade threefold (Table 8.4). As a result, the share of oil in the federal government's revenue rose from 17% in 1971 to 86% in 1975 and in turn made possible an increase in public spending from less than 20% of GDP in 1970–1973 to 35% in 1974–1977 of a much larger GDP—an increase in absolute (money) terms of over 500% (Oyediran, 1979).

Not only did oil revenue permit Nigeria to stave off the fiscal crisis of the postwar years, but it made possible a period of rapid economic growth as well. Between 1970 and 1976 the GDP and GNP per capita grew at a real annual rate of 7.4% and 5.4% respectively.

The Nigerian state itself was the major beneficiary of this large and rapid growth (Table 8.5). Not only was the state able to undervalue the massive growth of its defense and internal security budget, but in absolute terms the bureaucracy was able to enormously expand its size and the extent of its operations. This expansion gave birth to a huge construction boom embracing roads, housing, public buildings and basic infrastructure, which, in turn, unleashed a major demand for imported consumer and capital goods and generated a rather spectacu-

TABLE 8.4 Petroleum Production and Revenue
1973–1979

Year	Crude Petroleum Production (1975 = 100)	Crude Petroleum Exports (millions)	Volume of Crude Petroleum Exports (1975 = 100)	Crude Petroleum Export Price (1975 = 100)
1973	115	1,933	116	33
1974	126	5,665	128	94
1975	100	4,593	100	100
1976	116	5,894	116	108
1977	117	7,046	120	122
1978	106	6,033	108	118
1979	129	10,034	130	174

SOURCE: International Financial Statistics, Vol. XXXIII #12 (1980: 288).

lar proliferation of domestic, component, assemblage, and intermediary goods industries (Table 8.6).

Moreover, the rapid growth of oil revenue also centralized the Nigerian state apparatus. Whereas prior to the civil war the political and fiscal strength of the federal center was relatively weak in relation to the regions, federal control over the new economic base—oil— permitted a consolidation of state ownership and the genesis of a powerful, centralized bureaucracy. The twelve new state governments created by the dissolution of the old regions in 1967, in conjunction with a renovation of the system of revenue allocation, became increasingly dependent on transfers from the swollen federal pool.

In turn, state centralism in conjunction with rapid economic growth enabled the federal government to consolidate its power by literally buying off regional discontent. These same forces generated the emergence of an identifiable national bourgeoisie that increasingly came to see politics in pan-regional terms, a trend registered in the 1979 and seemingly continued by the elections of 1983 which witnessed the accession of the representative of this united, if still fragile, alliance to state power. Oil, then, not only permitted the successful prosecution of the war itself but allowed Nigeria to shed its regionally fractured political carapace and to emerge in the late 1970s as an aspiring member of the semi-industrialized Third World.

These developments, however, had a dark side as well, for by 1975, agriculture that still occupied some 64% of the population accounted

TABLE 8.5 Nigerian Imports 1974–1979

Principal Imports (million nairas)	1974	1975	1976	1977	1978	1979 Jan.–Aug.
Food and live animals	155.2	232.0	441.8	790.3	1,108.6	699.0
Drink and tobacco	9.1	19.6	63.7	146.8	57.7	5.0
Crude materials	63.4	67.0	79.3	70.7	113.6	92.5
Mineral fuels, etc.	50.9	92.0	181.2	136.8	181.2	111.6
Oils and fats	3.6	6.8	24.7	46.8	81.8	60.2
Chemicals	188.7	284.0	398.4	464.9	680.4	392.0
Manufactured goods	512.1	888.0	1,135.7	1,581.9	1,970.2	973.6
Machinery and transport equipment	608.3	1,306.0	2,447.4	3,528.8	3,759.4	1,720.6
Misc. manufactures	113.4	208.0	351.4	516.8	668.2	197.8
Other	10.7	8.2	8.5	13.0	13.8	12.0
Total imports	1,715.0	3,717.0	5,140.0	7,100.0	6,524.0	4,264.5

TABLE 8.6 Expenditure on Agriculture, by Major Expenditure Category*

	1977–78 Estimates (Recurrent & Capital)				3rd Plan 1975–1980 (Capital exp.)	
	Federal	States	Total	Percentage	Total	Percentage
Extension service and input supply	34.0	89.1	123.1	(16.0)	305.6	(10.0)
Fertilizer purchases		43.0	43.0	(5.6)	313.3	(10.2)
Mechanization	0.9	33.7	34.6	(4.5)	71.5	(2.3)
Direct production schemes	11.1	47.2	58.3	(7.6)	432.6	(14.1)
Seed multiplication	2.8	18.9	21.7	(2.8)	62.9	(2.1)
Credit	16.0	11.2	27.2	(3.5)	194.9	(6.4)
Irrigation	182.4	45.2	227.6	(30.0)	701.5	(22.9)
Training	1.2	15.9	17.1	(2.2)	47.3	(1.5)
Marketing and storage	15.4	15.5	30.9	(4.0)	73.1	(2.4)
Miscellaneous	5.1	13.7	18.8	(2.4)	132.8	(4.3)
Total Crops	268.9	333.3	602.3	(78.8)	2335.8	(76.4)
Livestock	20.3	77.4	97.7	(12.7)	487.7	(15.9)
Forestry	7.6	35.1	42.7	(5.5)	135.7	(4.4)
Fisheries	8.5	15.2	23.7	(3.1)	99.4	(3.3)
Total Agriculture	305.3	461.1	766.4	(100.0)	3058.3	(100.0)
Less federal grants to states			12.6			
Total (net)			753.8			

SOURCE: *The Green Revolution*, Volume 2. Lagos: Federal Ministry of Agriculture

*In millions of naira.

a. Includes special programs—Operation Feed the Nation (OFN), National Accelerated Food Development Project (NAFPP), Agro Service Center Programs (ASC), and Agricultural Development Projects (ADP).

for only 28% of national output. The dramatic change in the relative sectoral contribution of agriculture reflected not merely the growth in the importance of oil and other non-farm activities but a stagnating agrarian economy compounded by a deteriorating distribution of income both between and within sectors.

Although agricultural performance suffered as a result of wartime dislocation, the more crucial problems of the agricultural sector were both long term and structural. These problems were now to be intensified by the rapid structural transformation that accompanied the oil boom.

In particular, the massive growth of petroleum revenue accelerated the already present trend toward the commoditization of relations of production and reproduction in the rural sector while simultaneously increasing the demand for food. Since in the absence of any development of the means of production in agriculture the expansion of agricultural output was necessarily sluggish, there was no avoiding an agrarian crisis. Both domestic food production *and* export production sectors quite literally fell apart. Since labor remained the major input to food production and food the major input to the reproduction of labor, an increase in the market price of food was insufficient, in the absence of increased productivity, to generate an increase in agricultural output.

The result has been an emerging crisis of capitalist accumulation which has resulted from an inability to increase the rate of the appropriation of *relative surplus value*. The contradictions, then, which first arose in an industrializing Europe of the nineteenth century, have now become Nigeria's own. The inability to cheapen wage goods and, most crucially, food, in conjunction with rising pressure for a higher standard of living, have now come to haunt Nigeria's hopes of industrialization just as they haunted the emerging British capitalism of the early nineteenth century.

The oil boom and an overvalued currency have, until recently, allowed the effects of this crisis to be mitigated through the massive importation of food. Underpriced North American rice and wheat imports have, of course, further undercut domestic production. And it is here that the analogy with early nineteenth century Britain ends. For Nigeria, unlike the Britain of that period, has nothing to sell to the world besides its oil—at present a wasting asset in a glutted market.

Nor has the policy of importing cheap food reduced prices. On the contrary, the price of domestically produced food has increased dramatically (by 600% between 1971 and 1980 in Kano, for instance). To compound matters, attempts to control the price of food through a policy of cheap imports has been marked by scandal with imported rice at a landed cost of N 15 per bag fetching in excess of N 100 due to speculative licensing and hoarding.

Moreover, if oil has permitted Nigeria to escape the immediate consequences of the agricultural crisis, it has simultaneously deepened that crisis as well (Wells, 1983). Not only has cheap imported food undercut domestic production but the construction boom generated by the oil economy has distorted rural labor markets, where wages had reached twice the government minimum in the mid-1970s with the state itself often outbidding rural smallholders for access to rural labor. Moreover, the disintegration of the rural economy had created a class of individuals who are in Polly Hill's (1972) term "too poor to farm." The exodus of these unfortunates, in turn, increased the burgeoning demand for cheap food in urban areas. These then have been the central elements in the making of Nigeria's current agrarian crisis.

THE THIRD AND FOURTH NATIONAL PLANS: A NEW PHASE OF ACCUMULATION?

The Third (1975–1980) and to a much greater extent the Fourth (1981–1985) Nigerian National Development Plans have marked an attempt to institute a new phase of capitalist development in Nigeria. Agriculture holds a central place in this agenda. Although the proportion of expenditure devoted to agriculture in the Third Plan remained low—roughly 5%—expanded oil revenues permitted a huge increase in government spending (Table 8.6). The Fourth Development Plan envisions a huge total expenditure of N 82 billion, of which some 15% of the capital resources will be devoted to agricultural production and processing which are expected by the planners to grow at an annual rate of 4%. The 1981 capital estimates alone allocated N 1.62 billion to agriculture and the appropriation to the Agricultural Credit Guarantee Scheme has doubled in October 1981 to N 208 million.

Not only is the expenditure on agriculture in the Fourth Plan greater, but it reflects a renewed concentration of effort as well. In particular the Nigerian state has embarked on a two-pronged strategy funded by both domestic and international capital, which encourages large-scale, mechanized agriculture through subsidized inputs, and also promotes differentiation in the countryside by attracting urban and administrative elites into agriculture while attempting to transform rural merchants and petty officials into "progressive farmers." Both tendencies are central to the state's attempt to end reliance on independent smallholder production of agricultural commodities. Such producers are confronted by a combination of large-scale, highly capitalized agricultural production directly under the control of the state and/or international capital *and* smaller scale production controlled directly or indirectly by the state and/or international capital through the manipulation of subsidized inputs.

In theoretical terms, the nature of the attempted transformation can best be expressed as an attempt to transform an agricultural regime characterized by an absence of ruling class control over the conditions of production and extraction (based upon the appropriation of the *absolute surplus product* of rural producers). The new regime is characterized by a greater degree of ruling class control in which the dominant forms of surplus appropriation will be a combination of the *relative surplus product* of subsidized smallholders and the *relative surplus value* produced by agricultural wage-labor on projects dominated by rural or urban elites in conjunction with the Nigerian state and/or international capital. Thus, the paths of agrarian transformation by which this is achieved are conspicuously diverse and contradictory.

Direct state intervention in agricultural production is not new to the Nigerian scene, but the previous results have not been inspirational. In the early 1960s, for example, a series of 1500 acre farms were established in Western Nigeria. Expenditure on these farms by the then Western Regional Government amounted by 1971 to N 16.4 million or some 55% of its total capital expenditure on agriculture with virtually no productive success. Notwithstanding this dismal history, the Fourth National Plan envisages that production of wage foods on schemes directly involved in agriculture will account for 16% of the projected incremental increase in agricultural production. Government food companies alone have been allocated N 114.2 million and in the southern states, government plantations and food companies will absorb N 67.35 million from a total of N 131.38 million to be expended on food crop production. Three parastatals—the National Livestock Production Company, the National Grains Production Company, and the National Rootcrop Production Company—are charged with accelerating food production through large-scale, heavily mechanized production units. By 1980, the Grains Company had established 4,000 ha. farms, which include storage and processing facilities, at Mokwa (Niger State), Jema (Kaduna State), and Ilero (Oyo State). Similar enterprises are under construction in Bauchi and Kano state and are projected to be completed in the remaining 14 states by 1982. The Livestock Company's most significant program is to establish three poultry hatcheries that, using factory methods, aim at the production of 5.4 million chicks annually. State-funded broiler chicken factories are under construction at Agege and Port Harcourt.

The most dramatic state intervention in agriculture has been and will continue to be in large-scale irrigated agricultural projects (Palmer-Jones, 1980). Such projects, by virtue of their size and complexity, frequently have been joint ventures with international finance capital, especially the World Bank, or with private European-based firms. In addition to such state-run schemes as the Kano River Project in Kano and the massive Bakalori project southeast of Sokoto which is run with a Fiat-backed consortium, three huge projects planned for completion in 1991 have been initiated in the Chad Basin and the Hadeija-Jemare River Valley area at a projected cost of N 2.2 billion. The drive for irrigated agriculture is justified in terms of drought risk, but it is closely linked as well to the drive for wheat and rice import substitution. The Nigerian state has also become heavily committed to estate sugar production with the huge Savannah Sugar Scheme at Numan being linked to the N 144 million Hiri Dam and an expenditure of $558 million projected for the planned Sunti Sugar Estate.

Although in the past Nigerian state capital has been supplemented by foreign government or international finance capital in agricultural development, the Nigerian government has recently encouraged investment by private, foreign capital in the agricultural sector. Nineteen joint ventures are already planned by companies from Brazil, Canada, and Europe (African Business, November 1981).

European firms, in particular, have been quick to enter into agricultural production in Nigeria. The Bokko poultry farm is a joint venture between the state government and the German firm Rao-Imex, while Danish and British firms have established pig farms near Kuru. In both instances, such investment has encouraged the integration of local farmers as producers of hybrid maize livestock feed. In an attempt to encourage such activities, the Federal Commissioner for Agriculture informed a Dutch delegation in 1978 that the recently promulgated Lands Use Decree was a means by which the large amounts of land required by foreign capital could be easily and cheaply made available for international investors.

Meanwhile, in July 1980, the United States and Nigeria signed a memorandum encouraging American agribusiness in conjunction with the United States Department of Agriculture to increase investment in Nigerian agriculture. The memorandum provides for the opening of Nigerian trade and investment centers in the United States, the development of a United States Department of Agriculture Trade Office in Lagos, and the creation of an intergovernmental working group to design and implement specific agricultural projects in Nigeria. The United States members of the committee represent giant farm equipment manufacturers, financial concerns, and agribusiness such as FMC Corporation, Allis-Chalmers, and the Ford Motor Company; fertilizer, pesticide, and seed producers such as Pfizer, Occidental Petroleum, and Whittacker; food processing operations (Carnation, Pillsbury, and Ralston Purina); and financial institutions including the First National Bank of Chicago and Chase Manhattan. Forming one of the strands of the Reagan administration's policy, the committee has been hailed by Assistant Secretary for African Affairs Chester Crocker as a prime model "of the contributions and benefits of private sector involvement in Africa to which we are giving encouragement."

In addition to directly intervening in agricultural production, the Nigerian state has also reacted to the agrarian crisis by attempting to stimulate production through the provision of subsidized credit, fertilizers, and tractors and through changes in land tenure. These efforts have been characterized by an explosion of parastatal organizations and government programs.

The National Accelerated Food Production Programme (NAFPP) is emblematic of this strategy. The program has concentrated on increasing the production of rice, maize, wheat, millet, sorghum, and cassava through the integrated use of high yielding seed varieties, chemical inputs, credit, and improved marketing made available in "packages of improved practices" ostensibly for the use of the small-scale producer. In conjunction with this strategy, seed laboratories have been completed in Ibadan and Kaduna, 380 agro-service centers have been created, and a National Mechanisation Centre is under construction in Ilorin.

This indirect approach was strengthened in April 1980 with the establishment of a National Council for the Green Revolution, a coordinating body that seeks to "boost agricultural production and to ensure agricultural production through . . . agro-based industries (and) the construction of feeder roads" (Africa Now, October 1981, p. 181). This Green Revolution strategy relies heavily on the continued expansion of World Bank intervention in Nigeria, and as a result bank involvement in Nigeria has grown rapidly. Whereas by 1978, the bank had loaned $295 million for agricultural projects in Nigeria, during 1980 alone loans were made by the World Bank for the establishment of projects in Sokoto ($168 million), Bauchi ($132 million), Kano ($142 million), and Ondo ($59.6 million) states. Moreover, the Federal

Director of Rural Development has apparently been assured that the bank will assist in the multiplication of Green Revolution projects to all states in Nigeria by 1983. These bank-sponsored projects, known officially as Agriculture Development Projects, are projected to grow from 629 families in 1980 to 3,831,000 families in 1985. In addition, a modified Green Revolution package will be supplied to so-called Residual Accelerated Development Areas, which will include two-thirds of all Local Government Areas by 1983.

CONCLUSION

The civil war and the growth of petroleum exports have clearly opened up the historical possibility of a transformation of the nature of the political economy of the Nigerian state. Moreover, the lynch-pin of this transformation is to be the agrarian sector. The crucial question, however, is whether Nigeria's newly unified ruling class alliance, assisted by oil revenue, international capital, and a powerful centralized bureaucracy, is capable of managing its way out of this historic transformation.

There are good reasons for skepticism. The first of these, ironically, lies in the uncertain nature of the future reliability of the oil revenue itself. In 1977–1978, Nigeria faced a minor crisis when crude oil output fell by 29% from 2.23 billion b/d to 1.57 billion b/d. Far more serious, however, has been the recent slump in the demand for oil which witnessed a cut in Nigerian production from 2.09 billion b/d to 0.64 billion b/d over the period January to August 1981. As a result, Nigeria actually reduced the price of its oil by $4 per barrel. During this period, Nigeria's foreign exchange reserves supported the import bill. Since oil revenue is the foundation of the Fourth National Plan, the crisis generated a $1.5 billion cut in planned expenditures. Most publicity has been given to cuts in the civil service, but the bulk of the reductions in government spending must come from the delaying of capital projects central to the transformation of the agrarian sector, with one-third of the planned projects likely to be held up. Significantly, the River Basin Development Authorities have already seen their allocation reduced from N 1.55 billion to N 0.21 billion. Though Nigeria has the capacity to borrow greatly on the international market, it is already some $10 to $15 billion in debt. It remains unclear what the long-term implications of the vulnerability of the oil economy will be for the attempt to transform the agrarian base.

A second reason for skepticism is what has been termed the "managerial incapacity" of the Nigerian state bureaucracy. Specifically, the circulation of oil rents through the state provided the principal means by which federal patronage allowed merchants, bureaucrats, politicians, and businessmen to directly appropriate revenues. As Joseph (1978) points out, the 1970s were a huge and thoroughly disorganized spending spree in which civil servants, technocrats, and indigenous merchant capitalists channeled state revenues into their own coffers. In the course of events, millions of naira mysteriously disappeared into Swiss bank accounts and endemic patronage and corruption have colored the vastly inflated federal and state bureaucracy. In 1979, for example, the Public Accounts Commission reported that the Nigerian Customs and Excise Department was unable to account for N 8 million in missing vouchers while the Ministry of Finance had no record of some N 2 billion in state investments for the period 1970–1974.

This pathology of corruption is firmly rooted both in the historical antecedents of the Nigerian state as well as in the uncertain future of the oil economy. While the genesis of oil has permitted the emergence of a national ruling class, it has not abolished the regionalism of the pre-oil period. Quite the contrary: While the creation of nineteen states in place of the old regions has lessened the relative political significance of each state in particular, it has given rise to nineteen competing state bureaucracies, each of which on the basis of its own agenda strives to increase its share of the oil rents.

The impaired competence of the Nigerian bureaucracy in turn gives rise to a third source of skepticism regarding the possibility of a successful transformation of the agrarian sector—its ability to implement and manage the state interventions essential to that transition. The recently completed Bakalori irrigation project 150 km southeast of Sokoto provides a case in point. The impetus for Bakalori came from a Fiat-based bank consortium now in the hands of an Italian contractor (IMPRESIT). Two contracts for construction totaling N 154 million were to have been completed by March 1980; however, by January of that year, costs stood at N 350 million. The experience of Bakalori is not unusual. Wallace (1981) and Palmer-Jones (1980) have shown how the first phase of the Kano River Project at Kadawa south of Kano, which involved the construction of the Tiga Dam in 1974, has suffered from similar defects. Technical and labor difficulties have severely constrained the operation of the Kadawa project with the result that production of wheat on the scheme is much more costly than imported wheat. High subsidies will be required to cover even recurrent costs. In particular, the untimely provision of tractor ploughing, fertilizers, and the inadequate maintenance of irrigation canals have made yields low and uncertain. Moreover, all of this must be seen in the light of the massive costs per hectare of irrigated agriculture—N 2,000 at Bakalori; N 1,750 at Chad (Phase I); and N 8,000 at Kadawa.

A similar set of problems has arisen with regard to estate sugar production. In the vast Savannah Sugar Project, inflated technology prices, infrastructural bottlenecks, and poor financial and technical management have been responsible for huge delays and massive overspending. Expenditure on the Savannah Sugar Company alone stands at $412 million, yet the irrigation works remain uncompleted and "there appears little likelihood of sugar ever being competitive on the world market" (Quarterly Economic Review, 3rd quarter, 1981: 20). Undeterred by these difficulties, the Nigerian state has proceeded with the creation of the $568 million Sunti Sugar Estate.

Nor have managerial and associated technical problems been confined only to large-scale mechanized and/or irrigated projects. On the Funtua Integrated Rural Development Project many of the purported "service benefits" such as water and electricity supplies, post-primary schools, and maternity centers have failed to materialize. More crucially, only 520 km of road had been built by 1980, and cash flow problems, budgetary overexpenditure, poor marketing, and low disease resistance among Green Revolution "high yielding varities" have limited growth in agricultural output.

The fourth, and in the long term perhaps the most crucial, reason for skepticism regarding the outcome of the attempted transformation of Nigeria's agricultural sector lies in the potentially politically explosive implications of rural differentiation that has been engendered not only by state intervention itself but by the effects of oil dependence, "managerial incapacity," and corruption. The generation and heightening of class cleavages is inherent in the nature of the attempted rural transformation.

Thus, for example, at Bakalori, angry farmers fearful of losing their land for a time blocked construction on the project and engaged in armed conflict with the authorities. The reasons for such resistance are clear. On the scheme at Kadawa, resettlement of 12,000 farmers at Tiga has resulted in a deterioration of material conditions for 43% of all settlers, most particularly felt as a loss of good farm land. Farmers living downstream have lost fishing and lucrative vegetable production as a result of dam construction. The production of wheat and tomatoes for urban markets conflicts with the farmers' desires to produce sorghum for rural consumption. Moreover, the Kadawa Project and others like it, if inefficient, can function to the benefit of scheme workers, locally influential farmer traders, and rich outsiders through massive price subsidies. Thus, at Bakalori following local protests a constructing firm, MASDAR, in conjunction with the state has encouraged the creation of a wealthy farmer class and 350 ha. "development farms" with the result that within a year of the project's completion, some indebted smallholders have sold out to businessmen, teachers, and officials.

The Green Revolution as well, despite its purported populist or smallholder focus, has imported social and economic consequences that threaten the existence of smallholders. In attempting to transform the forces of production through subsidization, the high demand for inputs (such as fertilizer and insecticides) coupled with supply limitations, favors bureaucratic elites and influential merchant farmers. For example, of the N 30.9 million expansion of rural credit by the Agricultural Credit Guarantee Scheme in 1980, only 42.5% of loan applications were approved; 68% of these went to livestock and poultry production and 10% to mixed farmers using ploughs and bullocks, thus excluding the vast majority of small grain producers.

This focus on the well off is in part a continuation of a historical trend. Thus, Matlon (1981) documents that village elites have a substantially above-average rate of participation in government programs and his estimate that 20% of the inputs supplied to the three villages that he studied in Kano were "diverted for the personal use of selected members of the elite" comes as no surprise to those familiar with the history of the cooperative movement in Nigeria.

Yet if this focus on the well off is historically consistent, it is also a matter of unavowed policy. The World Bank Projects are oriented toward large-scale mechanized production. The average farm size in the Funtua Project is 4.1 hectares but the project aims to transform "all progressive farmers into large scale (100 ha.) farmers." In 1979, there were 186 large-scale farmers, 19,562 progressive farmers, and 66,438 traditional cultivators. Of all extension visits, 60% were concentrated on the progressive class, while large-scale farmers received intensive advice on farm plan design, implementation, and supervision. It is clear that the "traditional" cultivators who receive little assistance face the possibility of being reduced below competitive levels and transformed into the rural labor force necessitated by nonmechanized operations such as weeding. According to World Bank data (Vol. 1, 1981), between 1976 and 1979, the percentage of farm holdings of less than 2 hectares on the Funtua and Gusau Projects increased from 36% to 47% and from 36% to 41% respectively. As D'Silva and Raza (1980) put it, "the emergence of a landless class is a possibility for the first time in the area."

The immediate consequences of the increased relative impoverishment of the rural poor generated by the attempted agrarian transformation has been to increase the already fierce competition for work, housing, and social services in urban areas, with problematic political results. In this regard, the "Yan Tatsine" rebellion may well be a harbinger of things to come.

The setting for the rebellion was the ancient northern city of Kano. In 1963, with a population of just over a quarter million, Kano was a classical mercantile city specializing in the groundnut export trade. By 1980, it was estimated to have a population in excess of 2 million, including an industrial labor force of some 50,000. During the intervening years, Kano received a huge influx of foreign capital and state sponsored industrialization. These, in turn, attracted a vast number of impoverished rural dwellers from Nigeria and beyond. The results have been the internationalization of consumption styles among the urban rich, the increased commoditization of urban social relations, the creation of a disenfranchised and increasingly militant "floating population," and a corresponding increase in urban violence.

In December 1980, a militant Islamic sect, 'Yan Tatsine, under the leadership of their "prophet," Alhaji Mohammed Marawa, attempted to take over the Kano Friday Mosque with the further intention of seizing control of Kano itself. Blocked from reaching the mosque by police, the 'Yan Tatsine took over a school, fought a pitched battle with the police, and then retreated into the 'Yan Awaki section of the old city. There they fortified the area and seized some 50 to 65 hostages while preparing to do battle with the authorities. After ten days of widespread disorder marked by vigilante violence, fire fights with the police, and the breakdown of public order, the Nigerian Army was called in on December 28th. The army leveled the area and drove the rebels to a village outside of the city where a large portion of their number were either killed or captured. While a tribunal of inquiry is in progress, estimates of loss of life vary from 1,000 to 10,000.

Although couched in millenarian terms, it is clear that the 'Yan Tatsine revolt involved an overt criticism of the materialism and exploitation that has characterized both the petroleum boom and the attempted transformation of the Nigerian economy. The followers of

Alhaji Marawa were largely recruited from a section of the lower classes know in Hausa as *gardi.* Although classically the term *gardi* refers to any unmarried man who wanders from community to community to study the Koran, in contemporary terms, *gardi* have become a major source of ill-paid, casual industrial labor. Many of these individuals have come to Kano and other major cities in Nigeria as a result of having been displaced from the rural economy. In order to hide the shame and disgrace of their itinerant vagrancy, they have often assumed the guise of wandering Koranic students. The burgeoning mass of such individuals faced with the rapid increase in the price of food set the stage for the 'Yan Tatsine rebellion. Under the leadership of Marawa, they damned the affluent consumers of Western manufactures and seized property. 'Yan Tatsine, in other words, was expressive precisely of the despair and frustration arising from the post-oil transformation and is emblematic of the extent to which the Nigerian state will increasingly have to confront and/or mediate glaring class antagonisms.

Yet, if the 'Yan Tatsine rebellion is illustrative of the intensification of class conflict in Nigeria, it is also suggestive of the forms through which this heightened hostility is likely to be expressed. Religious schism and cleavages based on linguistic or regional identification are all a part of the heritage of the Nigerian past and class conflict is likely to be expressed in a language consonant with them. Moreover, it seems clear that if the present crisis intensifies, appeals to these forms of identification may well once again be made by those who see the risks inherent in their mobilization as a matter of lesser importance than the threat to their own position of privilege.

Thus, if there are grounds for skepticism regarding the ability of the Nigerian ruling class to manage a major transformation of Nigeria's political economy (See ILO, 1981, and Bienen and Diejomaoh, 1981) there should be little doubt that the nature of Nigeria's future lies in their ability to do so. We have suggested that Nigeria is currently pursuing several contradictory paths toward agrarian capitalism, all of which have their own relative strengths and weaknesses in relation to state power and popular dissent. The sorts of political forms that may emerge in such a situation are not wholly predictable of course; but a failure to manage those political contradictions may well spell economic and political chaos for a country that ten years ago was seen by many to hold all the promise of a new African future.

REFERENCES

BIENEN, H. and V. DIEJOMACH [eds.] (1981) The Political Economy of Income Distribution in Nigeria. New York: Holmes and Meier.

D'SILVA, B and M. RAZA (1980) "Integrated rural development in Nigeria." Food Policy 5: 282–297.

Federal Government (1980) The Green Revolution: A Food Production Plan for Nigeria. Lagos: Federal Ministry of Agriculture.

FORREST, T. (1981) "Agricultural policies in Nigeria 1900–1978," pp. 222–258 in G. Williams et al. (eds.) Rural Development in Tropical Africa. London: Macmillan.

HELLEINER, G. (1966) Peasant Agriculture, Government and Economic Growth in Nigeria. Homewood, IL: Irwin.

HILL, P. (1972) Rural Hausa: A Village and a Setting. Cambridge: Cambridge Univ. Press.

ILO (1982) Nigeria: First Things, First. Addis Adaba: International Labor Office.

JOSEPH, R. (1978) "Affluence and underdevelopment: the Nigerian experience." J. of Modern African Studies 16: 221–239.

MANN, S. and J. DICKINSON (1978) "Obstacles to the development of a capitalist agriculture." J. of Peasant Studies 5: 466–481.

MATLON, P. (1981) "Production and rural incomes in Northern Nigeria," pp. 323–372 in H. Bienen and V. Diejomach (eds.) The Political Economy of Income Distribution in Nigeria. New York: Holmes and Meier.

ONITIRI, H. M. (1971) "Nigeria's external trade, balance of payments and capital movements," in A. Ayida and H. Onitiri (eds.) Reconstruction and Development in Nigeria. Ibadan: Nigerian Institute of Social and Economic Research.

OYEDIRAN, O. [ed.] (1979) Nigerian Government and Politics Under Military Rule 1966–1979. New York: St. Martin's Press.

PALMER-JONES, R. (1980) Why Irrigate in Northern Nigeria? Oxford University. (mimeo)

SHENTON, R. (1984) The Development of Capitalism in Northern Nigeria. Toronto: University of Toronto Press.

WALLACE, T. (1981) "The challenge of Nigeria's Approach to agriculture 1975–1980." Canadian J. of African Studies 15: 239–258.

WATTS, M. (1983) Silent Violence: Food, Famine and Peasantry in Northern Nigeria. Los Angeles: Univ. of California Press.

WELLS, J. (1974) Agricultural Policy and Economic Growth in Nigeria 1962–1968. London: Oxford Univ. Press.

WILLIAMS, G. (1980) "Inequalities in rural Nigeria." Report prepared for the ILO, Oxford University, 1980.

World Bank (1981a) Accelerated Development in Sub-Saharan Africa (Berg Report). Washington, DC: World Bank.

——— (1981b) Farm Technology Adoption in Northern Nigeria, Vol. 1. Washington, DC: World Bank.

9

LABOR, COMMUNITY, AND PROTEST
IN SUDANESE AGRICULTURE

TAISIER ALI and JAY O'BRIEN

PRIVATE PUMP SCHEMES AND
THE INDEPENDENCE TRANSITION

In Sudan, the main goal of the colonial state's agricultural policies was the increased production of export crops, mainly cotton. The pursuit of that goal led to the modernization of irrigation by shifting the emphasis away from water wheels to pumps, flood works, and dams. The British cotton interests that formed the Sudan Plantations Syndicate and organized the Gezira Scheme in 1925 introduced new methods of irrigation, cultivation, management, known as the Zeidab-Gezira model. From the early period to the present, this model and its pattern of owner-tenant relations have been reproduced in all of the government as well as privately owned schemes.

Until the early 1950s, the great expansion in modern agriculture occurred almost exclusively in the state sector. Thus the Gezira started with 240,000 feddans, reached 670,000 feddans in 1931, and covered nearly a million feddans by 1954 (1 feddan = 1.038 acres). In addition, there were irrigation schemes in Tokar and Gash as well as rain cultivation in Equatoria, Gadambaliya, and the Nuba Mountains, all of which were under state control (Sudan, 1972: 7–8).

This trend was altered in the early 1950s as private pump schemes were established at an accelerated rate. The number of these schemes grew from 372 covering 170,000 feddans in 1944 to 2,229, utilizing over 770,000 feddans by 1957. The most phenomenal increase in private pumps took place in the mid-1950s, during the transition from colonial rule, through internal self-government to independence. Between 1952 and 1956, the total number of pump schemes more than doubled, while the area reserved for cotton production in the Blue Nile region alone almost tripled from 43,000 feddans to 114,000 feddans. A similar expansion took place along the White Nile where the total area under cotton increased from 20,000 feddans in 1949–1950 to 198,000 feddans in 1958–1959, a tenfold increase (Sudan, 1967).

In the literature on Sudanese agriculture, this rapid growth is attributed to the modern irrigation techniques employed by the colonial state and the international demand for cotton. Most of these studies stress the technical benefits of the Gezira and its Sennar dam, while the expansion of private pumps is related to the construction of the Jebel Awlia dam along the White Nile in 1937. In addition, much emphasis is placed on the high cotton prices that accompanied the Korean War. Although such insights are useful for understanding the overall expansion in cotton cultivation, they do not explain the specific phenomenon of explosive growth in the numbers of private pump schemes. The answer to this latter concern lies in certain broader socioeconomic and political considerations, which in turn reveal the long-lasting and far-reaching importance of this key development for the character of Sudanese peripheral capitalism.

The ultimate significance of the expansion of private pump-irrigated agriculture lies in its formative role in capital accumulation by one of the fractions of the Sudanese bourgeoisie that has figured centrally in all subsequent political struggles. During the decisive phase of the expansion of pump-irrigated cotton production in the 1950s and 1960s, this fraction of the bourgeoisie succeeded in articulating an enduring class alliance, one that has at times exercised hegemony through capturing control of the state (i.e., 1956 to 1968) and at other times has provided the principal opposition to its rival alliance when the latter has assumed hegemony (1972 to the present).

This agrarian bourgeoisie, formed in large part from precolonial religious and political elites, established its position in the modern Sudanese political economy initially on the basis of its investment and accumulation in private irrigated cotton production, from which base it staged its early struggles to capture the postcolonial state. In the 1960s, the profitability of pump schemes declined and combined with other relatively unattractive characteristics of such investment to lead these agricultural capitalists to seek more attractive forms of investment. At a time (1968) when the richest agricultural capitalist in Sudan (Sadig Al Mahdi) was the Prime Minister, the state carried out an "agrarian reform" program that freed up their private capital for investment in mechanized rainfed farming. In this way, pump schemes lost their earlier significance and the agrarian bourgeoisie transformed its economic base. Nevertheless, the politically and economically formative role played by the expansion of private pump schemes, including the conflicts the process involved, is the single most important key to understanding the formation of the principal power blocs whose struggles continue to shape the Sudanese political economy to this day.

A sample study of private pump schemes along the White Nile indicated that over 60% of the schemes were set up in the short period of 1953–1957 (El Hadari, 1968). But these were also the years during which self-rule was initiated and independence obtained. It was a period characterized by intensive political jostling, particularly within the capitalist class with economic interests in the agricultural sector, and this contestation was mirrored in the state and its policies. In short, a direct correspondence existed between the political developments of that period and the rapid growth in private pump schemes. This connection was not simply a by-product of the self-rule era and the transition to independence (cf. Awad, 1972: 14): The pattern had been initiated earlier by the colonial state when private licenses were granted to the religious aristocracy (Bakheit, 1972: 123–126).

An Economic Base for "Indirect Rule"

Up until the 1930s, the colonial state ruled the country in a centralized military fashion that included the imposition of martial law for much of that period. Most of the administrators were themselves British army officers who had no desire to delegate authority or involve Sudanese in the power structure. The memory of the Mahdist Revolution was still alive in their minds. But after more than two decades in the Sudan, the British finally discovered allies in the leaders of indigenous political institutions. They could, as the then Governor-General, Sir J. Maffey, put it, offer "a shield between the agitator and the bureaucracy . . . protective glands against the septic germs [of nationalism] . . . [and would] sterilize and localize the political germs which spread from the lower Nile to Khartoum" (Beshir, 1974: 110). He also thought that native administration would be a good investment:

> Be prepared to grant a worthy scale of remuneration to the Chiefships
> we foster . . . in order to give them dignity and status

. . . we shall therefore be saved in the long run from costly elaborations of our own administrative machinery [Duncan, 1952: 148–149].

Following the inauguration of "Indirect Rule" in the 1920s, the British began to issue licenses for private pump schemes on the Niles. Many tribal and religious leaders obtained the largest of these schemes. In fact, the first beneficiary of this policy was Abdel Rahman Al Mahdi, none other than the son of the Mahdi—the arch-enemy of British imperial rule. According to Henderson, during World War I when the Ottoman Sultan declared a *Jihad*, Sayed Abdel Rahman stressed to

his father's followers that the Turk was after all their traditional enemy. . . . After the war he was given the wood contract for the Sennar dam (built to irrigate the Gezira), and with the capital so acquired laid the foundations of a considerable fortune from pump-irrigated cotton grown on Aba Island [Henderson, 1965: 60].

In addition to virtual ownership of this 60 square mile island in the White Nile, Sayed Abdel Rahman acquired more schemes which were

financed by the government at a cost of 28,000. . . . Even in the Jazira [Gezira] . . . he had managed by 1931 to lay his hands on some 9,000 acres of cultivable lands. To these considerable profits from cultivation, one should add the zakat which since 1919 had been collected annually from all the Ansar (followers of the Mahdi), and the presents brought to the Sayyid by his richer adherents. . . . Thus by 1935 Sayyid Abd al-Rahman was . . . an affluent man by even the most conservative standards [Warburg, 1978: 33].

Sayed Abdel Rahman was the *primus inter pares* of the religious leaders who were granted licenses for private schemes, and along with Sayed Ali Al Mirghani and Sharif Yousif Al Hindi was one of the three pillars of the Sudan's religious aristocracy. Al Mirghani commanded a wide following through his Khatmiya religious sect. All three sectarian leaders, who were knighted by the British, later sponsored the country's political parties—the Umma, the People's Democratic Party (PDP), and the National Unionist Party (NUP), respectively.

The decision to grant licenses to Sayed Abdel Rahman was based on political considerations explicitly spelled out in the directives of the Governor-General in 1928 who specified that "as the Sayed is behaving reasonably in the religious and political field we ought, as a measure of political expediency to bind him to us by economic fetters" (quoted in

Warburg, 1978: 32). The colonial state handed Sayed Abdel Rahman the economic base to launch a new version of Mahdism, the leadership of which he had inherited. This "neo-Mahdism" proved its ability to command the following of the Ansar masses, but it was totally bereft of its original anticolonial content. The same strategy was also applied to the other religious leaders and tribal chiefs. In reality, then, private pump schemes were used as prizes to win the support of native administrators and religious shepherds to reward them and to strengthen their commanding positions.

Sudanese businessmen together with foreign finance capital were also deeply involved in these schemes. Their participation added an economic significance to the important political functions of this pattern of capitalist agricultural development. Almost all of the capital expenditure, which was estimated to have reached about LS 30 million by 1963, came from the private sector.[1] Among those who owned schemes were the country's wealthiest capitalists. Most of the financial outlays for these schemes originated from foreign commercial banks with branches in the Sudan, particularly from the British Barclays D.C.O. Some foreign capitalists operating in the country were also involved. In general, the banks shunned direct investment of this type mainly because of its long-term nature. The common practice was for them to provide the capital for agents who would later deal with the scheme owners. One result of this type of operation was the rise of Sudanese financiers, most of whom were themselves landowners.

The number of private pump schemes rose from 13 in 1904 to 244 by 1939 and had reached 1331 during the early days of self-government in 1954 (Sudan, 1967: 71; Shaw, 1966: 177). In this manner, not only were the cotton exports of the government and therefore its income enhanced, but, more important, support for the colonial state's policies was purchased.

Owners and Tenants

This dual function of the private schemes was unchanged by the postcolonial state and "people openly discussed the huge schemes allotted to individuals with close connections to the ministers and the Prime Minister himself" (Sudan Parliament, 1956). The postcolonial state also retained unaltered the colonial mold of capitalist economic relations within those schemes.

In its efforts to maintain a favorable price structure, the colonial state formulated a variety of laws to control the distribution and cost of land, water resources, and the labor of Sudanese farmers. Hence, the Nile Pump Control Ordinance of 1939 governed irrigation matters, the Nile Pumps Control Regulations of 1951 established the types of licenses, and the Nile Pumps Control Regulation of 1947 dictated the terms for the sharing of proceeds between tenant farmers and licensees (or owners). The licensees were given full control over management, ginning, and marketing of cotton. Their obligations included provision of water, advancement of loans and responsibility for 50% of the joint cotton expenses. The tenant farmers were responsible for the performance of all agricultural operations including maintenance of canals, harvesting, and clearing of fields. Tenant and licensee shared equally the expenses covered in the joint account: sacks, ginning, and marketing. If unsatisfied with a tenant's performance, or on some pretext, the licensee could evict him or hire extra laborers.

Moreover, rental and license fees were nominal in order to encourage agricultural operations. Licensee overhead costs were further reduced by the absence of any provision for schools, health clinics, housing, or any social services or other benefits, such as a reserve fund, which were available in the Gezira Scheme. There were no legal obligations for licensees to use agricultural inputs in order to maintain soil fertility. Auditing of accounts was not mandatory and since the licensees themselves prepared their own financial statements, they often tended to inflate marketing or ginning expenses that were paid for by the joint account. After the deduction of the joint account and other charges, the proceeds were divided between the licensee and the tenant in the ratio of 60% to 40% respectively. Finally, the interest of the colonial state in the continued cultivation of cotton was also evident in the cost structure of water charges. These charges discriminated against the cultivation of the important cereal dura (sorghum) in favor of cotton. In most schemes, dura, which could be grown locally, was bought from other regions.

The terms of this arrangement have remained to date the single most important issue confronting tenant farmers, private landowners, and the Sudanese state. The same tenant-owner relations, an integral part of the Zeidab-Gezira model, were reproduced, with only a few cosmetic changes, throughout all of the other state and privately owned irrigation schemes (see Barnett, 1977; Sørbø, 1977; O'Brien, 1980, 1984). They are inseparably related to subsequent events, particularly the gruesome incident at Jouda described below, the agrarian reform movement of the mid 1960s, and the general strike of July 1979 in the Gezira. Hence, an analysis of this pattern of the division of the proceeds is essential not only for the study of the private cotton estates, but also for any examination of agricultural development in the Sudan as a whole.

Mainstream social scientists suggest that the terms of the tenant/ owner relationships are on the whole reasonable, a veritable partnership (Awad, 1972: 15). However, the moment that all the provisions and their actual implementation are scrutinized, the picture that emerges is substantially different from that implied by the term partnership. In the case of the licensees, it is often suggested that they were "burdened" with such obligations as soil tests and payment of taxes. In fact, as subsequent events showed, "many of the schemes . . . were hurriedly set up . . . without adequate soil testing" (Awad, 1972: 15). Furthermore, by 1966 unpaid Business Profit taxes of scheme owners had exceeded LS 3.6 million, with even larger amounts of outstanding loans from public as well as private facilities (Adam, 1973: 40). The power of the licensee over the tenant farmer was immense, for the former could impose fines or ultimately requisition plots, while the latter was obliged to surrender all of his cotton produce. Most of the "sharing" was confined to the transportation and ginning expenses that were charged to a joint account. Even then the licensee had the unquestionable right of ginning the cotton wherever he pleased and at whatever cost. This often meant that landowners would process cotton in their own ginneries at higher costs rather than in other nearby establishments that they did not own. Moreover, since the grading of cotton excluded any tenant participation, tenants were routinely quoted prices for grades that were inferior to their produce. Monopoly over the marketing process allowed landowners to settle personal financial obligations by dispensing cotton at lower prices to their creditors without any regard for the tenants' rights or interests (Hamied, 1965: 33–37).

Not only were the tenants responsible for the basic agricultural operations—land clearing, plowing, seeding, picking of cotton, and the maintenance of all canals as well as roads—but they were also saddled with the expenses of dredging the main canals and installing pipes, and all of this in addition to the cost of the cotton seed. As for the provision for growing food crops free of rent and water charges, on most schemes this right remained a mere privilege. More often than not, licensees discouraged tenant farmers from this practice by delaying the pumping of water in order to (a) increase the area under cotton, (b) avoid exhausting the land, and (c) save the cost of pumping water. The tenants' tolerance was tested even further by the agonizing delay in the settlement of their accounts and in the receipt of their shares in the cotton proceeds, for which the average waiting period was over two years (El Hadari, 1968: 17–21). As a result, tenants were forced to resort to trader-moneylenders to obtain the basic necessities.

Implementation of the profit-sharing arrangement and the arbitration of disputes in these schemes were supervised by joint boards comprised of government agricultural inspectors, licensees, representatives of native administration, and tenants selected by the government after consultation with scheme owners. As the meetings of these boards were irregular and infrequent, power rested almost exclusively with the agricultural inspectors. However, since these inspectors shared many more mutual socioeconomic interests with the licensees than with the tenants, they invariably ruled in favor of the former group (Hamied, 1965: 35–37). Given this state of affairs, it is almost natural that:

> Evictions . . . became quite common. The tenants complained of high-handed behaviour by the licensees, undue delay in the settling of their accounts, arbitrary evictions for the sake of turning tenancies into (tax-free) experimental farms, irregular flow of water to their private plots, etc. They also claimed that they found no protection from the Agricultural Inspectors, whom they accused of conniving with the pump scheme owners [Awad, 1972: 16].

The condition of the licensees, on the other hand, has been succinctly summed up by Barbour, who observed that:

> Along the Blue and White Niles . . . a major transformation was taking place . . . profits . . . were so high that the usual period for the return of the capital sum was three years only, and some lucky and skilful scheme owners were clear of debt within one year [Barbour, 1961: 269–270].

and,

> For the man with £s5000 to £s50,000 or more to invest, a pump scheme has afforded a safe and extremely profitable venture that does not involve too great a delay. . . . While it might be argued that . . . the state should have imposed very stiff license fees to secure to itself some portion of the element of increased land value . . . this has not occurred. The license-holders pay the normal rate of business profit tax . . . their licenses are normally of a nominal ten years' duration, but in fact when these lapse they are renewed as a matter of course [Barbour, 1959: 253–254].

Against this background of uneven obligations and rewards, prevalent in private and public schemes alike, the tenants in their struggle to redress the balance began to form unions.

The Tenants Organize

The modern history of Sudanese tenant-farmers' organizations dates from 1946. Due to tenant defaults on loans during the cotton blights and the depression in the 1930s, the Sudan Plantations Syndicate, which administered the Gezira Scheme, had decided to retain a percentage of the tenants' share of the cotton receipts in order to create a tenants' reserve fund to cover bad debts. It was not until 1946 that the tenants discovered the existence of this fund—together with the fact that it had amassed a surplus of LS 1 million. This discovery triggered a widely supported strike by the Gezira tenants, who refused to plant cotton that season. The movement was led by local religious and tribal chiefs and it was based solely on economic considerations to the exclusion of all political motives. The strike was short-lived and after the mediation of national leaders a compromise about the handling of fund was reached. This event was significant in that it alerted the colonial state to the need for a body to represent the tenants. Accordingly, a Tenants' Representative Board was created with a purely advisory capacity (Haj-Hamad, 1980: 315).

Nevertheless, the lesson of the strike was recognized by tenants elsewhere, and by the early 1950s tenants in various parts of the country were struggling to form unions. In the private pump schemes, the tenants' movement began in 1952 but took several more years to establish itself. This was on the whole due to the fact that most of the schemes were held by religious dignitaries and their families as well as by tribal leaders and wealthy businessmen, and that many of the tenants were their loyal sectarian followers. In short, this area was the bastion of the dominant social class.

From the early days of the transitional period in 1953, before the election of the first parliament and the formation of a self-rule government in 1954, the movement toward unionization among Sudanese tenants had accelerated. The movement was widespread, encompassing tenants in Northern Province, the central area of the Gezira, the Blue and White Nile schemes and farmers as far west as the Nuba Mountains. In all of these regions tenants demanded recognition for their own unions in place of government-sponsored Tenants' Associations, which were dominated by traditional sheikhs or their sympathizers. However, it was mainly in the fertile triangle between the two Niles, on the Gezira and private cotton schemes, that the unionization movement was the most vigorous.

While the British colonial administrators officially ignored the unions and left their petitions unanswered, unofficially the colonial state used all possible means to stifle such organizations. District commissioners actively solicited the support of traditional leaders for the state-sponsored Tenants' Associations, while government loans for scheme owners were made available on more attractive terms by nearly doubling the grace period, extending the repayment time from three to five years without raising the interest rate from its 0.6% level (Al-Saraha, 17 August 1953). In comparison, tenants in Northern Province, who had had a poor winter harvest of wheat and beans and who had requested a reduction in their irrigation tax, were denied access to water until the tax had been paid in full; others who requested loans to recondition run-down water wheels were completely ignored (Al-Saraha, 7 July 1953). Also, in the Gezira, the colonial state reactivated a 1925 Land Settlement Act and requisitioned over 250,000 feddans from landholders who held less than five feddans each (Al-Saraha, 25 August 1953). At about the same time, several private pump schemes averaging between 15,000 and 30,000 feddans each were licensed to Umma Party leaders, tribal sheikhs, retired civil servants and business-men (Al-Saraha, 10 July 1954, 28 August 1954). Such schemes, the tenants argued, were harmful not solely because they allowed a few individuals to control huge tracts of land, but mainly because they monopolized water resources, the scarcity of which the government itself often claimed had obstructed the growth of cooperative schemes.

Toward the closing months of 1953, tenants' unions in the Gezira declared their intention of merging into one representative body. Only then did the British administrators of the Gezira acknowledge earlier petitions, but they remained adamantly opposed to the union and reaffirmed their view of the official Tenants' Associations as sole representatives of the tenants. The tenants went on to organize well-attended mass meetings in which hundreds of union representatives embraced the idea of a unified organization. Impressed by the huge gatherings, about three-quarters of the Tenant Board's membership publicly resigned from the government sponsored bodies and joined the Gezira Tenants' Union (GTU), itself born a few weeks prior to the formation of the first self-rule government in 1954 under NUP leadership (Al-Saraha, 10 November 1953).

By mid-1955, tenants' unions in the White Nile schemes had overcome the handicap of their fragmentation and amalgamated themselves into one organization for the whole region, with their counterparts in the Blue Nile schemes following along the same path. It was during this period that tenants in the private schemes first began to brandish the strike weapon. In certain areas—around Sennar, El Sheikh Talha, El Massarra, El Gomirat, and El Bousata—the weapon was used, though unsuccessfully, with tenants demanding, among other things, payment of overdue accounts and recognition of their committees (Al-Saraha, 1 June 1957). Most significant of these strikes was the one in Kassab Scheme that was owned by none other than Sayed Ali Al Mirghani, patriarch of the Khatmiya sect.

Considering the semi-divine status of the leading sectarian families, the strike at Kassab connoted a challenge that went far beyond local economic or political concerns and threatened the very fabric of the age-old national social order (Bechtold, 1976: 76). Hence, earlier calls by the religious aristocracy and agricultural capitalists for the formation of a coalition government grew more insistent. Finally, in the closing months of 1955, the two sacrosanct patrons of the Khatmiya and Ansar sects met for the first time in decades and publicly enunciated their desire for a national unity government (Haj-Hamad, 1980: 320, 359–360). The Khatmiya-Ansar rapprochement has been presented merely as "a marriage of convenience of two partners with opposite foreign and domestic political interests save one: to exclude their NUP rivals from office" (Bechtold, 1976: 188). However, these "interests" are rarely examined and the social forces behind them are never delineated. Instead, political developments are divorced from the complex contexts in which they take place and are conveniently reduced to the shallow confines of personal vendettas or the myth of ethnic rivalry. The interests in question were shockingly manifest in the incident at Jouda.

Jouda: The Explosion of the Class Struggle[2]

Once the independence celebrations of January 1956 were over, the Umma Party moved from the opposition benches and entered the cabinet, the premiership of which was retained by the NUP. Thus, the coalition government that the religious aristocracy had demanded turned out to be a coalition of agricultural capitalists with other fractions of the bourgeoisie. This was the sole instance to date when the cabinet appeared to represent the political interests of the various fractions of the power bloc in unison. As such, the government of February 1956 showed a great capacity for virulent abuse of political power to safeguard the bloc's economic interests, particularly in the agricultural sector.

The immediate challenge that faced the NUP-Umma government was that posed by the rising tide of union agitation in the private pump schemes. Shortly before independence, the White Nile Tenants' Union (WNTU) had submitted to the authorities a memorandum detailing their demands. Among other changes, they asked for (a) effective and meaningful partnership in scheme management by reversing the division of cotton proceeds, that is, granting the tenants a 60% share instead of the customary 40%; (b) the appointment of independent chartered accountants to review scheme accounts; (c) the participation of tenants in decisions concerning the ginning and marketing of cotton; and (d) official recognition for their union.

Once again the government adopted the position of earlier times and the tenants' demands were ignored. Nor did the regime budge at the union's warning of the possibility that ongoing sporadic strikes might lead to a massive stoppage. All subsequent calls for negotiations were met with official silence. Moreover, with the installation of the new government, intransigence gave way to a more aggressive policy by local authorities. Thus, early in February, leaders of the WNTU who were touring private schemes urging tenants to postpone strike action pending an attempt to set up negotiations were themselves arrested. These and similar acts set the stage for a chain of profoundly tragic events that left a lasting impression on agrarian relations in the whole country.

The backlash to the arrest of the union leaders was phenomenal. No fewer than 4000 tenants swarmed into Kosti, the administrative center of the White Nile, and demanded the release of their leaders from detention as well as the opening of negotiations on the items presented by the WNTU. The tenants warned that failure to comply with these demands would lead to their withholding of the cotton crop from the scheme owners. In an attempt to defuse the tense situation without losing face, the government representatives released the union leaders while simultaneously ordering the arrest of 150 tenants who had struck. Of these tenants, a first group of 53 were summarily tried and received sentences ranging from 18 months' imprisonment to ten whip strokes. Feelings were inflamed even further by the fact that the native administrator who presided over the trial owned a private scheme and held partnerships in two additional ones. Understandably, tensions mounted and following a union-sponsored rally, more tenants as well as workers and a representative of a government employees' union were detained, while all public gatherings were banned. In an effort to avoid further complications, not to mention the unwelcome attention of the Khartoum newspapers, the authorities moved the trial of the remaining 97 tenants out of Kosti to the adjacent village of Jouda.

At Jouda, there was also a major private pump scheme whose tenants had threatened to strike. The owner of this scheme, one of the Sudan's foremost financial capitalists and a brother of the post-Sudanization Managing Director of the Gezira Scheme, welcomed the court as a sign of law, order, and stability. Instead of subduing and dissuading the Jouda tenants from supporting unionization, setting up court in their midst had the opposite effect: the tenants demonstrated against the court and refused to pick cotton or deliver what had already been picked to the licensee pending the settlement of their share in the annual cotton proceeds that, by then, had entered a third year of delay.

Reaction to this situation by government officials and agricultural capitalists was harsh and uncompromising. The latter warned against a communist conspiracy, while the former moved in police reinforcements and announced that the Jouda tenants would be charged with the unlawful and criminal possession of goods, that is, cotton, which did not belong to them. The tenants, however, refused to give in or surrender the cotton, and in an attempt to disband them, a police contingent was moved in. In the confrontation that ensued, the spears and axes of the tenants proved no match for the fire power of the state's apparatus of violence. Government communiques held that three policemen had lost their lives and three had been injured, while attempting to minimize the extent of the tenants' casualties, which were "difficult to assess since they had fled into the fields." The WNTU, on the other hand, claimed that 150 tenants had been killed and over 500 wounded.

Controversy over these numbers was quickly overshadowed by developments of even greater horror. Following the clash in Jouda, the security forces rounded up about 680 tenants for further interrogation in the administrative center of Kosti. Of these, 281 were interned in a disused armory without proper ventilation, food or water. Because of these conditions, 189 people were discovered the morning after to have died of suffocation during the night, and the final death toll reached 195 (Al-Sudan al-Jadid, 20 February 1956).

As expected, a state of emergency was declared in the Blue and White Nile areas, in which all meetings and processions were made illegal. More troops were rushed into the region, which was declared a "closed district" that could only be entered with a government pass. All of the WNTU leadership was arrested together with representatives of various workers' trade unions, who were charged with fomenting hatred and who received sentences of several months' imprisonment. Fifteen Jouda tenants were also taken to court, some of whom were jailed for 18 months. Victims who died in the armory were buried in mass graves while each family was paid in compensation a maximum sum of LS 20, and the government assured everyone that justice would take its course.

In the aftermath of these hideous events, religious and tribal leaders fanned out among the schemes and "succeeded in convincing mourners that what happened was dictated by destiny and fate and asked everyone to submit to the will of Allah" (Al-Raie al-Aam, 25 February 1956). A few of the minor state functionaries responsible for using the armory as a detention center were at first charged with negligence and were suspended from their official duties, but shortly thereafter charges were dropped. An inquiry into the whole Jouda tragedy was promised but no evidence of its work exists. In fact, existing evidence suggests that, far from being punished, the individuals who held positions of direct administrative responsibility for the events were in fact rewarded. The commissioner in charge of the province at the time was promoted to the rank of Permanent Under-Secretary of a major ministry within about three years and eventually became the managing director of a major state trading concern.

The Changing Equilibrium of Class Alliances in 1956

After Jouda, the NUP-Umma coalition came under fierce criticism from every trade union organization in the country. A national strike was declared by the militant Sudan Workers Trade Union Federation (SWTUF) in which students and the press joined and there were renewed calls for a genuine national unity government with representation from workers, farmers, and the left-wing Anti-Imperialist Front (AIF). Representatives of tenants' unions from Gezira, Nuba Mountains, Northern Province, and Blue and White Niles decided to present the government with the common front of a Sudanese Farmers' General Union (SFGU).

Throughout these events, agricultural capitalists and the religious aristocracy maintained as low a profile as the situation would permit. On the whole, and not unexpectedly, the former spoke of a communist plot, while the latter attempted to distance themselves from the government. The sectarian leadership of the Khatmiya and Ansar, in what must have been a calculated prelude to future moves, consoled tenants' families and made vague remarks concerning government inefficiency, focusing on the Ministry of Interior. In consequence, the NUP leadership, which held both the premiership of the coalition government and the portfolio of the Ministry of Interior, bore the brunt of the criticism and the party's prestige was dealt a severe blow.

The fact that the Khatmiya sect chose not to shore up the NUP underlined the extent of the schism between that party's leadership and the combined forces of agricultural capitalism. The cumulative effects of these contradictions brought about the split of the NUP. Thus, in June 1956, Khatmiya loyalists among the tribal leaders, religious agents, and fractions of the bourgeoisie with economic interests in rural areas of northern and eastern Sudan broke away from the NUP and formed the Peoples' Democratic Party (PDP) (Haj-Hamad, 1980: 359–360). Within days of receiving the public endorsement of Sayed Ali Al Mirghani, the PDP joined forces with the Umma Party of Sayed Abdel Rahman Al Mahdi and voted the NUP-Umma government out of office (Beshir, 1974: 203). Far from being spontaneous, this defection from the NUP was a calculated act that had been in the offing for quite some time. According to the new Umma Prime Minister who headed the coalition with the PDP, plans for this alliance were prepared even before the Umma-NUP rule. In an affidavit the Prime Minister later acknowledged that Khatmiya Members of Parliament had been for several months on the payroll of the Umma Party before they bolted from the NUP (Hamad, 1980: 260–261).

Less than a year after the independence that the NUP had boasted of realizing, this party, the political vehicle of the one-time hegemonic fraction of the bourgeoisie, was reduced to the meek status of a shadowy opposition group. Deprived of the religious aristocracy's patronage and deserted by the most powerful fractions of the bourgeoisie, the NUP from this period on appeared as "the party of merchants, civil servants and other professionals with strong roots in the urban areas" (Bechtold, 1976: 20).

The Umma-PDP government was very much the creation of the most powerful indigenous social forces, a fact that ensured it a longer life-span than its predecessor. The relationship of the coalition parties with the religious aristocracy was stronger than mere spiritual guidance, financial backing, or political support through directives to the sectarian followers. Direct control was ensured through the appointment of the eldest sons of the Khatmiya and Ansar leaders to the presidencies of the Umma and PDP, respectively. This, however, does not imply that these parties were merely family institutions. Far from it—they were class organizations in a society that was dominated economically as well as ideologically by a religious aristocracy in alliance with agricultural capitalists.

These class organizations have taken various institutional forms in the years since the period discussed here, and relations of dominance have undergone shifts. Moreover, with the Umma-inspired and organized Agrarian Reform Act of 1968, the economic base of the agrarian bourgeoisie was transformed. This transformation was more than merely a matter of crop selection and techniques of production; rainfed farming centered on the production of sorghum—the main staple of the diet of the Sudanese masses—for the home market rather than on production of export crops. This profound change at the level of production served to sharpen still further the boundaries and incompatibility between established fractions of the Sudanese bourgeoisie in alliance with their affiliated subordinate classes. Indeed, the material basis for the orientations of various subordinate classes toward the dominant power blocs was altered through this transformation. This is particularly true of tenants in the irrigated schemes. The shift of private agricultural investment out of the pump schemes and into rainfed (non-tenant) farming relieved the explosive antagonism between the agrarian bourgeoisie and the tenantry and enabled the former to use state power to appease sections of the tenantry. This in turn gave increased scope to processes of social differentiation within the tenantry (see O'Brien, 1984).

With the shift to food production, the interests of the group dominated by the agrarian bourgeoisie took on the characteristics of what de Janvry calls an "articulated alliance," identified with the expansion of the domestic market and in opposition to the interests of its rival "disarticulated alliance" dominated by the externally oriented commercial bourgeoisie—since the mid-1970s in alliance with foreign Arab capital (de Janvry, 1981). Thus, the political divisions analyzed here have in later years become deeper and sharper.

SEASONAL LABOR MIGRATION AND ITS IMPACT ON PEASANT AGRICULTURE

The development of capitalist agriculture in Sudan on the basis of tenant cultivators in the Zeidab-Gezira model had as one of its explicit aims preventing the emergence of a large and turbulent landless proletariat. However, experience in the Gezira quickly showed that large supplies of wage labor would nevertheless be required on a seasonal basis, especially to pick the cotton. The result was the formation of a vast system of seasonal labor migration of peasants and pastoralists who continued to pursue their traditional productive activities at home during the rest of the year. These supplies of seasonal wage labor did not evolve spontaneously in response to the demand, but were created as the result of British policies devised to stimulate them (O'Brien, 1980, 1983).

Colonial Labor Policy

The policies of the British regime in Sudan that stimulated seasonal supplies of labor were heterogeneous and included policies that had other aims as well. The cornerstone of all such policy was, as in other African colonies, taxation of the indigenous population. The British government that ruled Sudan until 1926 under martial law had been preoccupied with problems of pacification and security, and had consequently taxed the population cautiously and at relatively low levels. But, once control over the northern provinces had been firmly established and resistance had subsided, the pressing need for labor in the Gezira, as well as the British desire to stimulate the cash economy generally, led to the revision of the tax laws in the 1920s. The British raised taxes and pressed their collection more vigorously throughout the country. The specific mix of taxes assessed varied from district to district according to local conditions, but generally included some form of crop, animal, and house or poll taxes.

Aggressive marketing of key consumer goods, including manufactured cloth, tea, coffee, and sugar, helped expand cash needs further— not to mention expanding markets for British industry and commerce. In some areas, such as the village of el 'Igayla discussed below, presenting such goods on local markets was sufficient to stimulate a demand. Elsewhere, such as along the middle reaches of the Rahad River, more forceful methods were required (see below). There, for example, peasants preferred the cloth produced by their traditional methods from cotton they grew themselves to the more expensive Manchester cloth. As a result, the British banned private cotton cultivation in Blue Nile Province (and others nearby), and when peasants persisted by moving their cotton plants inside their fenced compounds, the police searched them out and burned them.

In either case, the result was the substitution of a regular cash need for a key indigenous handicraft industry. Subsequently, government could manipulate prices of cotton piece goods, the supply of which it monopolized, in response to fluctuating economic conditions in the country. Government monopolies of tea, coffee, and sugar supplies were used in the same way. Thus, the Governor-General's annual reports regularly included a section in which pricing policies were related to crop yields and rural livestock prices for the year. Government also regulated amounts and distribution of supplies of these key consumer goods to the same ends. This occurred perhaps most dramatically in 1942–1943 when exceptionally bountiful peasant harvests resulted in a very poor turnout for cotton picking in the Gezira. At the recommendation of the Labour Board, supplies of cloth, tea, coffee, and sugar to rural areas were cut off and channeled through the administrative offices of the Gezira Scheme (Labour Board, 1943).

The offices of the colonial administration were put to use in other ways to help stimulate the flow of labor to the Gezira Scheme. District commissioners and their staffs toured the villages of their districts to propagandize on behalf of the Gezira Scheme and served as rural recruiters for picking labor. Sudan Railways periodically offered reduced fares for migrant labor traveling to the scheme area during peak seasons when labor supplies fell short of demand.

Additional supplies of wage labor were provided by immigrants from the west. In response to upward pressures on cotton-picking piece rates in the early depression years, the government adopted a policy of encouraging the settlement in and around the Gezira area of West African Muslim immigrants. Small villages of the Takari settled,[3] with official encouragement and assistance, in suitable vacant land throughout much of the scheme, where they supplied a year-round pool of virtually landless labor. Other groups of Takari settled in areas adjacent to the scheme, many of them in the Native Administration *dar* (tribal homeland) assigned to the Fulani sultan Mai Wurno southeast of Gezira (Duffield, 1979, 1981). There they cultivated their own family plots, working for wages in the Gezira Scheme during the cotton-picking season.

The British regime in Sudan protected labor supplies by rigorously restricting the development of other enterprises that might generate demands for labor that could compete with the Gezira (Gaitskell, 1959; O'Brien, 1980, 1983). It was not until the transitional period leading up to independence that the colonial government promoted investment by Sudanese private capital in mechanized rainfed cultivation. However, the rapid expansion of both irrigated and rainfed capitalist agriculture following independence led to rapid expansion in demand for seasonal wage labor.

The Expansion of Seasonal Labor Markets

Until the 1950s, regular supplies of seasonal labor to the Gezira Scheme came mostly from areas surrounding the scheme and from central Kordofan along the rail line. Takari settlers in and around the scheme formed the stable core of the labor force. Much of the seasonal labor force was composed of irregular migrants who sought wage labor occasionally, as the result of crop failures in the villages, unfavorable fluctuations in prices, and the incidence of special expenditures such as for marriage. Such irregular migrants participated in wage labor in varying ways and with varying frequency (see O'Brien, 1980, 1983).

During the colonial period there was widespread capitalist penetration of village productive systems through stimulation and expansion of cash needs. Although altered by this penetration, many peasant and pastoral systems remained basically self-sufficient in the limited sense that local production of subsistence and cash goods, irregularly supplemented by seasonal wage labor, generally sufficed to reproduce the community from one year to the next. However, wholesale disarticulation of domestic economies was not widespread, and was generally restricted to the core labor supply areas. Instead, there were a variety of responses to the pressures of partial incorporation into the capitalist economy based on differing internal characteristics and local conditions, including traditional divisions of labor (particularly productive roles of women) and attitudes toward work.

Within the range of variation, two broad patterns of response were particularly important: (1) many nomads and recently settled former nomads, among whom women took prominent roles in agricultural production, became regularly involved in cotton picking in family groups; and (2) members of strongly patriarchal groups and others in which women did little or no agricultural work most frequently sought to intensify local agricultural production and produce cash crops rather than seek wage labor (O'Brien, 1980, 1983). Among the latter type of groups, seasonal labor migration tended to be irregular, with only men migrating while women and children remained at home.

What is of central importance in this context is the fact that the development of the colonial political economy, and the agricultural labor force in particular, proceeded in such a way that the manner and extent of incorporation of individual communities depended largely on their location and internal characteristics. Initial stages of incorporation were achieved not through any profound transformation of existing production but through tapping potentials existing, in various forms, within precolonial productive structures for expanding production, either directly within the village through extension and/or intensification of production, or indirectly through drawing off surplus labor for work elsewhere. Thus, the early stages of capitalist penetration took place on the basis of absolute rather than relative surplus value.[4]

The British authorities in Sudan were explicit about preventing class formation on the European model that could produce an economically independent local dominant class or a volatile landless proletariat (O'Brien, 1980). Moreover, large supplies of cheap labor were needed only seasonally, and the maintenance of peasant and pastoral productive systems as the sites of their reproduction was necessary.

A crucial consequence of this condition for the colonial labor force was a diversity of forms of incorporation that allowed participation in wage labor in ways that were compatible with the continued reproduction of the varying organizing social relations in specific communities. This does not mean that colonialism did not foster specifically capitalist processes of class formation in the countryside. Indeed it did, as the following two case studies of villages with distinctly different patterns and histories of incorporation into agricultural labor markets indicate. Um Fila, in Blue Nile Province, preserved for decades a degree of productive autonomy that allowed irregular seasonal migration of adult men only. On the other hand, el 'Igayla, in central Kordofan, was deeply involved in regular wage labor, migrating in family groups to pick cotton, from the opening of the Gezira Scheme in 1925.

Um Fila: A Case of Marginal Incorporation[5]

The people of Um Fila belong to a Muslim Zabarma clan that came to Sudan from West Africa in the nineteenth century. After temporary settlement in various areas of Sudan, the core of this clan settled in three villages, including Um Fila, along the Rahad River in the early 1930s. This area had previously been sparsely populated and was included in the *dar* for West Africans granted to Sultan Mai Wurno in the Native Administration framework (Duffield, 1979, 1981).

The Zabarma came from an area with a long history of state formation based on tax/tribute-paying peasant farming, and were long accustomed to disciplined agriculture under conditions of regular exploitation. According to elders in Um Fila, their fathers had brought the group to its current remote location in order to escape influences, such as schools and urban markets, which they deemed threatening to their strong patriarchal authority.

Social Organization. Most of the village population is organized in large extended family production/consumption units composed of a father, his married sons, and their wives and children living together in fenced compounds. The men and boys work common fields together and their families consume from common stores and a unified treasury managed by the patriarch. Fathers control their sons' access to marriage partners, but post-marriage controls over sons are based on the favorable production mix and efficiency possible only for large units, and on a network of ideological supports, such as conventional expressions of respect for age. The ability of men to build and maintain large extended family production units has always depended on their reproductive success—particularly, their luck in fathering an appropriately spaced group of sons. Such reproductive success is consolidated through strategically timed polygynous marriages (see Gruenbaum, 1979; O'Brien, 1980).

Married women do not participate in the work in the main agricultural fields, but remain in strict seclusion within the family compound. Some women do perform some agricultural work, but this is generally confined to small plots within the compounds of poorer households.

Agricultural Production. Agricultural land is relatively abundant and is accessible to all members of the community by virtue of their membership in that community. The soil is heavy cracking clay, and the main crops cultivated are sorghum for household consumption and sesame for sale. In addition, small areas of millet are occasionally planted as a way of combatting the spread of *strega*, a weed parasitic on sorghum. Small amounts of other crops such as melons and okra may be intersown with the main crops or grown on small separate areas as well. The main plots are cultivated on a semipermanent basis using an internal rotation based on the primary alternation of sorghum and sesame, but usually without fallow. Yields under this regime seem to be remarkably stable (see O'Brien, 1978, 1980).

Since 1963, an increasing number of units hire tractors from local merchants or contractors to plow their fields. The use of tractors for plowing and planting has resulted in a more extensive pattern of cultivation by removing the labor demand bottleneck on cultivation previously imposed by the arduous task of hand tilling the heavy soil. Thus, the normal working day has been shortened from a virtually season-long dawn-to-dusk regimen to about 7 or 8 hours for the members of units hiring tractors. Most units do not hire tractors every year, but only periodically, as the soil compacts and hand tilling becomes more difficult again. Nevertheless, the regular use of tractors has created an important recurrent cash need that leaves farmers more vulnerable to inflation.

In addition to cultivating the main rainfed fields, some units also cultivate river bank/bottom vegetable gardens along the seasonal Rahad and a nearby tributary, and herd animals (mainly goats and sheep, with some cattle). However, successfully combining all three activities requires a large unit able to spare an adult (preferably aided by a boy) from the main cultivations for each garden and herd. Such large units are thus able to afford a much more balanced diet all year round and greater security for their members than are smaller units.

Wage Labor. For most households, migration for wage labor only occurs following poor crops or in order to meet some extraordinary expense, such as for marriage of a son. Only men work for wages, and among them it is most frequently the young and the demographically less successful who most frequently must migrate in search of work. When migrating, men of Um Fila virtually exclusively seek work in the higher paying but more arduous sorghum harvest and threshing, preferably in schemes nearby.

Wage labor within the village and a neighboring related village has recently been replacing cooperative labor parties for redistributing labor in peak season activities (such as weeding). However, most men participate in this type of wage labor both as employer and as employed. Also, such labor exchange between close relatives or friends, as well as in fields that lie close to the village, still takes place on the basis of compensation in meals and tea while working (cf. Abdel Ghaffar, 1974; Barth, 1964).

Internal Social Differentiation. Recently, the complex production units in Um Fila have begun to break down. The economic advantages of larger units over nucleated units continue to be enjoyed by some very large and successful units, but pressures on the patriarchs' management abilities and responsiveness to the needs and demands of their sons have been increasing as wage-earning opportunities in the area expand. In this context, inflation, the constant threat of sons breaking away, and the instability of the higher consumption standards of complex units lead some patriarchs to attempt to convert group assets to cash for trade, additional polygynous marriages, and so on. They thereby often precipitate conflicts with their sons that sometimes lead to a split.

Social differentiation among the people of Um Fila had previously been principally cyclical and demographic, an approximation of the Chayanovian model (Chayanov, 1966). Consumption standards generally rose with age and the number of productive sons a man had. A failure to have several sons resulted in the persistence of this situational poverty throughout life. The accelerated penetration of the village productive system by capital in recent years has begun to alter these conditions of differentiation. Inflation, expanding cash needs, and the fragmentation of extended family units have brought increasing pressure on people to adopt the calculus of returns to individual labor time. Thus, for example, the poorest and richest families now tend to drop millet, an unprofitable crop employed mainly for its role in the rotation, as they seek to maximize immediate returns to their labor time and cash investment. Increasingly, the only options for the more prosperous farmers are to establish self-sustaining cycles of accumulation, or to risk decline in their living standards. But the impossibility of sustained, expanding accumulation within agriculture leads them to convert assets into some form of trade. Group assets thus tend to become individualized in the hands of those who head production units.

At the same time, differentiation has begun to appear within the incipient local labor market. A few gain the ability to participate exclusively as employers of others; some find themselves having to neglect their own crops in order to earn cash through wage labor for their neighbors in order to meet immediate consumption needs. The reciprocal character of labor exchange is breaking down. However, within the existing framework of the village, there are limits to this process as none have yet become landless or face landlessness as an imminent prospect. Instead, crop mortgaging and crop speculation increase.

These differences within the village are still largely quantitative and reversible. A number of men in the village have in the past established themselves in trade only to lose their accumulated assets to crop failure or fire. There is no clear demarcation of internal class relations. However, class relations do play a crucial role in the life of the village.

To understand their nature requires a wider perspective than can be obtained by looking at the village in isolation.

Relations to Capital. Capital has penetrated village production processes from outside in a number of ways apart from the long-standing marketing of cash crops and the purchase by villagers of an increasing array of consumption goods. Through tractor hire, crop mortgaging, and direct investment in non-land agricultural inputs, capital from outside the village have moved beyond simple market relations with village farmers to play a role in the production process itself. As these external elements of the agricultural production processes of Um Fila have increasingly become systematic prerequisites for production to take place, that production has come to presuppose capital as an integral factor of production. For all but the small group of poorest families, successful cultivation of their fields requires hiring tractors (at least occasionally) from regional merchants or contractors, which in turn requires cash or credit. The poorest units subsist through the agricultural season on advances in grain from merchants and local crop speculators who generally demand a return at a rate of two sacks at harvest for each one advanced. They thus approach a condition of becoming *de facto* wage earners employed by capital in their own fields. In such circumstances, village agricultural production has come to produce capital directly for capital without the mediation of commodity markets. That is, to the extent that these new economic forms have spread in the village productive system, the character of the relationships village producers have with capital has been transformed from the indirect market relations of the sale of products to direct relations of production with capital—that is, the direct production of surplus value for capital (see O'Brien, 1979, 1980, forthcoming; Banaji, 1977; Bernstein, 1977).

Yet, for the most part, the villagers of Um Fila are not direct wage laborers working for capitalist employers, except insofar as they do work for wages part-time or short term through seasonal migration to places of employment outside the village, and in more limited ways in wage labor within the village. They maintain possession of their land and retain formal independence from capital in their disposition of family labor power and in the management of the production process. The control capital can exercise over the production process is thus limited by this formal independence. Nevertheless, villagers are increasingly becoming direct producers of surplus value for capitalists as their production increasingly posits capital as a starting point as well as producing it. The villagers thereby enter at the level of their own production processes into cycles of expanded capitalist reproduction on a regional and national scale. This aspect of incorporation into capitalist political economy is clearer, as well as much more developed, in the case of el 'Igayla.

El 'Igayla: A Case of Disarticulated Accumulation[6]

El 'Igayla is located in the region that has come to be known as the "Joama' belt" along the rail line in central Kordofan. The village was founded in its present location in 1898, shortly before British conquest of Sudan. El 'Igayla is located near the end of the great seasonal watercourse of Kordofan, Abu Habil, where the sandy ridges of northern Kordofan meet the heavy clay of southern Kordofan. In el 'Igayla this Joama' group initially cultivated millet and small amounts of cotton for local consumption on long-fallow shifting forest plots.

Sudden drastic changes in the village economy occurred as the result of a combination of factors in the 1920s. The east-west rail line linking el Obeid with Khartoum and the Gezira passed within a few kilometers of the village and, when the Gezira Scheme Scheme opened in 1925, large numbers of migrant laborers began to pass through the area. Some of these migrants were immigrants from Chad and West Africa looking for places to settle permanently. Also in this period, the British government began to pursue taxation more aggressively in rural areas, including el 'Igayla, in order to stimulate cash needs and a flow of labor to Gezira. At the same time, consumer goods, particularly manufactured cloth, appeared in local markets. Coincidentally, el 'Igayla was hit hard by the drought and famine that affected most of Sudan in 1925–1926 and again the following season.

The people of el 'Igayla responded to these conditions in a number of ways. Apparently regarding Manchester cloth as both superior to and cheaper than their own (especially in the context of complete crop failure), they rapidly abandoned the cultivation of cotton and production of cloth, buying imported cloth instead. During the disastrous 1925–1926 season, according to the old men, the District Commissioner visited the village and told them that food and cash wages were abundantly available in the Gezira Scheme to those willing to pick cotton. Accordingly, most the villagers went to Gezira that season and in the following season of drought.

The new source of cash income also gave the villagers another idea. They set about clearing the forest surrounding their cultivations and began to use the cash earned in the Gezira to hire some of the migrant labor circulating through their area to cultivate new fields. As production decisions came increasingly to be made on the basis of returns to labor and cash inputs—rather than on the basis of simple household consumption needs—farmers began to convert the millet plots to sorghum and sesame (and later groundnuts), which enjoy higher returns to labor and higher prices than millet. Cash cropping assumed rapidly increased importance, to the extent that most families now directly produce only a portion of their own food. Instead, much of the grain crop is itself marketed now, and families purchase a substantial portion of the food they consume.

Social Organization and Agricultural Production. El 'Igayla exhibits much more extensive and complex social differentiation than Um Fila. After the original settlers cleared and parceled among themselves all available cultivable land, groups of migrant families were encouraged to settle in and around the village to provide a pool of wage labor for the landowners. Some families received small grants or loans of land in exchange for working in the fields of the landowners, while others sharecropped small parcels and worked for wages on their benefactors' fields part-time. After the local harvest, these settlers generally went to Gezira to pick cotton, returning afterward for the following season of work in el 'Igayla.

As a result of this individualization of landownership and the distribution of small plots to settlers, el 'Igayla now has a significant permanent population of landless families and other families with only small holdings. In our 1977 survey, we found that 13% of the men in el 'Igayla owned 50% of the land owned by men, while 9% of all married men were landless (O'Brien, 1980). At the same time, 95% of all surveyed married women cultivated separate plots from their husbands, with 70% of married women individually owning their own plots, while the balance rented or sharecropped the land of others. Most of the landless men, and many other men who owned only small plots, also rented or sharecropped land.

With the emergence of a local wage labor market in addition to the more distant Gezira in a context of an increasingly skewed distribution of land in the village, extended family relations broke down. Children (or spouses) dissatisfied with their rewards for participation in family production activities had the opportunity of working for a wage in the fields of neighbors and obtaining their own independent supplies of cash. By 1977, we found that children of about 12 years of age and older could and often did demand the going wage from their own parents for their work in the fields. Thus, money had come to mediate most relations with the village, even within the nuclear family.

The local wage labor market in el 'Igayla and surrounding villages obviously differs substantially from the largely redistributive character of wage labor in Um Fila. Women and children, as well as men, frequently and systematically engage in wage labor locally as well as in migrations to schemes. They work primarily in agriculture, but in some other activities as well. The most prosperous—a well-defined and stable group—enter this market only as employers of wage labor, never as laborers, while most must work for wages at some point in the annual cycle. The landless among both men and women, as well as the young who may later inherit land, work for wages regularly, some of them for brief periods during the rainy season and some for half or more of each day of the agricultural season.

Labor Migration. Many families in el 'Igayla regularly migrate in family groups for wage labor in cotton picking. Women and children work along with the men and with comparable levels of productivity. In the 1970s, the size and viability of family groups migrating to pick cotton was declining. In part, this results from the increase in schooling, especially of boys, and the fact that schools are in session through the peak period of cotton picking. But the greatest role has been played by the increasing pressures on individual labor time and its returns in cash terms that lead individuals, especially men, to seek the highest paying work available. Accordingly, many young men, for example, seek the higher paying work in sorghum harvesting instead of accompanying their families to pick cotton. Similarly, many teenage boys go to towns for several months each year to work. More generally, wage-earning opportunities, especially for the young, have expanded to such an extent that families find it increasingly difficult to command the labor of all members for central household accounts. Generalized individualization of economic responsibility and activity has tended to fragment families to the extent that each member of the nuclear family tends to have his or her own source of income as well as specified areas of responsibility for household expenditures. Thus, in general, husbands are responsible for supplying the family with food, wives with meeting kitchen and furnishing needs, teenage sons with supplying clothes for smaller siblings, and so forth.

Social Differentiation and Relation to Capital. It should already be apparent that social differentiation is relatively advanced and that capital penetrates village production processes extensively in el 'Igayla. Crop mortgaging and analogous transactions in other goods, both with village-based entrepreneurs operating on a regional basis and with outsiders, are everyday features of life for most villagers. Conventional sharecropping and land rental are widespread.

In addition to these simple economic forms common to much of Sudan, there are a number of more complex forms that bind producers to capital. Cash-poor smallholders who cannot set production in their fields in motion independently may find a merchant to finance production. This may take various forms. The merchant may supply seed and cash to employ wage labor, even paying the landowner a wage for the work he does in his own field, in exchange for a share (usually a half share) of the crop at harvest after deduction of expenses. Alternatively, the merchant may formally pay a cash rent to the landholder in return for full rights to the crops produced. In such cases, the landholder usually hires on for a wage, perhaps supervising other wage laborers working his own fields, but without any claim on the harvest. A similar variety of forms exists in the employment of labor in the fields owned by larger, more prosperous landholders.

The village wage labor market in agriculture is also well developed. Individuals generally do not sign on as permanent or season-long employees of landholders. Instead, most engage in wage labor at intervals, especially in peak land preparation, weeding and harvest operations, for periods varying from a single morning or afternoon of work to a week or two of daily work. Commonly, an individual will agree to work for his or her employer each morning or each afternoon for such a period, spending the other half of each day in his or her own cultivations (which may be on rented or sharecropped land). Others, especially the landless who may be cultivating very small rented or sharecropped plots (or no land at all), may work full-time in wage labor for longer periods after completing each operation quickly in their own plots.

El 'Igayla exhibits a relatively extensive secondary occupational specialization by labor-skill and handicraft production. There are water carriers, herders, bed makers, house builders, employees of the village flour mill and diesel pump well, and others who spend part or all of their work time in nonagricultural activities. The work in such occupations takes an analogous variety of forms to those found in agriculture, from independent handicraft production to direct wage labor. Corresponding to this occupational specialization are a wide variety of cash needs integral to household consumption in the village.

The "merchants" active in el 'Igayla are not only engaged in trade, but, as evident in the forgoing, are involved in production processes in manifold ways. Not only are they owners of productive property and direct employers of wage labor, but they set production in motion in various other direct and indirect ways, such as crop mortgaging, sharecropping and land rental. These rural capitalists are not just operating in one village, but are operating over a wide region, as are other nonresident capitalists who are also involved in el 'Igayla.

In fact, the village of el 'Igayla has little social meaning—in the sense that Um Fila still does—except as a residential cluster. El 'Igayla residents work for outsiders, employ outsiders, trade with outsiders, and enter credit relations with outsiders on a daily basis and in systematic ways. The people of the village are integrated as nuclear family units and, increasingly, as individuals into the regional and national political economies through the mediation of cash relations unfettered by mediating cycles of social reproduction.

Differential Processes of Capitalist Penetration

The character of the formation of the colonial (and postcolonial) agricultural labor force had to allow communities to participate in wage labor in ways that were compatible with the short-term requirements of local social reproduction. This resulted in the segmentation of labor markets along largely ethnic lines according to different patterns and intensities of work and other variabilities corresponding to the operation of absolute surplus value in a heterogeneous social environment. In this way, expansion on the basis of absolute surplus value defined a substantial economic space within which social and cultural processes determined specific economic forms of capitalist incorporation. The preceding two case studies illustrate the range of variation that occurred in the manner and extent of incorporation of village productive systems into colonial markets under such conditions.

Such processes of differential capitalist penetration and incorporation into market systems on the basis of absolute surplus value are contradictory. On the one hand, they promote dissolution of village-based processes of social reproduction and the subsumption of village production units by a generalized process of expanded reproduction of capital—whether rapidly as in el 'Igayla or slowly as in Um Fila. On the other hand, once the limits of expansion on the basis of absolute surplus value are reached through differential incorporation, capitalist reproduction requires more homogeneous processes of relative surplus value. This contradiction in Sudan has resulted in the emergence of processes based on the conversion to the dynamic of relative surplus value—primarily through intensification of labor effort rather than new techniques. By the late 1970s, this had resulted in an escalating crisis of the agricultural labor force in particular and the entire Sudanese political economy in general.

The consequences of this recent (and ongoing) crisis for agricultural labor markets in Sudan are many and far-reaching. There has been a marked intensification of processes of individualization of market relations generally and labor market participation most especially, leading to increased calculation of individual labor time as the central criterion of work. These pressures are intensified by accelerating processes of "backdoor" proletarianization, by which rural producers are increasingly incorporated into consumer markets as peasant productivity declines and cash needs proliferate (cf. de Janvry, 1981). Reflecting these pressures, the mid-1970s witnessed strong tendencies toward equalization of wage rates across the boundaries of the previous market segments, and thus the breakdown of the segmentation itself. This does not mean that wage rates have become or can be expected to become uniform throughout capitalist agriculture in the country. Instead, the emerging pattern of wage differentials in agriculture is coming to reflect differential transport costs, physical differences in work activities, and a new range of social variables.

Specifically, wage rates in cotton picking seem unlikely to stabilize at a level as high as for sorghum harvesting wages—toward which they were moving in the late 1970s—because of the different physical requirements of the two tasks. While more women can be expected to begin joining the men in harvesting sorghum, children and women who have small children or are pregnant generally cannot attain satisfactory levels of productivity in this heavy work. Such people, together with the aged and less robust, are therefore likely to continue to provide pools of smaller family groups for cotton picking. Thus while cotton-picking wage rates necessarily rise as the size of migrating family groups declines, a ceiling relative to sorghum harvesting wages remains immanent in the continued availability of these smaller family groups.

These changes in agricultural labor markets in Sudan amount to nothing less than a complete transformation from ethnic segmentation to social differentiation of the labor force. In 1970, knowing an individual's age, sex, and ethnic identification was a reliable predictor of the type, frequency, duration, intensity, and other important characteristics of that person's involvement in wage labor. By 1980, ethnic identification had become virtually irrelevant in such prediction, and factors such as location and opportunity cost had become more important.

This transformation in the dynamics of the agricultural labor market—indeed, this formation of a *national* labor market for the first time—has created increasing pressures on employers of agricultural wage labor to slash nonwage and fixed-cost components of the wage bill. As wage laborers increasingly recruit themselves to work where the wage rate is highest, employers have cut their involvement in the previously dominant elaborate systems of recruitment and their payment of workers' transport costs. The result is broadening scope within the emergent national wage labor market for the operation of standard capitalist market forces, such as competition and unemployment.

However, the unfettered unfolding of these recent trends would be disastrous for the cheap labor agricultural economy of Sudan, particularly insofar as competition for labor emerges and wage rates are forced to rise to a level that could cover the transport costs of workers traveling greater distances. Not surprisingly, capital and government have been fighting the damaging aspects of these trends. It is this context that makes certain otherwise puzzling government policies of the late 1970s and 1980s understandable. Thus, for example, current patterns of mechanization, though often uneconomical by direct cost-benefit criteria, create structural unemployment and underemployment, as well as reinforcing and concentrating seasonal demand for labor. Still more clearly, the settlement of refugee populations from Eritrea and Ethiopia as landless labor without full civil rights in key scheme areas provides off-peak season cheap labor and wage-busting super-cheap core labor supplies in peak season operations. On the other hand, the shift from a culturally defined association to a socially defined confrontation between capital and labor in combination with these sorts of policies also raises the prospect that labor resistance and struggle may take increasingly direct class forms.

NOTES

1. The LS 30 million is an approximation of different figures obtained from the Agrarian Reform Corporation in 1976–1978.

2. The following account is based on reports during February and March 1956 in the Khartoum newspapers Al-Raie al-Aam, Al-Saraha, Al-Sudan al-Jadid and the article "The Anniversary of Jouda" in Al-Sahafa (Khartoum), 24 March 1970.

3. Takari is the term many of these groups, most of them Hausa speaking, use to refer to themselves. Arab Sudanese generally refer to them as Fellata, a term that has come to have pejorative connotations (see Duffield, 1979, 1981).

4. For the development of the concepts of absolute and relative surplus value, see Marx (1967). Appreciation of the importance of this conceptual distinction in analyzing colonial penetration of precapitalist modes of production is only recent. See Banaji (1977), Bernstein (1977) and O'Brien (1977, 1979, 1980).

5. The account of Um Fila given here is based on fieldwork carried out there by O'Brien in 1976–1977, 1978, and 1979 funded by grants from the Ford Foundation-sponsored Manpower Research Project of the Faculty of Economic and Social Studies, University of Khartoum, and the Economic and Social Research Council, National Council for Research (Khartoum) S. E. el Shazali, H. M. Kuku, and M. Y. Ahmed el Mustafa assisted in various stages of this research. Use has also been made of the results of research in Um Fila by Ellen Gruenbaum. See O'Brien (1978, 1980) and Gruenbaum (1979).

6. The account given here of the village of el 'Igayla is based on fieldwork there carried out by O'Brien in 1977 with the help of the grants listed in Note 5 above. M. Y. Ahmed el Mustafa, M. A. Abu Sabah, and M. A. el Dukhari assisted in this research (see O'Brien, 1980).

REFERENCES

ABDEL G.M.A. (1974) "The relevance of indigenous organizations of production to development." Bulletin 11, Khartoum: Economic and Social Research Council.

ADAM, F. H. (1973) "Asalyeeb al-intag al-zeraie fi al-Sudan" (Modes of agricultural production in the Sudan). Bulletin of Sudanese Studies 4, 1, 2.

AL-RAIE Al-AAM (Khartoum).

AL-SAHAFA (Khartoum).

AL-SARAHA (Khartoum).

AL-SUDAN AL-JADID (Khartoum).

AWAD, M. H. (1972) "Sudanese agriculture." Unpublished paper. Khartoum.

BAKHEIT, G.M.A. (1972) Al-Idarah al-Baritaniyah wa-al-harakah al-wataniyah fi al-Sudan 1919–1939 (British Administration and Sudanese Nationalism 1919–1939). Beirut: Dar al-Thaqafa.

BANAJI, J. (1977) "Modes of production in a materialist conception of history." Capital and Class 2(3): 1–44.

BARBOUR, K. M. (1961) The Republic of the Sudan. London: Univ. of London Press.
——— (1959) "Irrigation in the Sudan: its growth, distribution and potential extension." Transactions and Papers of the Institute of British Geographers, N. 26.

BARNETT, T. (1977) The Gezira Scheme: An Illusion of Development. London: Frank Cass.

BARTH, F. (1964) "Economic spheres in Darfur," in R. Firth (ed.) Themes in Economic Anthropology. London: Tavistock.

BECHTOLD, P. K. (1976) Politics in the Sudan: Parliamentary and Military Rule in an Emerging African Nation. New York: Praeger.

BERNSTEIN, H. (1977) "Notes on capital and the peasantry." Rev. of African Pol. Economy 10: 60–73.

BESHIR, M. O. (1974) Revolution and Nationalism in the Sudan. London: Rex Collings.

CHAYANOV, A. V. (1966) The Theory of Peasant Economy. Homewood, IL: Dorsey.

DE JANVRY, A. (1981) The Agrarian Question and Reformism in Latin America. Baltimore: Johns Hopkins Univ. Press.

DUFFIELD, M. R. (1981) Maiurno: Capitalism and Rural Life in Sudan. London: Ithaca Press.

——— (1979) "Hausa and Fulani settlement and the development of capitalism in Sudan: with special reference to Maiurno, Blue Nile Province." Ph.D. dissertation, University of Birmingham.

DUNCAN, J.S.R. (1952) The Sudan. London: Blackwood and Sons.

EL HADARI, A.E.R. (1968) "The economics of agricultural production in the private pump schemes: Part I." Research Bulletin of the Department of Rural Economy, University of Khartoum, No. 13.

GAITSKELL, A. (1959) Gezira: A Story of Development in the Sudan. London: Faber and Faber.

GRUENBAUM, E. (1979) "Patterns of family living: A case study of two villages in the Rahad Area (Sudan). Monograph 12." Khartoum: Development Studies and Research Centre.

HAJ-HAMAD, M. A. (1980) Al-Sudan: Al-mazaq al-tarikhy wa affag al-mustagbal (The Sudan: The Historic Crisis and Future Horizons). Beirut: Dar al Kalymoh.

HAMAD, K. (1980) Al haraka al wataniya al Sudania: Al istiglal wa ma badu (The Sudanese National Movement: Independence and After). Al-Shariqa: Matbat Sawt al Khalij.

HAMIED, B. M. (1965) "Qadaya al-islah al-zerai" (Problems of agrarian reform). Al-Fejer al-Jadid 9.

HENDERSON, K.D.D. (1965) Sudan Republic. New York: Praeger.

HOLT, P. M. (1967) A Modern History of Sudan. London: Weidenfeld and Nicolson.

——— (1958) The Mahdist State in the Sudan, 1881–1898. Oxford: Clarendon Press.

Labour Board (1943) Minutes of the eighth meeting of the Labour Board, August 1943. Contained in unnumbered file of minutes of the meetings of the Labour Board, in the Archives of the Sudan Gezira Board, Barakat.

MARX, K. (1967) Capital, Vol. 1. New York: International Publishers.

NUGDALLA, S. A. (1972) "Elite formation and conflict in a modernizing society." Ph.D. dissertation, Manchester University.

O'BRIEN, J. (1984) "The social reproduction of tenant cultivators and class formation in the Gezira Scheme, Sudan," in B. Isaac (ed.) Research in Economic Anthropology, Vol. 6, Greenwich, CT: JAI Press.

——— (1983) "The formation of the agricultural labor force in Sudan." Rev. of African Political Economy 26: 15–34.

———— (1980) "Agricultural labor and development in Sudan." Ph.D. dissertation, University of Connecticut.

———— (1979) The Political Economy of Development and Underdevelopment. (With the assistance of S.E. el Shazali). Khartoum: Development Studies and Research Centre.

———— (1978) "How traditional is 'traditional' agriculture?" Sudan J. of Economic and Social Studies 2, 2: 1–10.

———— (1977) "Primary export production and the structures of underdevelopment," pp. 33–56 in A. M. el Hassan (ed.) Essays in the Economy and Society of Sudan, Vol. 1. Khartoum: Economic and Social Research Council.

———— (forthcoming) "African labor forces in historical perspective." Unpublished manuscript.

ROBERTSON, J. (1974) Transition in Africa. London: C. Hurst.

SHAW, D. J. (1966) "The development and contribution of irrigated agriculture in the Sudan," in D.J. Shaw (ed.) Agricultural Development in the Sudan. Papers for the Thirteenth Annual Conference of the Philosophical Society of the Sudan in conjunction with the Sudan Agricultural Society, 2 vols., Khartoum.

SØRBØ, G. (1977) How to survive development: The story of New Halfa. Monograph 6. Khartoum: Development Studies and Research Centre.

Sudan (1972) Gezira Board. Information and Publication Section. The Gezira Scheme: Past and present. Barakat.

———— Ministry of Agriculture and Irrigation. Reports.

———— (1967) Sudan Almanac. Khartoum: Government Press.

Sudan Parliament (n.d.) List of the Honourable Members of the Constituent Assembly 1954–57.

———— (1956) Weekly digest of proceedings. Session Number 927.

WARBURG, G. (1978) Islam, Nationalism and Communism in a Traditional Society: The Case of Sudan. London: Frank Cass.

10

ZAMBIA'S CAPTURED PEASANTRY

WILLIAM COWIE and JOTHAM MOMBA

The 1981 strike
by 55,000 copper mineworkers in Zambia was described as "the most
severe political crisis in post-independence history" to face that country
(Africa Report, 1981). As an incidence of collective action by Zambia's
workers, it was distinguished by its open challenge to the government
on the one hand and its failure to elicit support from the rural masses
on the other. However, given that it is rural producers who have gained
least, both absolutely and relatively, from state policies since 1964, the
situation appears somewhat paradoxical. On average, the plight of the
rural producer has worsened as a consequence of deteriorating terms of
trade between urban and rural areas (Fry, 1975); shortages of basic
producer and consumer goods; continued urban bias in development
plans and resource allocation (Young, 1973); and institutional weakness, especially among rural production support services, stemming
from poor coordination, low quality and inadequately trained and
motivated staff and inadequate capitalization and funding (Honeybone,
1979). Furthermore, there is evidence of ongoing social disintegration in
the rural areas caused by continuing outmigration of the young and
educated, and the erosion of the more traditional bonds of social
cohesion that centered on kinship and "tribal" status.

Yet as Barrington Moore and others have noted, immiseration need
not breed protest, especially of an organized fashion (Moore, 1973;
Paige, 1975). This is so, they argue, because political action and

inaction arise not from indexes of GNP or even from relative deprivation, but from specific social structures and historical situations. This chapter shows how the existing structural situation of the Zambian rural producers has led to their collective, if not individual, passivity at a time of political turmoil.

The first section of the chapter situates rural producers in Zambia's distinctive political economy. The most significant ideological and material forces are outlined, and the role and place of rural producers are defined.[1] The second section discusses the methods and tactics employed by UNIP and the state in its attempts to incorporate or otherwise neutralize opposition groups, despite deteriorating economic conditions. The third section presents two cases illustrating how production organization divides rural producers and how state-party manipulation of resources and local ideologies limit their capacity collectively and assertively to promote their interests even where cohesion exists. The conclusion evaluates the stability of the present structure and its implications for political action and economic progress in the near future.

The two geographic areas signaled out for discussion are Mazabuka and Monze Districts of Southern Province and Kanyanja Parish, Chipata District, Eastern Province. By Zambian standards, the agricultural systems in both locales are advanced: farmers produce and sell commodities *not only* to acquire consumer goods, *but also* to buy producer goods with which to expand production. Historically, these advanced areas owe their status to colonialism, and the kinds of pressures and dynamics that colonialism unleashed. In the case of Southern Province, commodity production expanded rapidly in the 1930s (Bayliss, 1979); in the case of Eastern, it followed World War II (Cowie, 1982). However, rural differentiation never reached a stage where the wage-labor relationship mediated human or social production relations. Rural producers were not separated from the means of production and many labor arrangements did not take the form of monetized transactions. In structural terms, the situation fits Bernstein's model of rural producers whose relations with capital and the state are mediated through "various forms of household production . . . [and] who are engaged in a struggle with capital/state for effective control of the conditions of production" (Bernstein, 1977). The focus of this chapter is precisely the nature and character of that struggle as fought out in the political arena.

THE POLITICAL ECONOMY OF REPUBLICAN ZAMBIA

The Mining Imperative

Since 1964, the material and political forces represented by the copper mining industry on the one hand—the doctrines, policies, and priorities of the national politicians of the ruling party UNIP (United National Independence Party) in conjunction with the state on the other—have given meaning and context to the role and place of the rural producers in Republican Zambia. The mining industry has given Zambia a mineral export base of some considerable dimensions (in African terms) from which the state, until recently, has been able to draw substantial revenues. In the words of Harvey, the Zambian state at independence was one with "an extremely limited supply of capital in the physical sense, but with an effectively unlimited supply of capital in the monetary sense" (Harvey, 1971). On the other hand, the political party UNIP, in its leaders' desire to maintain control and promote its version of "national" development, has attempted to expand and consolidate the position of the party as the leading national political organization, a position it established during the period of colonialism. Simply put, maintaining and expanding its legitimacy has been a foremost concern of UNIP's leadership since independence (Ollawa, 1979). As for the state, its role has been not only to serve the needs of administration and to implement party policy, but to promote development through active, extensive, and direct participation in the national economy. It is now also Zambia's major employer and an integral part of the still expanding patronage network.

At times, the interests surrounding these material and ideological forces have coalesced in such a way as to be mutually reinforcing, or supportive. This was the case for example when majority ownership of the copper industry by the state was welcomed, or at least tolerated, by private multinationals as a way of guaranteeing their investment (Seidman, 1974). At other times, state interests and private multinational interests have collided, as when the Zambian government failed to persuade companies to diversify their sources of supply away from Southern African markets following Rhodesia UDI in 1963 (Ndulo, 1979). At the same time, tension has not been confined to relations between the state and the private sector. The mine workers, whose "voluntarist" unions were formed in the colonial period, have long resisted incursions by the state into their domain; a resistance which became explosive before and during the aforementioned strike of 1981 (Fincham and Zulu, 1979).

Rural Producers

UNIP/state ideology and activity together with the large-scale and revenue earning capacity of the mining sector have kept the rural producers in a weak position both economically and politically. An enormous market exists for food in Zambia's cities, as nearly 50% of the Zambian population is urbanized (Simons, 1979), yet overall food production since independence has stagnated. Food imports far out-weigh domestic production in wheat, rice, flour, and until 1975 beef, making Zambia a heavy importer of foods.[2] As the revenue from the copper industry has declined in recent years, the food import bill becomes more difficult financially and more embarrassing politically. Furthermore, neither as a reservoir of labor nor as a source of investible surplus has the government viewed the rural sector as instrumental to Zambia's short- or medium-term needs. Rather, efforts at surplus extraction have centered almost exclusively on the mining industry (Daniel, 1979); a bias difficult to sustain in the face of recent low world prices for copper.

The rural population's lack of centrality in Zambia's economic structure and developmental priorities matches an equally peripheral role in party politics. Although rural producers gave mass support to the nationalist parties, neither the ANC (African National Congress), while it was leading the political struggle against Federation in the 1950s, nor the UNIP (United National Independent Party), after it became the majority party in 1960 and won independence, drew its organizational strength from rural producers. Both parties were rooted in and oriented toward urban areas. Only after 1958, in the form of a reconstituted ANC, and later within UNIP following the 1968 elections, did capitalist oriented rural producers gain an institutionally independent and expressive voice (Cowie, 1980; Momba, 1982). Their voice became increasingly muted and their organization incapacitated, however, as the single-party system evolved (Scott, 1974).

UNIP: FROM MASS ACTION
TO BUREAUCRATIC CONTROL

Nationalism and Development:
The Problem of Legitimacy

For the national leadership of UNIP, the party and its organization was, initially at least, both an instrument for achieving political hegemony (attaining a one-party state) through the ballot box and for implementing their developmental objectives. By 1973, it was clear the party had failed on both counts. UNIP by that year had fallen short of overwhelming popular electoral support and it had not been able to carry out the developmental initiatives of the party center. The declaration of one-party participatory democracy in 1973 was the leaders' response to failure. A new set of tactical difficulties faced the UNIP leadership, a leadership increasingly centralized around Kenneth Kaunda and a few advisers operating from State House. New political alliances had to be forged outside strict party organizational structures notably with bureaucrats and professionals, among others. The notion of party supremacy gave way to the new political ideology of "participatory democracy," and to the building and promoting of a new institutional structure that would implement State House directives. This new emphasis relied more heavily on popular mobilization through the state bureaucracy.

The party's failure to meet its political and developmental objectives was due in part to the continued inability of the party centre to control local branches. More fundamental were the party's political and developmental biases which increasingly alienated the rural populace and in particular the more commercially minded small producers and the traditional leadership. What were these biases?

In the first instance was the UNIP leadership's own preoccupation with political control. After UNIP's setbacks in the 1968 elections in which opposition parties maintained and enhanced their support in many regions, the concerns of leadership became "not (those) of economic development primarily, but those of legitimacy" (Chikulo, 1979). Secondly, and corresponding with the search for political hegemony was the promotion of a national developmental ethic in which the economic interests of the "nation" (as seen by the leadership) took precedence over local, ethnic, regional, or other factions or collective interests. In other words, on both the political and developmental fronts, the leadership presented the party as an instrument for the building of a national "classless" society (though not without inequality and privilege); the party was to represent the interests of all by virtue of its having incorporated, in one way or another, all levels and sections of society. This was the meaning of the slogan "One Zambia: One Nation": the party encompassing all interests in the nation and, by virtue of its monopoly over decision making, becoming the ruling force. In practical terms, such developmental priorities gave primary place to the establishment of large-scale, capital intensive, urban-based industry. In particular, new large-scale mining ventures were encouraged to diversify the economy away from copper (Seidman, 1974; Libby and Woakes, 1980). Neither the Central Committee nor Kenneth Kaunda believed that a competitive private sector market is intrinsically meritorious. Indeed, all major economic relations and transactions, industrial and agricultural, are controlled by the state, notably through parastatal bodies, and are subject to extensive political intervention (Turok, 1981). Prices are controlled by the state (as are investments, material inputs, and other expenditures), albeit with autonomy granted to responsible agencies themselves (Tordoff, 1980). Centralized state control of the economy is directed toward development of the urban centers; what does not yet appear to be in place, however, is central *planning* (Turok, 1980).

This urban bias is understandable given UNIP's organizational roots. Even in rural areas in the early 1960s, UNIP expressed, and tapped, the aspirations of the young and educated who perceived their futures as lying "in town" (Cowie, 1980). Likewise, the tendency of the Zambian state to undertake extensive state-party intervention into the economy, as witnessed in the building of the country's extensive parastatal structure, is not surprising given the colonial legacy of intervention and control by the state over economic activity. It is equally clear however, that such state control has resulted, as mentioned earlier, in price discrimination against rural producers (Dodge, 1977).

Together, and over time, such political and developmental biases were bound, perhaps inevitably, to alienate growing numbers of rural producers to the point that by the time of the introduction of the one-party state system "support for the ruling United National Independence Party was probably lower than at any time since before Independence" (Scott, 1980). Furthermore, the shift away from party to state as mobilizer is unlikely to alter the antirural nature of such a strategy. Recent development plans, for example, show little sign of coming to grips with the problem of agriculture. Promoting the potential of the richer peasants to become a truly independent commodity producing class is inimical to those who participate in, and benefit from, the party-state patronage structure. Consequently, where the rural areas are concerned, the issue is one of political control and the key object is to ensure that rural capitalist interests do not obtain a voice outside party-state control and do not ally themselves with urban-based opposition groups (Cowie, 1979b). This is not to suggest the UNIP leadership was faced with general consensus among urban groups especially outside the party. Quite the contrary, reliance on the bureaucracy in particular posed hazards. This was evident, for example, in 1975 when Mwanakatwe, a member of the Cabinet, issued the "Manifesto of the Right," criticizing extensive state involvement in the economy. Such a view might appeal to the private sector in the country that was weakened by the 1975 collapse of copper prices. Many of the most influential private entrepreneurs obtained their start as senior officials in the state sector, and they share similar ideologies not only with the more commercially minded rural farm population, but also with other free enterprise sympathizers employed by the state. Political-ly, these elements have had their hand strengthened in recent years, not only because of Zambia's current, and serious, economic difficulties (the per capita income of Zambia has fallen 54% between 1975 and 1981), but by transnational donor agencies and financial institutions that advocate more investment in smallholder agriculture and greater reliance on the private sector (World Bank, 1978).

Opposition Forces and UNIP Tactics
in the Republican Era

At the time of independence in 1964, the most visible manifestation of opposition was, clearly, the African National Congress, the opposition political party. The banning of political parties other than UNIP after 1972, however, clearly solved the problem of the ANC as a visible functioning organization. In a later section, the effect of one-party status on UNIP's branch organization and activists in rural areas will be discussed. In the urban areas, UNIP status among the poor was, and remains, solid. Elsewhere, however, UNIP was faced with consolidating its position among organized workers and with those employees of the state apparatus who were opposed to UNIP policies. It was also faced with curtailing the scale and scope of the private sector. In the latter instance, state control of the commanding heights of the economy has assured that, in the short term at least, the private sector would remain weak, ineffectual, and isolated. Vigilance over the state apparatus itself, originally facilitated by the setting up of a parallel party bureaucracy (Tordoff, 1974), has become internalized to the political system with the forgoing of the party-state alliance after 1973. Through all this and up to the present, (despite their all-important voting support for UNIP), the unionized work force, and above all the unionized miners, have remained the most worrisome and potentially threatening element to UNIP hegemony in the urban centers.

The support of the unionized workers for UNIP was crucial both to the party's achievement of national domination and to the party's surmounting of the critical period during 1972 when disaffection within UNIP led to the formation, under Simon Kapwepwe, of the UPP (United Progressive Party), a party that had links with rural areas. At the same time, however, the unionized sector, especially the rank and file, have strongly opposed political control of union affairs (Gertzel, 1975). Indeed, in the same year that UPP was formed, UNIP was faced with three serious strikes at government-controlled companies: an explosives factory, United Bus Company, and Zecco. The issues in these strikes were clearly economic, having to do with rising costs of living. Nevertheless, the implications for UNIP of a merger of these urban economic and rural-based UPP groups was not lost on the leadership. In the future, party-state/union relations would require a surer footing, not only to enable continued support for UNIP, but also to prevent any future merger of rural and urban opposition interests. Despite incorporative efforts and numerous arrests of union leaders, unions have maintained their identity, and have continuously managed to exact wage and other concessions because of their willingness to strike spontaneously and in defiance of the law. The 1981 strike itself was evidence of this continued propensity and ability to act independently.

Nevertheless, while UNIP and the Zambian leadership has failed to contain wage demands, prevent strikes, and press the mining workers into being a wing of the party or party-state, structurally and practically, workers and workers' grievances have remained isolated from others in society, particularly from rural producers. For instance, the stability of the work force is such that there is little turnover of labor between rural and urban areas. Evidence suggests that remittance payments to the rural sector are low, visits infrequent, and communication intermittent, though more thorough information is needed (Cowie, 1979c). Indeed, the workers feel little responsibility for the plight of their rural countrymen. For their part, rural producers recognize that present agricultural pricing policies favor urban residents, and in consequence have little sympathy for urban worker economic demands. Arguably, the ability of the unions to maintain their integrity and exact higher wages has been won at the price, politically speaking, of representing only themselves. It now remains to examine UNIP-state strategy and tactics with respect to rural producers.

The Decline of the Peasantry as a Political Force: The General Context

Efforts to undermine any form of independent (non-UNIP) political expression by Zambia's rural producers began as soon as the Republic was declared in 1964. Both indirect and direct means were employed. Among the former were the loan schemes, most notably those sponsored by the COZ (Credit Organisation of Zambia, 1966-1970) which provided generous (and poorly administered) loans to thousands of rural residents. It is generally recognized that these were not only a form of political payoff to UNIP supporters, but also testimony to those who were not that there was truth to the slogan "it pays to belong to UNIP" (Scott, 1978). Simultaneously, the position of chiefs and village leaders was undercut as a result of the dismantling of the Native Authority system and its replacement by a new structure operating under the Ministry of Local Government. By 1978, 43 districts or rural councils were created under the Local Government Act of 1965. All elected councillors belonged to UNIP, and among them were three senior officials of the council, a secretary, a treasurer, and a public works officer. At the sub-district level were Ward Development Committees (WDCs) and Village Productivity Committees (VPCs), with the number of WDC members averaging around twelve, but varying considerably. The VPCs on the other hand, consisted of a chairman and a secretary, with the chairman often being the village headman. Equally likely, however, was that both the position of chairman and secretary would be UNIP members (Tordoff, 1980).

The reorganization of rural institutions created other offices as well, including those in marketing cooperatives, youth and community organizations, parent-teacher associations, and the like. Having a position in the old Native Authority structure represented no claim to these offices, though the position of chief remained recognized by the government. Responsibility for local courts was removed from the chiefs' authority, and with it control over revenues therein earned from fines, dues, and the like. The new offices served not only to undermine

traditional authority, particularly with youth, but also provided opportunities for ambitious, nontraditional elements.

At the same time, especially in the earlier years, more coercive and
intimidatory tactics were employed. For example, membership drives
were launched in non-UNIP areas with great vigor and often employing
pressure tactics ("Mazabuka tactics"). Under these, opposition party
members and leaders were, for example, harassed by elements of the
UNIP Youth Brigade in particular (Tordoff and Molteno, 1974). Often
these activities led to open violence, even causing death. Another tactic
was to allow only those who possessed a party card to sell their produce
to state marketing agencies. Such instances on occasion reflected the
inability of the party center to control local organizations.

Despite these tactics and changes, political problems ensued. It
became clear that replacing the old colonial institutional structure had
not created loyalty to UNIP, at least not to the party center. As the
cases discussed below illustrate, the erosion of the old leadership had
little real political consequence. In some instances, as among the
Gwenbe Tonga, where no chiefly authority had existed until the
colonial government imposed one, the ex-colonial chiefs had little
power to undermine. Elsewhere, as in the Southern Province in general,
such leadership had long been displaced by well-to-do commercially
oriented agricultural producers whose party loyalties lay with the ANC.
On the other hand, where traditional authority and structures remained
resilient, as among the Ngoni of Eastern Province, a complex interplay
between traditional leadership, well-to-do producers, and political
activists ensued in a way that was not always beneficial to UNIP or to
central control by the party. Indeed, the undermining of traditional
leaders at best left a vacuum for new leaders to emerge, leaders whose
concerns, while nontraditional, were nevertheless local, and geared to
gaining markets and access to the state distribution and resource
networks. From the perspective of UNIP, the modernization of
administrative structures, rather than providing the framework for
promoting UNIP's development initiatives, instead entrenched and
consolidated social relations based on the economic forces built under
colonialism.

For rural producers, the capture or contestation of local political and
economic institutions by market oriented local leaders had a twofold
effect. First, it enabled them effectively to resist and undermine UNIP's
initial strategy of support and promotion of production cooperatives
and by 1968 this strategy was abandoned by the party. Second, it forced
UNIP into a piecemeal revision of its approach to rural development

and to focus on reestablishing institutional control and legitimacy for the party (or at least the party leadership) under the ideological rubric of "one-party participatory democracy." At the same time, the low producer price of maize had the effect of undermining the economic well-being of commercial producers everywhere in the country (Muntemba, 1978). Partly to combat absentee landlords and expatriate domination in land purchase areas, the 1970 Land Acquisition (and subsequent) Acts placed all land under the authority of the Office of the President. Henceforward, all land tenure became conditional tenure, an idea quite alien to most rural producers (Momba, 1982; Bayliss, 1977).

The Land Acquisition Act provided UNIP with the legal framework for establishment of a settlement scheme program that, as Ray has noted, promoted "encapsulation" of a peasant elite where party-state instruments of control and patronage could be more effectively utilized (Ray, 1979). Thus, a technocratic program taken from the colonial administration's files helped form a small select class of loyal and productive farmers. Outside these schemes, investment in rural infrastructure by the state has tended to concentrate on social services, both as a way of preventing further rural differentiation built along the old colonial lines, and as a means of tempering the obvious discrimination that was occurring in other spheres and particularly in pricing (Cowie, 1979b). Despite their various origins and purposes, the above policies together separated out groups of privileged elites subject to some manipulation by the state's control of access and incentives.

In the case studies that follow, events and circumstances are examined in an effort to evaluate the relations between politics and economics in modern rural Zambia. While it is clear that in its efforts to maintain control the UNIP leadership has had to turn, more and more, to the state and bureaucratic apparatus, its ability to effect control was also facilitated by the kind and pattern of economic differentiation that was occurring (and being promoted) in rural areas following independence. In the case of Kanyanja Parish, the post-independence pattern of differentiation was distinct from that of the colonial period, and it prevented rural producers from acting as a cohesive force. In the case of Southern Province, the colonial pattern of economic differentiation was accentuated in a way that maintained social cohesion but led to little desire to support worker-led actions against the state. The cases cover two very different zones from somewhat different perspectives with field-research carried out a few years apart. The Kanyanja field research was done in 1975–1976, a few years after the declaration of the one-party state, when some of the major new policy initiatives of the government, such as marketing cooperatives, were only beginning to appear. The focus of study is on villagers and farmers, some of whom are among the poorest people in Zambia. The case of Southern Province has settlement schemes as a major component of analysis and pays more attention to richer and more successful farmers in a more favored region. The field data were collected in 1979–1980 (Momba, 1982).

THE CASE STUDIES

Southern Province: The Politics and Economics of Control

The Colonial Legacy. Commercial farming by Africans first made its appearance in colonial Zambia in the 1930s in the Tonga-speaking region of Southern Province. While colonial attitudes discouraged African marketed production and the scale of activity was not great, by the 1940s commercial practices were firmly entrenched and the process of economic differentiation well rooted. That such should appear in Southern Province before anywhere else, despite the lack of state support, is understandable given its location—both geographically and economically—in the colonial order. Midway between the white settler farming areas of Southern Rhodesia and the copperbelt to the north, Southern Province was traversed by a railway line that was not only colonial Zambia's sole outlet to the sea, but the focal point of white farming settlement in colonial Zambia itself. The markets this rail line facilitated, together with the demonstration effect (and in some instances, support) of European farmers, gave Africans in Southern Province a head start into the marketplace—a head start that has had enormous influence on politics and production in Zambia to the present day.

The period between the end of World War II and independence in 1964 saw some radical changes in the attitude of the colonial administration in favor of African agriculture. Emphasis was increasingly placed on the creation of a small but dynamic stratum of African small-scale commercial farmers. Several schemes were introduced to facilitate this process. They included, among others, the Peasant Farming Scheme (which, because it was concerned with creating new commercial farmers, did not operate in Southern Province); the Livestock Scheme; and the African Farm Improvement Schemes (AFIS). The latter was first introduced into Mazabuka District in 1946 and rapidly spread to other provinces: Eastern Province in 1950 and Central Province in 1952. In Southern and Central Province, the schemes were financed by a fund that was accumulated out of the maize sales of African producers. Because the responsible agency, the Maize Control Board, paid a reduced (i.e., less-than-European) price for all purchased maize, it had the effect of subsidizing, through a bonus program, scheme farmers at the expense of farmers not belonging to schemes. The effect of these measures, together with a selection procedure for schemes that gave preference to the better educated, more skilled, and more prosperous elements of rural society, accentuated the pattern of economic differentiation that was started in the 1930s. These inequalities are expressed in the production statistics of this period. For example, production of maize per acre by such improved or scheme farmers was over twice that of non-scheme (unimproved) farmers by the late 1950s. Similarly, they cultivated almost three times as much land, largely because they had equipment such as ploughs, oxcarts, and the like, which unimproved farmers did not have in the same quantity. For example, about 30% of unimproved farmers in the two districts had no plough, while all improved farmers did. In short, the period 1945 through 1964 was one of promotion of an emergent rich peasantry under the tutelage of the colonial state. Ultimately, such significant economic change had its implications for the emerging politics of nationalism, and later republicanism.

Two often-conflicting themes emerged in Southern Province as this increasingly differentiated rural population responded to nationalist agitation. The first was strong support for the ANC (African National Congress), then Zambia's main nationalist party; the second was the tendency by rich producers to defend their particular interest within the overall context of nationalist politics. Indeed, among the well-to-do, ANC support took second place to defence of these particular interests. They refused, for example, to participate in boycotts of colonial agricultural programs, which they viewed as beneficial to themselves. Nevertheless, despite such instances, the rich producers supported the ANC in its early struggles against Federation, and they helped mobilize the rural population to that end. Particularly active were Seventh Day Adventist Church members of Rosangu Mission, who maintained a form of political organization in Mazabuka West long before the urban-based ANC thought of opening branches in the countryside.

The fuel for rural-based activism, as it was so often elsewhere, was land and price discrimination. Africans in Mazabuka had lost more land than any others in colonial Zambia with the exception of the Lamba of the copperbelt, yet they were engaged in commercial farming more than any other group. New white settlement, and Federation, threatened further land alienation. African farmers wanted better (European) prices for their crops, and better marketing facilities. Around these issues, emergent nationalism and farmers' grievances merged, at least for a time. By 1958, however, with a lull in nationalist agitation following the creation of the Federation of Rhodesia and Nyasaland, the alliance proved difficult to sustain.

Initially, in its nationalist campaign, the ANC, and its activists and supporters, developed a tradition of anti-state agitation and cooptation. Native authority messengers, for example, who were supposed to be agents of the state against the ANC, at times were agents for the ANC itself, notifying the public of meetings and the like. At the same time, the practice of interrupting meetings, and defying central authority, also became more commonplace. The growing tensions between state and rural producers ultimately carried over into the Republican period as rural producers grew increasingly aware that their interests as farmers were not defended. Even the ANC itself, between 1948 and 1958, was not seen as particularly sensitive to the interests of African farmers vis-à-vis European farmers. For example, the rich peasants generally resented the attack on the African Farming Improvement Scheme and its members. Among the rich peasants was a feeling that the fight against the Federation and for an independent black government should not be at the expense of the benefits they were accruing from colonial schemes.

A split in the ANC in 1958, which led to the formation of the forerunner of UNIP, the Zambia African National Congress (ZANC), clarified and harmonized the relationship between the ANC and rural producers in Southern Province. The subsequent ANC reorganization led to the appointing of leading Tonga men with strong links to the rich producers of Southern Province, including members of AFIS Schemes. As a result this agricultural improvement scheme was no longer severely criticized by the ANC (Momba, 1982).

Well before independence, then, the political battle lines between the African commercial agricultural producers and the emergent republican state were drawn. While such producers had not gained leadership in the wider national cause, and indeed had, before 1955, found themselves at odds with all nationalist parties over key issues, they had captured for themselves the remnants of the ANC organization in Southern Province and elsewhere. From 1958 to 1972, efforts by UNIP to break the grip of the ANC, and hence, the independent political expression of rich peasants (an effort that was particularly vigorous in Southern Province) failed. As in the country generally, UNIP tactics toward these producers consequently changed as UNIP party support flagged, fragmented, or otherwise failed to undermine partisan opposition. Tactics of political confrontation gave way to economic and institutional cooptation, as the central leadership shifted its organizational and patronage emphasis away from party confrontation to party-state patronage.

In the years 1964–1973, Southern Province was Zambia's "bête noire" politically speaking. Because the opposition ANC had control and because even local UNIP representatives were sympathetic to ANC objectives, it was difficult for the party apparatus, and its individual members, to influence the region in any direct sense. In focusing on developments in Southern Province after 1964, then, greatest attention in this chapter is paid to the overall thrust of UNIP policy and practice as it affected the economic position of rural producers. To its advantage, UNIP's task was made somewhat easier by the reality that withdrawal from the marketplace was an unpalatable option for producers so long engaged in commercial production. Whenever possible, farmers sought to forestall measures that would be harmful to commercial agricultural production.

Changing Patterns of Differentiation in Southern Province: The Republican Period. Colonialism had left, roughly, a three-tiered class system in the rural areas of Southern Province. At the top were the large-scale European commercial farmers, many of whom left Zambia at independence. Below them were the African commercial farmers, the most significant of whom belonged to the African Farm Improvement Schemes (AFIS). The third was the group of cultivators largely village based who produced almost exclusively for consumption.

By 1980, Southern Province farmers could be divided into similar classes and strata, albeit with notable differences. Once again at the top are the large-scale capitalist farmers. They constitute the remnants of the colonial European farming community together with a few indigenous Zambians who have purchased large farms. As a social group, these farmers are well served with agricultural credit facilities (both from commercial and state banking sources). They are a very self-conscious elitist class.

Another identifiable and important group is farmers resident and producing in settlement schemes. They enjoy a great deal of government support in the form of agricultural credit, extension advice, marketing services, soil surveys, plot demarcation, access roads, water supplies, cattle dipping facilities, paddocks, and favored treatment by loan agencies. Scheme farmers are granted 14-year leases and must perform satisfactorily. They must practice crop rotation, growing two other crops besides maize. There is a required minimum yield, which is subject to modification from year to year. Failure to comply may mean termination of the lease, though no instances are yet known of this. Since the recruits for the schemes are the well-to-do village farmers, none of these provisions appear to act as a deterrent. Despite the lease, the settlement farmers perceive themselves as independent producers whose access to land is not conditional.

A study of scheme farmers (Momba, 1982) illustrates three important points. First, there is little question that the schemes accentuate colonial class divisions, further enlarging the production of the farmers who had prospered under colonial capitalism. Second, the study shows that the Republican state can implement measures and build institutions that promote agricultural production by independent producers. Third, and most significantly, these measures and institutions have remained highly concentrated socially and geographically, and circumscribed economically and politically. Access to state support services and resources is limited and conditional. While Zambia may "promote the strong," largely out of its need to legitimize itself and temper opposition, it is not a generalized policy of "betting on the strong" in any Stolypin-like mould. A closer examination of the practice of agricultural support policy will show how conditional access is used.

Following the collapse of the Credit Organization of Zambia in 1970, the responsibility for administering loans to farmers fell to the new Agricultural Finance Company. Since its inception, most AFC credit has been advanced to small-scale farmers on a short-term basis. Access to this credit is biased against the less wealthy farmers. The AFC requires detailed reports from agricultural extension officers. After 1975, the Ward Development Committee became involved in loan applications. Those having no cattle or implements were usually denied credit.

Only the wealthiest farmers qualify for medium- to long-term AFC loans. The majority of loans are issued on a seasonal basis with full repayment expected at the end of the agricultural season. No further loans are granted if there is a debt outstanding, or if the repayment record is poor. Farmers ineligible for AFC loans are not eligible for loans from other agencies. Furthermore, owing money to the cooperative union disqualifies one for AFC credits. The consequence is that many are excluded from further agricultural credit after only a year or so. Many do not approach AFC at all because the regulations are so stringent. Nor is such stringency and limited accessibility solely confined to the AFC. Southern Province Co-operative Marketing Union (SPCMU), for example, also offers credit facilities. Such credits are limited to full members—full membership being relatively costly (20.00). While lending restrictions are not as tight as AFC, inability to pay back loans has made many ineligible for further assistance.

The private and state commercial banks, led by the Zambia National Commercial Bank, extend most of their loans to large-scale farmers. Like the AFC these banks favor short-term loans. Individuals must pay back in full before receiving another loan. Access to such loans is conditional upon having an ongoing account with the bank, something only the very rich farmers have. Other sources of funding are available, such as the Cattle Finance Company. But here too, entry is highly restricted. To qualify for a loan that is designed to assist in breeding and fattening, a farmer must have a dipping tank, sufficient water supply, fencing material, and enough pasture. Clearly, only the very well-to-do and settlement scheme farmers qualify. Furthermore, since 1975, price inflation for seeds, fertilizer and implements has further accentuated the effects of limited access to funds.

Among other farmer support services, evidence suggests that extension personnel tend to favor the well-to-do farmers over the poorer farmers (Cowie, 1979c). In Southern Province, the majority of those farmers who owned tractors had frequent visits from agricultural personnel, while those with one plough had never seen an agricultural extension officer in ten years (Momba, 1982). Poor transport facilities, low skill and morale among extension officers, and the low pay for their work make the extension personnel ineffective in promoting production among poorer producers. In contrast, services pertaining to health, education, and community development are more equally enjoyed by all.

It remains now to evaluate how this accentuated and distinctive differentiation pattern in Southern Province has affected the political position of the rich producers both in relation to their poorer cousins in the villages and vis-à-vis the party-state system.

It was clear to UNIP at the time of independence that commercially oriented farmers had captured the remnants of the ANC organization in Southern Province after the 1958 split. It was also clear from the results of the 1964 general elections that the ANC enjoyed substantial support in that region. Therefore, UNIP's campaign to solicit support for the 1968 election was particularly vigorous with all the instruments and tactics at its disposal being applied. As noted earlier, these tactics included the liberal allocation of loans; the reorganization of rural administration structures; and the selling of former European farms to Zambians. Rallies and campaigns were sponsored throughout the Southern Provinces, and attempts were made to strengthen the party organization through recruitment campaigns and the establishment of branch offices.

All of this, however, failed to break the hold of the ANC. For, in response, the ANC asserted that UNIP was a socialist party that in its desire to reduce inequalities in Zambia was going to confiscate the herds of cattle-rich people. On this platform the ANC retained most of its seats in Southern Province. That such an ideology gained widespread credence among the general population is not, however, a function of what was said by whom, so much as a product of the sorts of ties, relationships, and commonalities representatives of each of the parties had with the local rural producers. In this, the ANC was at a distinct advantage when compared with UNIP.

The introduction of the one-party participatory democracy in 1972 caused significant changes in both the process and nature of rural politics in Southern Province. Most significantly, ANC and UNIP supporters allied following the merger of the two parties to defend rural producer interests, an alliance easily facilitated by their similarity of concerns. After the government declared one-party participatory democracy, the well-to-do abandoned active participation in party politics. From 1974, their efforts became increasingly concentrated on making demands on the state via their participation in ward development committees and marketing cooperatives.

Kanyanja: The Politics and Economics of Resistance

The Political Legacy of Colonialism. The area known as Kanyanja Parish lies some 20 kms. to the southeast of the provincial capital of Eastern Province, Chipata. At one time alienated European land, it has been continuously inhabited by Ngoni cultivators since before the colonial period. It was later purchased by the colonial government in 1941 as part of its efforts to relieve land pressure in the overcrowded Ngoni reserve that lay to the west and south. Several villages were relocated within the Parish in 1948, villages that have remained there to the present time. Despite these relocations, land pressure has remained a problem in the entire Chipata area.

The years that immediately followed World War II, as elsewhere in colonial Zambia, marked a turning point in the social and economic position of Kanyanja Parish. Under provisions of what was known as the "Kanyanja Betterment Scheme" the colonial government built wells, dams, roads, a ghee factory, an agricultural station, and later a school, all in an effort to make the locale a model for the colonial government's postwar rural development strategy.[3] The government also, by 1950, began to allocate allotments in a block to the east side of the parish that were to be the farmsteads for the new stratum of peasant farmers that were being supported under the colonial government's Peasant Farming Scheme (Kay, 1964).

In the section that follows, discussion will focus on the strategy and tactics by which UNIP attempted to establish its political legitimacy, and their effects on the attitudes and position of the Kanyanja's rural producers. Also examined is the way in which ensuing processes of economic differentiation affected the ability of the peasantry to act collectively.

Throughout the first decades of colonial rule, grievances and protest in Kanyanja went through traditional channels, or through the Native Authority system built by the British (Barnes, 1967). Even in the first years after World War II, when Kanyanja was undergoing major changes to its social and economic fabric brought about by colonial initiatives, nationalist sentiment was muted, as the Parish residents gained substantially from these colonial development efforts. Indeed, the headman of the largest and most influential village of the locale was considered a "model" headman by colonial officials because of his willingness to cooperate with the colonial regime in its efforts at building a more dependable subsistence base for the local people.[4]

With the formation of ZANC and later UNIP in the later 1950s, however, a major change was brought to the nature and character of politics in Kanyanja. A branch of the ANC was established for the first time in the Parish under the encouragement of the Provincial Treasurer for ANC in Eastern Province, a resident peasant farmer. His leadership, together with an economic and social composition of the Parish that facilitated a series of alliances between headmen, chief, and peasant farmers enabled the ANC to withstand UNIP pressures and enticements during the 1960s. The pressures referred to came both from surrounding UNIP party organizations outside Kanyanja (no visible UNIP branch existed in Kanyanja in the 1960s), which tried to sell membership cards, hold rallies, and build party organization in the area; and from state economic and social programs that made a point of assisting UNIP party members. Despite such efforts, Kanyanja continued to support the ANC in the 1968 election, and the branch leaders continued to figure prominently in the national organization of the ANC. Yet, even before that election, when it was clear to all where Kanyanja stood politically, even more direct and concerted efforts began to be applied by UNIP to break ANC power. Essentially, the ideas about using rewards, persuasion, and "absorption-through-better-organization" were abandoned, and the "Kanyanja war" was launched.

In a period of a year and a half surrounding the 1968 elections, the rural councillor for the South Chipata area, an ANC activist, was arrested and detained, allegedly for "corruption." The ANC Provincial Treasurer was hounded to the point where he was forced to leave, not only the locale, but the district. In 1968, he had built a store near the school, but could not get a license to operate it. One night, the store was raided and looted; the windows were broken and the doors smashed. Elsewhere, farmers and villagers, when going to market, had to show their UNIP cards or they could not buy or sell goods. Finally, there were open fights between gangs of youths who supported UNIP (many of whom came from surrounding UNIP villages) and those who supported the ANC.

On the economic front, all government-sponsored infra-structural development and maintenance ceased (1965–1973). The schoolmaster, who was an alcoholic, was never replaced, and few received visits from agricultural extension personnel. There was only one exception to this general pattern. A grazing area was fenced off for one peasant farmer so as to enable him to leave his cattle unattended. The funding for this fencing came from the short-lived Beef Scheme, a UN-supported program. Interestingly, this farmer's brother was a district governor in Northern Province, while other members of the family had been UNIP activists and among the best known teachers in Eastern Province. Otherwise, none of the social programs such as health, education, and water supply, which tempered the discrimination producers experienced with respect to crop pricing and production support structures, were made directly available to the people of Kanyanja. Two colonial services, the milk purchasing station and the ghee factory, were closed down. In response, peasant farmers of the locale, at one time the most productive in Eastern Province, were forced out of production. The economic impact of this on the well-to-do was devastating; income plummeted, land was abandoned, and buildings deteriorated.

By 1970, much of the will and organizational capacity that had made the ANC such a resilient political force in Kanyanja was broken. The jailed ANC rural councillor was reinstated as a ward councillor, having jointed UNIP. He also organized a UNIP membership drive, and worked to build further the branch organizations of UNIP both within and around Kanyanja. Interestingly, by 1975, this ward councillor had built up a network of small retail shops in the rural areas of South Chipata. Both the supplies and vehicle for servicing these shops came from an Asian businessman resident in the nearby provincial town. For his part, this businessman regained some access to a market area that had been closed off to Asian business interests after independence.

By the time the one-party state was declared in 1973, the people of Kanyanja had been through a difficult time in which life itself seemed in danger. They had been isolated from surrounding communities, and bypassed by "development." In time, especially after the banning of ANC, opposition to UNIP gave way to tacit acceptance, though not approval. Unhappiness and discontent, mixed with distrust and fear, were still to be found in 1975, but there was no longer interest—nor really any point—in maintaining organized partisan opposition. Old grievances were reformulated into new forms of expression, and a search began for the gains to be had from economic improvement and from cooperation with the state. Protest now took the form of wrestling with the state and party for control over the farm and the allocation of local resources. Examples of conscious opposition remained, however, as when former ANC supporters sabotaged officially sponsored Independence Day celebrations in 1976 by setting up a "counter" celebration at a nearby school. Yet, such incidental manifestations of informal opposition were themselves a reflection of a greatly altered social, economic, and political situation within the parish. It is to these changes that we now turn.

Changing Patterns of Rural Differentiation in Kanyanja. During the first years of independence, economic differentiation in Kanyanja slowed and its pattern changed from the strict colonial division between ordinary villagers and state supported peasant farmers. Changes that had a specific bearing on Kanyanja included (a) the new terms of conditional tenure after 1970, and (b) the emergence of new non-state supported rural producers. As shall be shown, these modifications in the pattern of differentiation had a bearing on the capacity of the more commercially minded producers to articulate their grievances and to act in any group fashion.

With respect to the issue of conditional land tenure, following independence Crown land and alienated freehold land became state land. Former native reserve and native trust land became local government land. Even before this, in 1967, it became illegal to rent land. While this change in tenure status left little conscious impression on the resident population of the former native reserve and native trust regions, it had a profound effect on farmers immediately to the east of the Parish, in an area known as Kagunda.

Kagunda was, and technically still is, the property of a Chipata Asian businessman since resident in Kitwe. Before 1967, he employed Africans to grow vegetables on the rich and moist land of the farm to supply the Asian community in Chipata. He also rented land to Africans who were either assisting in the growing of vegetables, working in town, or employed on nearby European farms. In 1964, local UNIP officials told the renters that they no longer had to pay rent and that they were free to remain on the land as it was now "Zambian."

The existence of these renters, or squatters as they were called, had a twofold effect. First, they gave strong support to UNIP, especially after 1969. Indeed, of three UNIP branches in and around the Kanyanja area, the Kagunda Branch was the most active and organized. Second, however, the existence of the squatters tempered and undermined the position of the richer producers of the locale, not only because they were UNIP supporters, but also because they provided a labor pool upon which many peasant farmers were dependent. To complicate matters, some of the more influential peasant farmers themselves benefited from the taking over of land by the state. They too had been renting acreage on the Asian farm (in addition to the farms they had), and under the new arrangements, they could continue to use the land rent-free.

The issue of squatters acting as a labor pool needs some explanation. One of the greatest complaints of well-to-do producers, both against the colonial and republican governments, was the lack of availability of labor. Indeed, during both periods, considerable effort was made by the state to prevent the creation of a landless class that ultimately might make its way to the cities (Cowie, 1979b). Consequently, most of the half dozen full-time farm laborers in the region were from Malawi, and many were Jehovah's Witnesses, who had come to Zambia to escape persecution (Minority Rights Group, 1975). The squatters' situation, however, was different. Although far from landless, they were land poor, and in consequence they sought occasional employment with nearby peasant farmers.[5]

For the commercial producers, then, Kagunda squatters represented both a resource and a threat; the squatters' land hunger made them a labor pool, but it also made them potentially hostile to the land-rich peasants. For UNIP, they were ideal clients from the perspective of political mobilization. Indeed, the ability of the party to influence the affairs of Kagunda squatters was apparent in 1974, when local party officials succeeded in consolidating the scattered homesteads of the area into two sizable villages. These villages became, in political terms, UNIP villages. For their part, UNIP and the local Chief Mpezeni (the latter, well-to-do and an ally of peasant farmers) were both aware of the political mobilization potential of this group, and constant appeals were made to their loyalties.[6]

Another cleavage in the cohesiveness of the peasantry occurred as a consequence of the emergence of a new group of relatively well-to-do farmers known locally as "independent farmers."[7] This group, scattered in isolated farmsteads, were few in number, and were different from the peasant farmers in several respects. Most had opted for commercially oriented farming after independence. For that reason, they had to rely almost solely on their own resources and devices to secure the land, capital equipment, and labor necessary for successful commercial farming. In these endeavors, they had not enjoyed the encouragement of the state, either colonial or republican, and at best were simply tolerated. As a consequence, they did not consider themselves as part of the party-state patronage system. They were fiercely proud of their independence, and considered nearby peasant farmers to be "in debt to the government." Ironically, many of them earned their investment capital as employees of the local government. Yet others had formerly been employed either in the colonial Native Authority or as relatively well-paid skilled workers in Lusaka and the copperbelt.

Geographically, independent farmers were widely scattered throughout the parish, as they occupied land deemed infertile by village cultivators. In an area as densely populated as Kanyanja, such land was scarce, and consequently independent farmers clashed *with each other* for possession of available land. Indeed, the only clear instances of disputes over land title were among members of this group. Furthermore, because as individuals they fell within uncertain jurisdiction, both in chiefly terms (the farmsteads lay on the borderlands of jurisdiction between two chiefs) and in state terms (they refused to participate in either village regrouping or farm settlement schemes), they were reluctant to appeal to *any* officials to resolve land claims.

Finally, although many improved farmers had been state employees, they sought less rather than more state involvement in agriculture and in the rural areas. They did not involve themselves as citizens in local or national state or party institutions or affairs. In consequence, they were not visited by agricultural extension personnel, despite good farming records; they were not selected to cooperatives and other bodies; and their economic and social ties were limited to colleagues at work, or well outside the region. The focal points for their local activities tended to be within small sectarian churches. On the other hand, the old colonial peasant farmers formed a noticeable contrast. They had always been politically active in the ANC and remained active in another way after 1972. They were, for example, leading figures in the new wave of institution building that began to take place in Kanyanja following 1975, subsequent to the declaration of the one-party state. They comprised the executive of the marketing co-op established in that year, controlled the parent-teacher association, and succeeded in organizing their own Independence Day celebrations. One successfully agitated for a new tractor, even though he continuously challenged government officials at open meetings.[8] In other words, for colonial peasant farmers, partisan opposition gave way to the new politics of mutual co-optation and manipulation by state and rural producer. Nevertheless, the failure in Kanyanja of the "new" and the "old" commercial elites to unite in relation to the state weakened the position of both.

As for UNIP itself, 1975 also brought changes. Through new personnel, UNIP began getting involved in local affairs more effectively. The alcoholic teacher was replaced by a well-known UNIP activist from the North Chipata area, and efforts were made to introduce school and other programs long available elsewhere. Old UNIP supporters (notably the farmer who many years before had the fence built) took up new land on a nearby settlement scheme that was started in 1974. To what extent this new presence has facilitated new alliances, however, remains an open question.

CONCLUSION

In discussing the relationship between politics and production in rural Zambia, it is apparent that the recurrent problems of legitimacy for UNIP's leadership coalesced with an urban-biased development strategy in such a way as to place politics ahead of production where UNIP/rural producer relations were concerned. Nevertheless, despite strenuous efforts by UNIP to neutralize the effects that colonial production relations had on nationalist politics in the country, and despite the party and government having relatively abundant cash resources available from copper mining to finance its initiatives, commercial farmer interests proved too cohesive, entrenched, and articulate to be dislodged. Indeed, the head-on confrontation with the ANC that characterized UNIP tactics in the 1960s solidified party differences (as in Southern Province) and provoked rural producers to refuse to participate in UNIP and government development efforts (as with producer cooperatives in Kanyanja and elsewhere). Indeed, by 1968 it was increasingly evident that the party center had lost control over many rural party locals, even in UNIP areas. But UNIP maintained its hold over the urban centers through this difficult period. Through UNIP, the city retained an increasingly tenuous political and economic grasp over the countryside. What was evident by 1970 was that a patronage system based solely on the party, either as an instrument of incorporation or of mobilization, was inadequate to the task of nation building as defined by the UNIP leadership. The interest groups given definition under colonialism—state bureaucrats, union leaders, and rank and file, as well as rural producers—were hostile, in varying degrees, to the task. Consequently, a new basis for establishing hegemony and promoting mobilization was found under the slogan and principles of "one-party participatory democracy." Under it, new and broader alliances were formed, notably with the state, thereby widening the patronage network and hence the UNIP leadership's potential political base.

By the late 1970s, the national political-organizational climate had become more clearly delineated along lines of ideology (especially in economic affairs) rather than along the lines of the old colonial interest groups. Where differences were becoming more manifest was over the nature of national development strategy as a whole; whether to have more or less state involvement in the economy became an issue of great importance. This process of cleavage along ideological lines appears most advanced in the state/private sector of urban areas as witnessed by the "Manifesto of the Right" noted earlier. It seems to be least developed among trade unionists and the rural population. In the case of the former, a tradition of institutional independence together with willingness to take spontaneous action in defense of their economic concerns predominates in the entire sector. In the rural areas, the picture is complex in that in some areas, such as Southern Province, the political hegemony of the richer peasant farmers over the rural population has prevented ideological cleavages occurring. In other areas, such as in Kanyanja, rural producers are highly fragmented, with each fragment displaying distinct attitudes toward the state and the party. In both, patronage and incorporation maintain UNIP and government ascendancy and prevent any clear opposition from coalescing.

In Southern Province, the rich peasants have become more, not less, dependent on the state for their well-being. They can afford to make few mistakes in farm management or politics without risk of losing access to resources, especially financial resources, altogether. As inequalities grow and the well-to-do capture more and more of the development institutions for themselves, their need for labor will also grow. The rural poor are the most likely candidates for a growing rural proletariat. Such class division does not weaken the domination of UNIP and the urban classes for it enlarges the scope for state-party intervention and manipulation. To a degree, this has already been anticipated by the situation on the large commercial farms where the party and responsible ministries have frequently interfered on behalf of farm workers.

At the same time, however, the state-party is faced with the contradictions in its own policies and practices. To make patronage work, it cannot invoke the strict disciplinary measures that it has set out for farmers who fail to produce, especially where the farmers are UNIP activists in good standing. Similarly, the state-party is torn between using its hold over marketing outlets, prices, and distribution systems for maximizing production and popular support or for controlling the reactions against urban bias.

Ultimately, the capacity of the state-party machinery to maintain its grip on economic and political developments in the countryside will be determined as much in the cities as in the countryside. Zambia must continue to feed its urban population, and to this end it must find food supplies, whether from its own farmers, from outside countries or from MNCs managing production in the country. Zambia also must face the pressures from influential international circles that advocate the withdrawal of the state from agricultural marketing. Finally, it has still to cope with the pressure of urban capitalist elements in the private sector and inside the state. Thus far, UNIP's success at keeping potential rural and urban opponents politically, economically, and ideologically separated has been instrumental to its primary objective of maintaining power.

NOTES

1. The theoretical argument used here is further developed in Cowie (1979a).
2. In constant 1965 prices, agricultural output rose from K97.4 million in 1965 to K137 million in 1977, much of this in the sugar, poultry, and egg sectors.
3. As outlined in the Ten Year Development Plan for Northern Rhodesia, 1945.
4. Ongoing soil erosion and drought in the 1930s and 1940s had clearly shown colonial officials that the land area that they had allocated to Zambians was inadequate for subsistence purposes.
5. Over the 5 villages surveyed, the average land allotment per person was 0.73 hectares. For the squatters in Kagunda, it was 0.43 hectares.
6. At one meeting, attended by the Paramount Chief and UNIP representatives, both stated their concern for protecting the rights of Kagunda residents to the land.
7. Average hectarage available per person was 6.89 for independent farmers and 4.36 for peasant farmers.
8. Formerly a prominent ANC activist, this farmer continued to make efforts toward maintaining cohesion among rural producers as a class. At meetings, he would promote his role as general spokesman, addressing government officials in the name of "we poor people."

REFERENCES

Africa Report (1981) September-October.
BARNES, J. (1967) Politics in a Changing Society. England: Manchester Univ. Press.
BAYLISS, C. (1979) "The emergence of indigenous capitalist agriculture: the case of Southern Province." Rural Africana 5, New Series 5 (Spring-Fall): 65–81.
BERNSTEIN, H. (1977) "Notes on capital and peasantry." Rev. of African Pol. Economy 10: 55–73.
CHIKULO, B. C. (1979) "Popular participation and development: the Zambian model." African Q. 19, 2: 179–182.
COWIE, W. J. (1982) "Changing settlement schemes and economic development: the case of Kanyanja Parish, Zambia." Ph.D. dissertation, University of London.
——— (1980) "The peasantry, urban bias and nationalism in Northern Rhodesia/Zambia." Canadian Association of African Studies Conference, Guelph, Ontario. (mimeo)
——— (1979a) "Articulation, global-capitalism and the spatial organization of colonial society." Antipode 13: 47–54.
——— (1979b) "Rural underdevelopment in an urbanised mining economy." Rural Africana 4–5, New Series (Spring-Fall): 49–63.
——— (1979c) "Aspects of resource access among villagers and farmers in Kanyanja Parish: Chipata District, Eastern Province," in A. Marter and D. Honeybone (eds.) Poverty and Wealth in Rural Zambia. Communication No. 15, Institute for African Studies, University of Zambia.
DANIEL, P. (1979) Africanisation, Nationalisation and Inequality. Cambridge: Cambridge Univ. Press.

DODGE, D. (1977) Agricultural Policy and Performance in Zambia: History, Prospects and Proposals for Change. Berkeley: Univ. of California Press.

FINCHAM, R. and G. ZULU (1979) "Labour and participation in Zambia," in B. Turok (ed.) Development in Zambia. London: ZED Press.

FRY, J. (1975) "Rural-urban terms of trade, 1960–1973, Zambia: a note." African Social Research 19: 730–738.

GERTZEL, Z. (1975) "Labour and the state: the case of Zambia's mine workers union — a review article." J. of Commonwealth and Comparative Politics 13, 3: 290–304.

HARVEY, C. (1971) "The control of inflation in a very open economy: Zambia, 1964–9." Eastern Africa Economic Rev. 3, 43: 43–61.

HONEYBONE, D. (1979) "The impact of farmer training courses on Zambia's rural development," in D. Honeybone and A. Marter (eds.) Poverty and Wealth in Rural Zambia. Communication No. 15, Institute of African Studies, University of Zambia.

KAY, G. (1965) "Changing patterns of settlement and land use in the Eastern Province of Northern Rhodesia." Occasional Papers in Geography No. 2, University of Hull.

LEMARCHAND, R. (1972) "Political clientelism and ethnicity in tropical Africa: competing solidarities in nation building." Amer. Pol. Sci. Rev. 66, 1: 68–91.

LIBBY, R. J. and M. WOAKES (1980) "Nationalisation and the displacement of development policy (towards copper interests)." African Studies Rev. 23, 1: 33–50.

Minority Rights Group (1975) Jehovah's Witness in Africa. London:

MOMBA, J. (1982) "The state, peasant differentiation and rural class formation in Zambia. Case study of Mazabuka and Monze Districts." Ph.D. dissertation, University of Toronto.

MOORE, B. (1974) Social Origins of Dictatorship and Democracy. Gretna, LA: Pelican.

MORAN, T. (1974) The Multinational Corporation and the Politics of Dependence: The Case of Copper in Chile. Princeton, NJ: Univ. of Princeton Press.

MUNTEMBA, M. (1978) "Expectations unfulfilled. The underdevelopment of peasant agriculture in Zambia: the case of Kabwe Rural District, 1964–1970." J. of Southern African Studies 5.

NDULO, M. (1979) "Domestic participation in mining in Zambia," in B. Turok (ed.) Development in Zambia. London: ZED Press.

NZIRAMSANGA, M. T. (1979) "Domestic resource costs of investment projects in Zambia's Second National Development Plan." East African Economic Rev. 6, 2: 1–9.

OLLAWA, P. E. (1979) Participatory Democracy in Zambia: A Political Economy of National Development. Ilfracombe, Devon: A. H. Stockwell.

PAIGE, J. (1975) Agrarian Revolution: Social Movements and Export Agriculture in the Underdeveloped World. New York: Free Press.

RAY, D. I. (n.d.) "Bureaucratic encapsulation and rural development: the Zambian case." Calgary. (mimeo)

SCOTT, I. (1980) Chapter in W. Tordoff (ed.) Administration in Zambia. England: Manchester Univ. Press.

———— (1978) "Middle class politics in Zambia." African Affairs 77, 308: 321–334.

———— (1974) "The 1968 General Elections," pp. 155–196 in W. Tordoff and R. Molteno (eds.) Politics in Zambia. England: Manchester Univ. Press.

SEIDMAN, A. (1974) Natural Resources and National Welfare. New York: Praeger.

SHAW, T. M. (1982) "The political economy of Zambia." Current History (March).

SIMONS, H. J. (1979) "Zambia's urban situation," in B. Turok (ed.) Development in Zambia. London: ZED Press.
SOUTHALL, T. (1980) "Zambia: class formation and government policies in the 1970s." J. of Southern African Studies 7, 1: 91–108.
TORDOFF, W. [ed.] (1980) Administration in Zambia. England: Manchester Univ. Press.
——— and R. MOLTENO [eds.] (1974) Politics in Zambia. England: Manchester Univ. Press.
TUROK, B. (1981) "Control in the parastatal sector in Zambia." J. of Modern African Studies 14, 3: 421–445.
——— (1980) "Zambia's system of state capitalism." Development and Change VII, 3: 455–478.
——— [ed.] (1979) Development in Zambia. London: ZED Press.
YOUNG, A. (1973) Industrial Diversification in Zambia. New York: Praeger.

11

MAN AND BIOSPHERE
IN ZAIRE

BROOKE GRUNDFEST SCHOEPF

UNESCO's
Man and Biosphere (MAB) Program, officially launched in 1970, is an international research and training effort intended to improve the management of different types of ecosystems broadly defined as systems of human use of the physical and natural environment. The program aims to promote an integrated social and ecological approach to the reciprocal influences between people and their environments (Kartawinata et al., 1976). Internationally, MAB assumes that promoting research and training of host country nationals, support for planning and monitoring institutions, and increasing public awareness will result in improved ecosystem management and enhanced quality of life for the world's peoples. The international terrain is divided into regional programs providing technical advisory services to country programs (Whyte, 1982).

Author's Note: Data on the MAB program were obtained while the author participated in preparing the Phase II Country Environmental Profile of Zaire in July-August 1981. At this time, a visit was made to the Southeast Shaba copperbelt and to the rural Lufira Valley in the company of Zairian officials. Officials, researchers, and community leaders were interviewed and documents

Conceived as socially beneficial, there is no intent that ecosystem management programs should contribute to deepening social inequality. In Zaire, however, the Lufira Valley Man and Biosphere program, as it was planned in August 1981, could do just that. How and why this might happen, the sociopolitical, institutional, and ecological context of the program, are the subject of this chapter.

ECOLOGY AND PEOPLE OF THE LUFIRA VALLEY

The Lufira Valley MAB Reserve is located in Southeastern Shaba on a vast alluvial plain, part of a drainage basin traversed by small streams between the Lufira River and the Kundelungu escarpment. On its northward course from its headwaters near the Zambian border to the Lualaba River, precursor to the mighty Zaire River, the Lufira enters a broad, shallow manmade lake created as a catchment basin for the Mwadingusha Dam. Flooded in 1930 and enlarged several times since then, this Lake Changalele forms part of the hydroelectric supply network of the copperbelt (Goorts et al., 1961; Magis, 1961a, 1961b).

South of Lake Changalele, the Lufira basin lies within the open woodland or *miombo* of the southeastern plateau. Rainfall in Upper Lufira Valley averages between 1000 and 1200 mm annually with a marked dry season generally lasting for seven months, from mid-April to mid-November. A detailed survey of soils and vegetation undertaken in 1956–1958 found the valley to contain some of the most fertile soils of southeastern Shaba (Bourgignon et al., 1960). The researchers remarked upon the cultivators' detailed ecological knowledge.

were reviewed. Background research was undertaken in 1974–1978 while the author was Professor of Rural Sociology at the Université Nationale du Zaïre, Lubumbashi. Research was supported by the Social Sciences Division of the Rockefeller Foundation, Tuskegee Institute, and the U.S. Agency for International Development. Grateful acknowledgment is expressed to all these institutions, which are in no way responsible for the data or conclusions presented here. These remain the sole responsibility of the author. Professors Crawford Young, Michael Lofchie, and, especially, Harry Grundfest offered generous comments on earlier drafts; Claude Schoepf shared the labor of research. All remaining errors are mine alone.

Precolonial Farming

In the precolonial period, the local farming and social systems included ways of deploying resources to cope with immediate problems and also left reserves for future contingencies. Both properties are necessary for longterm group survival (Vayda and McCay, 1977). They retained their adaptive capacities by means of complex patterns of agricultural and social behaviors supported by networks of wider social ties. As in other areas of Africa, so in the Upper Lufira Valley, the preconquest farming system tended to conserve both soils and labor.

Several different niches were occupied by the Lemba, the main ethnic group in the region. On the better drained and more fertile valley soils, crops were grown in associations that maximized the use of available nutrients while they provided leafy cover against soil erosion and insolation. Shifting cultivation was integrated with more intensive practices, including formation of mounds and ridging over vegetal refuse and hand irrigation of dry-season stream border gardens. Termite hills and former house sites were used for garden patches and growing medicinal herbs. All of these were semipermanent sites used for as long as 10 years. Fields of lesser fertility supported crops of 1 to 3 seasons and were fallowed for up to 20 or even 30 years, by which time the trees, cut to waist height, had regrown. Weed growth was minimized by periodic burning and abandonment of fields. Dispersion and burning minimized the dangers from insect pests and plant diseases, as did the cultivation of several varieties of the same crop species.

In other words, here, as elsewhere in Central Africa, shifting cultivation was integrated into a complex system combining extensive and intensive farming methods (Allan, 1965; de Schlippe, 1956; Doke, 1931; Miracle, 1967; Reining, 1966, 1970; A. Richards, 1939; Trapnell, 1943; Trapnell and Clothier, 1937; Wilmet, 1963).

The Lemba, like other precolonial social systems in the area, incorporated flexible marriage and residence patterns, kingroup fusion, fission, and migration, all of which apparently adjusted population in relation to group needs for land and labor (Doke, 1931; A. Richards, 1939; Wilmet, 1963). Settlements were small—rarely exceeding 50 hearths—and dispersed (Grévisse, 1956: 149). Cultivated plots were shifted around the village sites. Social processes, such as the death of a chief, epidemics, and suspicion of sorcery, often led to the abandonment of villages before cultivable lands were exhausted (Wilmet, 1963: 24). Sociopolitical flexibility and endemic diseases apparently resulted in populations well below carrying capacity throughout the Congo-Zambesi crest area (Allan, 1965; Turner, 1967; Wilmet 1963).

Colonial Impact

In the late nineteenth century, the peoples of the area suffered heavily from the warfare and labor drain of the slave trade to both coasts, while in the late nineteenth and early twentieth centuries, they suffered the ravages of European conquests, plunder, and rape (Crawford, 1912; Campbell, 1929; Morrel, 1906; Springer 1926; Verdick, 1952). The problem for agricultural production was one of under rather than overpopulation.

Requirements of the colonial agricultural administration and the need for young male labor on the mines and railroads further disrupted the farming system. The absence of male labor remained a continuing problem in the villages (CPPI, 1951 in Guebels, n.d.) and rural women were much overburdened. This, rather than "tradition," was responsible for the creation of a "female farming system."

Villages and fields were relocated along roads to facilitate administrative surveillance. Since roads were generally built on the less fertile plateau soils, conflict arose. Obliged to plant cassava along the roads, cultivator families left these fields to themselves while concentrating their efforts on the grain staples, sorghum, finger millet, and maize grown in association with other foods on the richer alluvial soils. There was a high dependency ratio and fields were quite small (0.3 to 0.35 ha. per person) due to the absence of labor for clearing garden plots (Schoepf and Schoepf, field notes; Wilmet, 1963). Toward the end of the colonial period, the administration created large, consolidated villages and the field rotation system was disrupted.

The Lemba Today

The majority of the Lufira Valley's rural population is identified as Balemba, and is closely related to the Lamba peoples of Zambia (Doke, 1931). Although the Lemba chiefs claim descent from the Lunda Mwant Yav or emperor, the language spoken today is a dialect of Kibemba. Prior to colonial conquest, the Lemba lived in autonomous villages without states or rulers. They had clans without any corporate lineage organization. In anthropological terms, their society was ranked rather than stratified (cf. Fried, 1967 for elaboration); their chiefs were religious figures rather than rulers and all adults enjoyed access to productive resources and considerable personal autonomy. Descent was matrilineal and women were significant actors in kingroup and community affairs as well as in small domestic groups or families. Responsible for fertility of lands and people, some women were chiefs, priests, and healers.

Today there are perhaps some 20,000 to 25,000 Lemba living in Zaire and others in Zambia. Many Lemba are rural and most of these tend to live in small communities away from the main road that connects Kipushi to Lubumbashi and Likasi. Urban dwelling Lemba and Lamba work mainly in the mines, commerce, or "informal sector" occupations. Few Lemba have obtained secondary school diplomas, none are university graduates and none have attained commercial or political success and bourgeois status. Research on Lemba in Lubumbashi (1977–1978) was complicated by the tendency for urban Lemba to dissimulate their origins, reducing their visibility as members of a stigmatized, "backward" group.

Consequently, Lemba of the Lufira Valley lack a powerful broker to serve as an advocate for their interests, either within the MAB bureaucracy or at the university. In a political system conceived as based on patron-client relations and rife with exceptions to formal rules, this constitutes a serious handicap. For a group that perceives itself to be stigmatized by the central government for its participation in the Katangese secession of 1960–1962 and, perhaps more cogently, for its ethnic ties to the Lunda cluster and, hence, suspected of having supported the rebel forces that twice took southwestern Shaba in 1977 and in 1978, the handicap is doubly serious.

THE MAB PRESENCE

Officially established in Zaire in 1979, the national MAB program is overseen by a committee under the chairmanship of the State Commissioner for Environment, Conservation of Nature and Tourism (DECNT). Government reorganization in 1982 placed this department—scarcely three years old—under the Department of Agriculture and Rural Development. Within the DECNT in 1981, the program was administered by the Director of International Relations. Three regional projects have been established, each in a different ecological zone. Each is located close to a national university campus and is associated with researchers there.

Regional reserve projects are administered by DECNT staff trained to B.A. level in sociology and agronomy. In the case of the Lufira

Valley Reserve, the project head holds a diploma in family and population studies. Both he and his assistant are from areas with markedly different environments. Neither is familiar with the local ecology or farming systems, nor do they see any reason to study these *with* the inhabitants since they consider that the latter are poor agriculturalists, lazy and intractable ("dur"; interviews August 7, 18, and 19, 1981). They view their mission as involving regulating the activities of the local people and putting them to work at cultivating large fields, for in their opinion, "the people of Shaba do not work."

Each of the three projects is overseen by an interdisciplinary committee composed primarily of university faculty members. In the case of the Lufira Valley project, the University of Lubumbashi is the related institution and the Head of the Department of Sociology-Anthropology chairs the MAB subcommittee. This group does not have its own budget. When interviewed in August 1981, the subcommittee chairman had yet to make a field visit to the reserve area. He and others had merely accompanied officials on a ceremonial tour that did not depart from the highway.

The original project site was indicated by an expatriate ecologist who has worked in the area for many years (interviews August 7 and 10, 1981). It contains large tracts of *miombo,* or wooded savannah climax vegetation, including some excellent gallery forests. The reserve occupies 50,000 hectares situated between 50 and 80 kilometers from the university campus and is accessible by all-weather roads and tracks.

MAB Research

The reserve program is still in the planning stage and, according to officials, had not yet elaborated a research design or a comprehensive set of objectives and means for their realization. No project funds are allocated for research, which is done on a laissez-faire basis. That is, although the MAB has offered to provide recompense for each article published by regional committee members, individual researchers must obtain funds from other sources. This, in effect, leaves the direction of research in the hands of expatriate professors and their teaching/research assistants. To date, funds for ecological research have been supplied by the Belgian government. Botanical ecology is the dominant research interest and, in this context, the local peoples have been viewed as destroyers of the environment. At the present time, there is no ecological anthropologist on the faculty, no one trained in agricultural geography or farming systems research, and no one specifically interested in local ethnography or in the cultural survival of the people of the Upper Lufira Valley.

Such research does not constitute a high priority category in the national Department of Higher Education and Scientific Research. International support for university teaching, training, and research is concentrated in the "hard" sciences and engineering. Recent support of social sciences has gone solely toward quantitatively oriented agricultural economics. According to interviews conducted among Zairian officials and in the bilateral agencies, the reasons for these priority choices are political. The qualitative policy sciences are found to investigate issues that both sides prefer to ignore.

With respect to the case at hand, MAB officials displayed lack of familiarity with studies made of the Lufira Valley ecology and farming systems more than twenty years earlier, although reports of this work are readily available at the CEPSE library in Lubumbashi (FULREAC, 1958; Bourgignon et al., 1960; Wilmet, 1963). Similarly, papers presented at the 1981 MAB colloquium held in Lubumbashi make no reference to this work, nor do they indicate any first-hand knowledge of the local cultural ecology or efforts at agricultural intensification. Instead, the few papers that refer to the local inhabitants do so in terms reminiscent of an earlier era and propose to bring them "development" unspecified as to its form (cf. Bourgeois, 1981). Repeating colonial misunderstandings about "irrational" African agriculture, they appear unaware of work that provides more positive assessment. The newer work includes several doctoral dissertations publicly defended at the university in recent years, faculty seminars, and published works (cf. Bifuko, 1973; Kazadi, 1978; Lumpungu, 1974, 1977; Mulambu, 1974; N'Dongala, 1966). Thus, while it might appear that ecological research is to begin with a clear slate, in fact, the traces of colonial writing on irrational peasant traditionalism, on social and mental structures and customary land tenure rights, all of which are held to impede agricultural development, are unmistakable (see Ciparisse, 1978, for a recent example). The danger is that, as in the colonial period, these notions will be used to serve as justification for land alienation, forced labor, and crop planting quotas.

MAB Officials and Local People

As in the other two areas of Zaire in which it has been operating, the Lufira Valley MAB has designated what, in theory, are three concentric spatial zones for observation and experimentation. (Actually, two central zones originally had been designated by the ecologist, for he had been working in two areas, one on either side of the highway, but the zoning had been changed.) In the central zone of the reserve all productive activities will be forbidden. People will not be able to use the area for farming, fishing, hunting, or collecting wood, mushrooms, or medicinal substances. Surrounding this is a buffer zone, in which people may carry on their normal activities under MAB surveillance, but will be forbidden to introduce innovations that lead to environmental modification. In the outer, experimental zone, "the inhabitants will be able to pursue their activities, but the introduction of new technology will be regulated" (Mbusu, 1981: 3).

What types of regulation and experimentation are intended in the outer zone were not spelled out in Mbusu's paper, but officials indicated their plans during interviews. Both said that "the villagers will be required to cultivate larger fields," with crops imposed by territorial officials. In other words, obligatory cultivation still remaining in force from the colonial period (in this area 0.6 hectare of cassava and 0.5 ha of maize per married couple and half as much for single adults—men of 18 and women of 15 are considered adults) is to be extended without supplying any new means of production. This plan apparently had not been made known to the chiefs, for they made no mention of it.

The chiefs of the Upper Lufira Valley protested the designation of the MAB Reserve in what they claimed is an area occupied by their people. They addressed a letter of *doléances* to the Commissioner for Environment in December 1980 and attended the MAB Colloquium held in Lubumbashi in April 1981 to make the situation known. In their letter, they indicated that small farmers agree maize development is an important national goal and pointed to the overlap of programs with competing goals (MAB and the National Maize Program, PNM). They urged that the reserve be established in an uninhabited area.

MAB officials, however, refused to acknowledge the basis of the chiefs' complaint: "We flew over the region, we saw that there are no people in that region" (interview August 19, 1981). The chiefs, it is claimed, are uncooperative because they "have a low level of education and do not understand the problem" (Makwa, 1981: 5). MAB agents hold negative stereotypes of the people of the region as hard to deal with, uncooperative and against progress: "people who have always been against State authority" (interviews August 7, 10, 18, and 19, 1981).

The chiefs of the area dispute the claims of the MAB project head who found no people living in the central zones and only a few cultivating there. In support of their December 1980 letter, the chiefs had their registry officers draw up lists of people living in the central and buffer zone communities, using the census and tax records. While these probably are not fully accurate, they give approximate figures: some 2,000 inhabitants of one of the *groupements* live or cultivate in the central zone. Three other groupements are also affected in the 17,000 hectares comprising the central and buffer zones. In August 1981 neither the community leaders nor the researchers were aware that the second central zone had been shifted at the behest of the mining companies, removing some communities from the zone and adding others to it.

It would be incorrect to see regionalism or individual incompetence as the major causal elements in the MAB's strategy, for there are indications of a similar high-handed style, evictions from valued resource bases, and popular opposition at the other two reserves (interviews August 17, 1981). Nevertheless, regional stereotyping helps officials to justify the agents' actions and to dismiss the chiefs as "habitually obstructionist," when in fact they are attempting to articulate the interests of their people who have real cause for concern.

More serious, however, is the issue of extended planting obligations, which, if the MAB agents succeed, will be imposed under the guise of promoting ecological research and conservation. The MAB will not move the reserve to an uninhabited area because (a) this site is convenient for part-time research by university faculty; (b) the research is supposed to include study of the effects of human agency upon the environment; and (c) the MAB agents are caught up in the national effort to increase agricultural production. The goals of researchers and bureaucrats have converged in the reserve project. They need accessible areas that contain people to study and to put to work.

Why are the chiefs opposed to the MAB reserve? Are they irrationally obdurate? Do they misunderstand the program's aims? Their perspective must be considered in its historical context, for local skepticism with respect to the benefits of research is based on past experience.

Research and Expropriation

Geological research undertaken during the period of King Leopold's Free State was followed by the award of one third of the entire region, including sizable tracts of Lemba and Sanga lands, to the Compagnie du Katanga. Communities were dispossessed from areas propitious for mining, farming, and urban development. As early as 1916, local chiefs warned that soils were becoming exhausted in several areas to which African cultivators were restricted (Fetter, 1968: 170). The Lemba also were forbidden to mine and smelt malachite, the extremely high grade copper rock found on their lands, an interdiction that still holds today (Chief Katanga IX, interview April 1976; CDC interview August 1981).

In 1934, the administration began developing a wildlife park system, enclosing nearly 3 million hectares. In creating the Upemba National Park in Central Shaba, boundaries were drawn so as to detour the properties of large European ranchers and mining companies (Merlier, 1962: 61). African villagers, however, were evicted and forbidden to hunt in the park (cf. Ngirabakunzi, 1976: 4, for a similar situation in Rutshuru).

Toward the end of the colonial period, in 1956–1958, an interdisciplinary team from the University of Liège in Belgium studied the soils, vegetation, climate, and farming systems in the Upper Lufira Valley (cf. FULREAC, 1958; Bourguignon 1960; Wilmet, 1963). The chiefs were told that creation of a rural development center would enhance the quality of life of the people of the valley. They unanimously agreed to alienate 600 hectares of prime agricultural land situated between the main village and the mining concession (FULREAC, 1958: 12).

At the time the FULREAC limited its actual territorial request to 600 hectares for "reasons related to native politics," while neighboring lands outside the concession covering some 2500 to 3000 hectares were to be used as pasture and forest (FULREAC, 1958: 11). The major objective of the Mangombo station was not the development of the local rural economy but the resettlement of unemployed workers from the Copperbelt cities who could not be sent home to their regions of origin (FULREAC, 1958: 10). Both expropriation and immigration were included in the agreement. "The Great Chief signed in due form, according to law, the ruling by which he gave his approval to the installation in the designated area of foreigners to be presented to him by the FULREAC" (FULREAC, 1958: 12).

The village most intensively studied was the first to be expropriated. Subsequently other villages were similarly expropriated and regrouped in what is now a small town of 2,500 people under the Great Chief. The "notables" or lineage heads, formerly chiefs of those villages, interviewed in 1977–1978, reported that their people had been obliged to move without being able to harvest their standing crops and were forced to rely upon relatives for subsistence since their losses had not been compensated.

Over the years, the chiefs found their expectations of development unmet and the station directors found the chiefs' demands unreasonable. Whether those earlier expectations were reasonable or not, continuing relations between the communities and what is now the CEPSE farm are colored by the fact of continuing expropriation of lands from the local communities. There is also a thread of cultural persistence in the structure of the relationship developing between these and the MAB.

MAB officials state that the ecological reserve is an experiment that will last for only five years, after which the lands will be returned to local control. The chiefs point out that increased bureaucratic restriction, control, and surveillance are likely to result in lowering the already low incomes of the cultivators affected. Thus MAB activities would be likely to cause the departure of many young cultivator families, both from the area and from farming as an occupation. To the chiefs, whose sacred duty it is to safeguard the community patrimony and whose status and authority depend upon their ability to attract a large following, this prospect is understandably threatening. Hence, chiefs and people are united in their opposition to the use of their territory for research that holds no benefits for them and promises new restrictions on their attempts to adapt and survive as farmers and as a rural community.

MAB AND INTENSIFIED AGRICULTURE

Throughout much of human history, agricultural intensification has proceeded at the cost of intensifying the labor invested in production, without augmenting the returns per unit of labor invested. Sometimes this intensification has resulted from population pressure on available lands, sometimes from sociopolitical pressures (Boserup, 1965, 1970).

For the most part, land in southeastern Shaba has not been in short supply. However, fertile agricultural lands are extremely scarce. As a result, there has been some intensification of land use in response to new opportunities. With the availability of tractor-hire for plowing, some farmers are clearing plots of tree stumps—either laboriously by hand, or by hiring a tractor at great expense. They are reluctant to leave the land fallow to restore fertility, for they would risk losing the land to others. The only way to keep a plot of land is to cultivate it continuously and fertilizer must be used on continuously cropped land. In this way, agricultural intensification is taking place.

The availability of labor or labor-saving devices in peak seasons is a crucial factor in agricultural intensification. Often, they require new forms of organization. Cultivators in the largest farming community in the area have formed cooperatives supported by the Catholic diocese and a dedicated parish priest. The oldest of the cooperatives maintains a tractor, a truck, and a diesel-powered mill used by members and by the community at large. Another mill and two large trucks are privately owned. A cooperative of young couples has begun a commercial chicken farm and two community leaders are experimenting with pig raising, while others are raising goats. The senior cooperative leader attended a church-sponsored rural development training program in 1978 and a community development council has recently been formed to coordinate the various self-help efforts. The MAB officials do not appear to be aware of the changes introduced by the villagers themselves, nor have they spelled out what the effects of their proposed moratorium on the introduction of new technology will mean.

As the chiefs point out in their letter to the DECNT commissioner, the designated MAB reserve area has been the site of extension activities by an agricultural development project carried out by the National Maize Program (PNM). The project involved high yielding seed varieties bred to local conditions, fertilizer, and new planting methods. Apparently scale-neutral, it has had only limited success among the small cultivators who fear becoming indebted as a result of fertilizer purchases and who cannot mobilize sufficient labor to make increased maize production worthwhile. In addition, the new maize operations require labor for weeding and spreading fertilizer just as the government-imposed manioc crop must be planted on meter-high ridges. Since this seasonal demand absorbs the entire work force available to most families, more extensive maize cultivation is constrained.

Alternative Cropping Strategies

Villagers, understandably, are reluctant to abandon associated cropping methods in their gardens. Instead of devoting more land to maize, the peasants have worked out their own solutions, attempting to maximize cash incomes without jeopardizing their subsistence security. Those without access to tractors cultivate small plots of maize using the intensive methods for household consumption, while for sale they grow a variety of other crops that require less labor than maize in the peak seasons and are more readily transportable. These include sugar cane, hot peppers, tomatoes, and local eggplant, as well as leaves of the cassava—0.6 ha. of which must be planted in any case. Given the relatively low market price of maize and the manioc planting requirement, these locally devised solutions are the same as the optimal strategies devised by means of computer modeling (Schoepf and Schoepf, 1980).

This is not to say that peasant cultivators in the Lufira Valley would be prosperous and self-actualizing if only they were left alone. Cultivators here are not an "uncaptured peasantry" (Hyden, 1980). There is tremendous need for increased incomes, particularly among the poorest families, and for accessible services of all types, particularly quality health services, nonformal adult education, and agricultural credit adapted to small farm constraints. The most essential needs remain those related to developing agricultural technology adapted to the needs of small farmers that reduce drudgery and increase the returns to their labor. In order to achieve this, understanding of present production and decision-making processes is "of paramount importance in determining the relevance, practicality and potential success" of proposed changes (Norman, 1973: 2).

The great merit of the PNM project is that it sought to persuade the farmers to follow the proposed new method rather than requiring everyone to join in. The MAB plan to impose cultivation of large fields, whether of maize or of manioc, represents a serious threat to agricultural change beneficial to the local producers. Not only those who grow crops in the central zone, but peasant cultivators in the intermediate and experimental zones of the reserve as well, will be subject to MAB surveillance and control. Under the plan, peasants would be obliged to follow the directions of administrators who have never farmed, have no knowledge of the local ecology, do not speak the local languages, and demonstrate no particular interest in the survival of the local people. To the peasants, more administrative control signifies a heightening of already familiar abuses, including arbitrary fines and various sorts of payments to officials at various levels (cf. Schatzberg, 1980, for a similar situation near Lisala in Equateur Region).

Class Conflict Over Land

The chiefs and people of the area are aware that they, rather than the parastatal mining company, the charcoal company, and the large farms of the "politico-commercial bourgeoisie," are the ones to be affected by the MAB interdictions and experiments in the area. The representatives of industrial firms and large farms claim that their superior contributions to national development and local employment merit preferential treatment when competing interests are involved. The MAB, according to its national director, has responded to the expressed needs of these powerful institutions and their leading personalities. For example, one of the original central zones, to the west of Lubumbashi-Likasi road and encompassing an area of several thousand hectares, would have encroached upon an area of woodland being clearcut for charcoal by the parastatal mining company Gécamines, which had cut 5,000 hectares during the previous year and was expected to cut the same amount or more during the current, and subsequent years. The MAB director stated that at the request of the Gécamines, the central zone has been shifted so that the reserve now lies entirely to the southeast of the road, a total area of 50,000 hectares (interview August 18, 1981.)

In addition, the reserve boundaries have been traced so as to avoid the area in which a long-established expatriate firm has been cutting wood for charcoal on approximately 1000 hectares each year. Both firms, employing practices that are recognized to "entirely devastate the forest," operate under permit from the DECNT that plans to replant trees in the cut-over area at some future date.

The forest on the eastern side of the Lubumbashi-Likasi road is also being clearcut to widen the existing two-lane dirt road in preparation for tar surfacing. This road will accommodate trucks carrying maize from the large farms to urban mills. New large farms are being cleared on the fertile valley soils. Gécamines's former social service and agricultural subsidiary, CEPSE (Centre d'Exécution des Programmes Sociaux et Economiques), which took over the FULREAC station, farmed 2000 hectares of maize in 1980–1981 using mechanized monocrop cultivation. According to the farm manager, CEPSE, which is now independent of Gécamines, plans to add another 2000 hectares in the next two years and would like to go on enlarging their operation. This land, formerly part of the community estate, was excluded from the MAB central zone at the behest of the company (interview August 10, 1981).

Influential members of the politico-commercial bourgeoisie are also involved in land appropriations in the valley. The president delegate general of Gécamines was having a 1000 hectare concession surveyed at the time, and 600 hectares had been allotted to the president of the CEPSE, while a 100 hectare maize farm had been taken over by the former DECNT commissioner—now commissioner of agriculture.

These properties also were skirted in drawing the central zone boundaries. "After all, they constitute powerful interest groups," the MAB director explained (interview August 18, 1981).

The issue of forestry management offers further examples of the influence of big firms. The secretary of state for DECNT introduced the government's forestry policy as one of "management rather than conservation. . . . The goal is to increase production, so that wood exports can earn foreign exchange." The role of the state is to provide information and infrastructure for old and new firms seeking opportunities to exploit national resources (notes of July 1981). Lower level DECNT agents speak of controlling the activities of private firms, but the large companies have powerful friends and it is considered unwise to hamper their operations by exercising zealous surveillance. Some entrepreneurs are prepared to initiate officials posted to the regions (provinces) in the forestry business. The officials are university graduates with contacts in other ministries, the parastatals, and the business community who readily exchange facilitating favors, as they do in fishing, ivory, and other valuable products of the natural environment.

In the Lufira Valley project, woodcutting by both artisanal charcoal makers and a large privately owned firm are termed "anarchic" by the MAB's national director (interview, August 18, 1981). Artisanal cutters in the valley select the trees they fell, cut at waist-height, and move on, allowing spontaneous regrowth to occur. However, their burning methods are said to produce only half as much charcoal per unit of cut wood as industrial methods. The large firms cut all trees in their concessions and in 1980–1981 some 7,000 to 9,000 hectares were "entirely devastated" in the Lufira district.

Regulation by the DECNT consists in registering the areas to be cut by the companies and collecting a fee of $\bar{Z}98$ ($19) per hectare. The cut areas are left to be reforested at public expense. An official explained:

> An exploiter has no interest in doing the reforestation on land which does not belong to him. We are obliged to do it. The exploiter says: I give work to 2000 workers, so I work for the State. . . . They asked us not to put the central zone over there . . . where they are cutting.
>
> So you altered the project?
>
> Yes, of course.

He then condemned the activities of the artisanal charcoal makers (who are mainly not Lemba but later settlers): "They cut anarchically, without permission. They have to be stopped before the forest disappears totally." The artisanal charcoal burners probably will not be stopped. Instead, they will be harassed by officials intent on collecting unauthorized payments in lieu of fines.

The chiefs and other community leaders fear that progressive appropriations of land will leave them and their descendants landless. The president of the development council of one community expressed the perspective of those whom he represents:

> The Bakajika law [of 1973, nationalizing land] makes the land the property of the people (*udongo ya bantu*). We, too, are the people of the State. The state is the Mother of the people (*mama ya bantu*). The State must give us the means to permit us to live. In Europe, where land is private property, landless people are caught in unemployment. We Africans do not want that to happen to us or to our descendants. [Here we have] people who want to cultivate [the land], to develop themselves for their children and for the country by their production. . . . The State should encourage people to remain in the countryside and cultivate [interview August 10, 1981].

The suspicion that reserve lands will not revert to the community is a reasonable one. As noted, the valley's more fertile lands are successfully sought for both private and parastatal large farms. The ideology of officials supports the powerful interests. Large farms are conceived of by high government officials, agricultural technicians, and many Zairians educated in the western derived university system as "modern," "efficient," and "rational," in contrast to peasant cultivation which is "traditionalist," "backward," and "inefficient" (cf. Mukendi, 1979, for a recent version). The only claim communities can exert is their de facto occupation and use of lands. Once removed, their claims can be dismissed as being without any sort of foundation in "customary law." In addition, under the "Bakajika law" the Zairian State claims the right of eminent domain. While this measure, officially designated as "land reform" has made it possible to legalize land transfers from expatriates to Zairians, it has also weakened the land rights of rural communities where lands are held in common (Lumpungu, 1977). The legal and political weakness of the peasant communities undermines their internal unity, further harming their capacity for defending their basic interests. In their letter of *doléances*, the chiefs report that they are suspected by people in their communities of having sold the lands to the MAB and to the holders of private farms.

What Research for Whom?

Rather than asking how traditional knowledge and local adaptations might contribute to conservation and ecosystem management, MAB planning views peasant cultivators in the Upper Lufira Valley as enemies of the environment whose activities must be controlled. In contrast, the large firms and farms are viewed as both powerful and progressive in their contributions to development—as forces with whom alliance and accommodation are to be sought. This view is short sighted when management of the regional ecosystem is taken into account, for the activities of the latter set of actors are far more destructive than those of the former set. Furthermore, it is likely that only when peasant cultivators have an interest in preserving their patrimony will their cooperation in ecosystem management be possible. This requires security of community land tenure that can only be achieved when the rights of communities of small cultivators are accorded precedence over those of capitalist firms and individuals.

Research is needed to associate traditional knowledge (folk ecology or ethnoecology) with science in the effort to arrive at solutions for problems of agricultural development and ecosystem management (Brokensha et al., 1980; Franke, 1982; P. Richards, 1975, 1979, 1982; Vayda et al., 1980). It appears that both types of problems could benefit from adopting a farming systems research strategy including collaborative work between professionals and farmers, drawing upon the expertise of both sets of actors in the identification of problems and their solutions (Gilbert et al., 1980; Gilbert and Norman, 1981; Harwood, 1979; Hildebrand, 1979; Schoepf and Schoepf, 1980). Research could develop into a consciousness-raising experience for both professionals and communities. Once agreed upon the necessity of land-use controls, networks of local communities would probably be more effective in regulating their territories (Franke, 1982; Vayda et al., 1980). Unfortunately, there is little precedent for this type of approach in Zaire.

The MAB example demonstrates that a project entering the sociopolitical environment of Zaire enters a terrain contested by class forces already in motion. The Gécamines is Zaire's most important parastatal firm, producing copper, cobalt, and other minerals for the capitalist world market. It accounts for more than half the national output and garners more than three-quarters of the foreign exchange. The firm's continued expansion is considered crucial not only by the government of Zaire but by the consortium of Western governments and bankers that underwrites the present regime. Associated with its interests are a medium-sized expatriate enterprise and the holders of extensive agricultural concessions in the Upper Lufira Valley. The latter are members of the new class that has emerged in the post-independence period. The response of the MAB to these powerful interests is quite natural and, indeed, follows international recommendations for the creation of ecological reserves (Kabala, 1976: 105).

The state bourgeoisie—perhaps more aptly termed a "politico-commercial bourgeoisie" (Schatzberg, 1980)—composed of persons who circulate between and straddle positions in government, the parastatals, and private enterprise, can be seen coalescing into a class "for itself." Conscious of their own interests, they dominate the process of bureaucratic decision making. The lower and middle levels of the bureaucracy are occupied by men who look to the interests of the powerful to guide their actions, while at the same time they use their office and connections to further their own business interests (cf. Gould, 1980; Gran, 1979).

It would be inaccurate to portray the village as a homogenous, egalitarian community, lacking internal differentiation. Indeed, the chiefs and other leaders are in some ways an emergent class. Nevertheless, the most significant distinctions in wealth and the greatest access to strategic resources lie beyond the village, now, as they have for the past 100 years. In the face of powerful outside forces, community leaders represent the *vox populi*. There are indications that the bureaucracy is attempting to divide the chiefs by recognizing now one, now another as "more reasonable" and cooperative. The chiefs are beginning to be distrusted by the community. By shifting resources, officials may be able to co-opt some of the leaders, to cast doubt on others, and, eventually, to silence opposition to the MAB reserve. The effect would be to discourage community self-help efforts and entrepreneurship among an extremely disadvantaged group in Zairian society, thereby contributing to further rural exodus in an area where neither rural nor urban employment opportunities exist.

At present, there is no hope that communities of small cultivators can outweigh the national and international forces shaping bureaucratic decision making.

REFERENCES

ALLAN, W. (1965) The African Husbandman. Edinburgh: Oliver and Boyd.

BEZY, F.,J.P. PEEMANS and J. M. WAUTELET (1981) Accumulation et sous-développement au Zaïre 1960–1980. Louvain-la-Neuve: Presses Universitaires de Louvain.

BIFUKO, B. (1973) "Le concept de 'mode de production' historique et état actuel des recherches." Annales. Lubumbashi: Faculté des Sciences Sociales, Politiques et Administratives.

BOSERUP, E. (1970) Women's Role in Economic Development. New York: St. Martin's
——— (1965) Conditions of Agricultural Growth. Chicago: Aldine.

BOURGEOIS, M. (1981) "Quelques réflexions à propos de l'agriculture au Shaba." Paper presented at the MAB Colloquium, Lubumbashi, April.

BOURGUIGNON, P., J. CALEMBERT, and M. STREEL (1960) Prospection pedo-botanique des plaines supérieures de la Lufira (Haut Katanga). Université de Liège: FULREAC.

BROKENSHA, D., D. M. Warren, and O. Werner [eds.] (1980) Indigenous knowledge systems and development. Washington, DC: University Press of America.

CAMPBELL, D. (1929) Wanderings in Central Africa. London: Seely, Service.

CIPARISSE, G. (1978) "An anthropological approach to socioeconomic factors of development: the case of Zaire." Current Anthropology 19, 1: 37–41.

CONKLIN, H. C. (1961) "The study of shifting cultivation." Current Anthropology 2: 27–61.
——— (1954) "An ethnoecological approach to shifting agriculture." Transactions of the New York Academy of Sciences 17, 2: 133–142.

CRAWFORD, D. (1912) Thinking black: 22 Years Without a Break in the Long Grass of Central Africa. New York: George H. Doran.

deHEMPTINE, J. F. (1926) "Les 'mangeurs de cuivre' du Katanga" Congo 1, 3: 371–403.

deSCHLIPPÉ, P. (1956) Shifting Cultivation in Africa: The Zande System of Cultivation. London: Routledge & Kegan Paul.

The Economist (1981) "Zaire's debt: the hat goes round again." July 11: 71–72.

FETTER, B. (1968) "Elisabethville and Lubumbashi: The process of segmentary growth." Ph.D. dissertation, University of Wisconsin, Madison.

FRANKE, R. W. (1982) "Power, class and traditional knowledge in Sahel food production." Unpublished Manuscript.

FRIED, M. H. (1967) The Evolution of Political Society. New York: Random House.

FULREAC [Fondation de l' Université de Liège Pour les Recherches Scientifiques au Congo Belge et au Rwanda-Burundi] (1958) Mission interdisciplinaire d'étude du Haut-Katanga: Le territoire de Mangombo. Deuxième Rapport (June). Université de Liège: FULREAC.

GILBERT, E. H., D. W. NORMAN, and F. E. WINCH (1980) "Farming systems research: a critical approach." Rural Development Paper No. 6. East Lansing: Michigan State University, Department of Agricultural Economics.

GILBERT, E. and D. W. NORMAN (1981) "Farming systems research in West Africa." in B. G. Schoepf (ed.) The Role of U.S. Universities in International Rural and Agricultural Development. Tuskegee Institute: Center for Rural Development.

GOORTS, P., N. MAGIS and J. WILMET (1961) Les aspects biologiques, humains et économiques de la pêche dans le lac de barrage de la Lufira (Katanga-Congo Belge). Université de Liège: FULREAC.

GOULD, D. J. (1980) Bureaucratic Corruption and Underdevelopment in the Third World: The Case of Zaire. New York: Pergamon.

GRAN, G. [ed.] (1979) Zaire: The Political Economy of Underdevelopment. New York: Praeger.

GREVISSE, F. (1956) "Notes ethnographiques relatives à quelques populations autochtones du Haut-Katanga industriel." Bulletin Trimestriel du Centre d'Etude des Problèmes Sociaux Indigènes (CEPSI, Elisabethville) 32 (March): 65–207.

GUEBELS, L. (n.d.) Relation complète des travaux de la commission permanente pour la protection des indigènes. Gembloux: J. Ducolot.

HARWOOD, R. R. (1979) Small Farm Development: Understanding Farming Systems in the Humid Tropics. Boulder: Westview Press.

HILDEBRAND, P. E. (1979) "Generating technology for traditional farmers: the Guatemalan experience." Paper presented at the International Congress of Plant Protection, Washington, DC, August.

JEWSIEWICKI, B. (1977) "Unequal development: capitalism and the Katanga economy, 1919–1940," pp. 317–345 in R. Palmer and N. Parsons (eds.) The Roots of Rural Poverty in Central and Southern Africa. London: Heinemann.

KABALA, M. (1976) La conservation de la nature au Zaire. Kinshasa: Editions Lokole.

KABWIT, G. C. (1979) "Zaire: the roots of continuing crisis." J. of Modern African Studies 17: 381–407.

KARTAWINATA, K., A. VAYDA, and S. WIRAKUSUMAH (1976). "East Kalimantan and the Man and Biosphere Program." Unpublished manuscript.

KATWALA, G. (1981) "Blockage mechanisms, disincentives and economic crisis in Zaire: the role of the West." Les Cahiers du CEDAF No. 2.

KAZADI, T. (1978) "La problématique de l'agriculture paysanne en sciences économiques au Zaire." Revue de Recherche Scientifique 2: 285–300 (IRS, Kinshasa).

LEMARCHAND, R. (1979) "The politics of penury in rural Zaire: the view from Bandundu," in Guy Gran (ed.) Zaire: The Political Economy of Underdevelopment. New York: Praeger.

LEPLAE, Edmund (1913) "L'agriculture du Congo Belge. Rapport sur les années 1911 et 1912. Deuxième Partie, l'agriculture du Katanga." Bulletin Agricole du Congo Belge, 4.

LUMPUNGU, K. (1977) "Land tenure systems and the agricultural crisis in Zaire." African Environment 2, 4 and 3, 1: 57–71:

———— (1974), "Régime des terres et crise agricole au Zaire." Revue Africaine de Développement 1, 1: 50–58 (Kinshasa).

MAGIS, N. (1961b) La Pêche dans les Lacs de Retenue de Koni et de N'zilo I (Haut Katanga). Université de Liège: Editions FULREAC.

———— (1961a) "Nouvelle contribution à l'étude hydrobiologique des lacs de Mwadingusha, Koni et N'zilo." Bulletin du CEPSI 57: 92 (Lubumbashi).

MAKWA, P. (1981) "Les activités humaines, leurs incidences et l'attitude de la population vis-à-vis de la Réserve de la Biosphere Vallée de la Lufira." Document No. 11, Colloque du MAB, Lubumbashi, April.

MALAISSE, F., J. ALEXANDRE, R. FRESON, G. GOFFINET, and M. MALAISSE-MOUSSET (1971) "The miombo ecosystem: a preliminary study," pp. 363-404 in P. M. Golley and F. B. Golley (eds.) Tropical ecology. Athens.

MIRACLE, M. (1967) Agriculture in the Congo Basin. Madison: Univ. of Wisconsin Press.

MOREL, E. D. (1906) Red Rubber: The Story of the Rubber Slave Trade Flourishing on the Congo in the Year of Grace 1906. New York: The Nassau Print.

MULAMBU, M. (1974) "Cultures obligatoires et colonisation dans l'ex-Congo Belge." Cahiers du CEDAF 6–7, Série 2 Brussels: Centre d'Etudes et de Documentation Africaine.

N'DONGOLA, E. (1965) "Mutations structurelles de l'économie traditionnelle dans le Bas-Congo sous l'impact de la colonisation et la décolonisation." Cahiers Economiques et Sociaux (IRES, Kinshasa) 4, 1: 3–32.

NORMAN, D. (1978). "Farming systems and problems of improving them." pp. 318–347 in J. M. Kowal and A. H. Kassan (eds.) Agricultural Ecology of the Savannah: A Study of West Africa. Oxford: Clarendon.

——— (1973) "Methodology and problems of farm management investigations experiences for northern Nigeria." African Rural Employment Paper, No. 8. Department of Agricultural Economics, Michigan State University.

Programme National Maïs [PNM] République du Zaire, Département de l'Agriculture. (1980) Huitième rapport annuel. République du Zaire, Département de l'Agriculture.

——— (1975) Troisième rapport annuel.

REINING, C. C. (1970) "Zande subsistence and food production." pp. 125–163 in P.F.M. McLoughlin (ed.) African Food Production Systems. Baltimore: Johns Hopkins Univ. Press.

——— (1966) The Zande Scheme. Evanston: Evanston Univ. Press.

RICHARDS, A. I. (1939) Land, Labour and Diet in Northern Rhodesia. London: Oxford Univ. Press.

RICHARDS, P. R. (1982) "Ecological change and the politics of African land use." Paper presented at the Annual Meeting of the African Studies Association in Washington, DC.

——— (1979). "Alternative strategies for the African environment: 'Folk Ecology' as a basis for community-oriented agricultural development." Unpublished manuscript.

——— [ed.] (1975) African Environment: Problems and Perspectives. African Environment Special Report, No. 1. London: International African Institute.

SCHATZBERG, M. G. (1980) Politics and Class in Zaire: Bureaucracy, Business and Beer in Lisala. New York: Africana.

SCHOEPF, B. G. [ed.] (1981a) The Role of US Universities in International Rural and Agricultural Development. Tuskegee Institute: Center for Rural Development.

——— (1981b) "Introduction: agricultural research, problems of technology transfer," pp. 73–75 in B. G. Schoepf (ed.) The Role of US Universities in International Rural and Agricultural Development. Tuskegee Institute: Center for Rural Development.

SCHOEPF, B. G. and C. SCHOEPF (1981). "Zaire's rural development in perspective," pp. 243–254 in B. G. Schoepf (ed.) The Role of US Universities in International Rural and Agricultural Development. Tuskegee Institute; Center for Rural Development.

——— (1980) "Beyond farming systems research." Paper presented at the Annual Meeting of the American Anthropology Association, Washington, DC. December.

SCHOEPF, C. (forthcoming) "Small farmer maize cultivation in southeast Shaba: a linear programming analysis." M.S. thesis, Auburn University, Department of Agricultural Economics and Rural Sociology.

SPRINGER, J. M. (1927) Christian Conquests in the Congo. New York: Methodist Book Concern.

TRAPNELL, C. G. (1934) The Soils, Vegetation and Agriculture of Northeastern Rhodesia: Report of the Ecological Survey. Lusaka: Government Printer.

TURNER, V. (1967) The Forest of Symbols: Aspects of Ndembu Ritual. Ithaca, NY: Cornell Univ. Press.

VAYDA, A. P. and B. J. McCAY (1977) "Problems in the Identification of Environmental Problems," in T. P. Bayliss-Smith and R.G.A. Feachem (eds.) Subsistence and Survival: Rural Ecology in the Pacific. London: Academic Press.

VAYDA, A. P., C. J. P. COLFER, and M. BROTOKUSUMO (1980) "Interactions de l'homme et de la forêt dans le Kalimantan oriental." Impact: Science et Société 30, 3: 193–205.

VELLUT, J. L. (1977) "Rural poverty in western Shaba, c. 1890–1930," pp. 294–316 in R. Palmer and N. Parsons (eds.) The Roots of Rural Poverty in Central and Southern Africa. Berkeley: Univ. of California Press.

VERDICK, E. (1952) Les premiers jours au Katanga (1890–1903). Elisabethville: Comité Spéciale du Katanga.

WHYTE, A. (1982) "The integration of natural and social sciences in the MAB programme." Int. Social Sciences J. 34, 3: 411–426.

WILMET, J. (1963) Systèmes agraires et techniques agricoles au Katanga. Brussells: Académie Royale des Sciences d'Outre-Mer.

World Bank (1975) The Economy of Zaire. Volume II: Sectors. East Africa Regional Office Report No. 821-ZR (July 23).

——— (1980) Zaire: Current economic situation and constraints. Washington, DC: World Bank.

YOUNG, M. C. (1965) Politics in the Congo. Princeton, NJ: Princeton Univ. Press.

12

PEASANTS AND COLLECTIVE AGRICULTURE IN MOZAMBIQUE

OTTO ROESCH

Of those African countries pursuing a socialist path, few have sought to implement as ambitious and radical a strategy of rural development as has Mozambique. Since winning political independence from Portugal in 1975, after a 10-year guerrilla war under the leadership of the Front for the Liberation of Mozambique (FRELIMO), the government of Mozambique has pursued a far-reaching, nationwide program of voluntary agricultural collectivization. The aim of the program has been to gather the dispersed peasant population into concentrated settlements — known as "communal villages" — and to reorganize their productive

Author's Note: This chapter is a preliminary attempt to present some of the findings of 10 months of research that the author conducted in the Baixo Limpopo for purposes of a Ph.D. dissertation, between March 1982 and January 1983. I wish to express my thanks to all the Mozambican state and party structures that assisted me in my work, especially the Direcção Nacional de Habitação and the Centro de Estudos Africanos, Universidade Eduardo Mondlane. I am especially indebted to the Centro de Estudos Africanos and its staff, past and present, who first formulated some of the analyses contained in this study. I have tried to acknowledge this debt where possible.

activities along collective lines through the formation of state farms and cooperatives. As of 1981, more than 1500 communal villages had been established, involving more than 1½ million people, approximately 15% of the rural population (Direcção Nacional de Habitação 1981). The goal of the program is to have most of Mozambique's rural population in communal villages practicing collective farming by the end of the decade.

Though registering significant advances in the areas of health, education, habitation, and popular political participation, Mozambique's communal village-based strategy of rural development has not been an economic success. State farms have performed poorly, the cooperative movement has remained weak, and peasant agricultural production has declined. Agricultural production as a whole has stagnated, and the socialization of peasant family production has proceeded slowly. Peasant family agriculture has remained the productive base of all communal villages, and the reproductive base of the peasant family.

The Mozambican case is an instructive example of the kinds of problems that revolutionary socialist governments in Third World countries must grapple with as they attempt the transition from peasant to socialized agriculture. The difficulties of defining clear and effective policies on the interrelated questions of the role and relative importance of peasant family production in the transition process, and the form and pace that collectivization is to take, are well illustrated by the policy and practice of Mozambique's rural development strategy since independence.

This chapter outlines the general features of Mozambique's rural development strategy, and examines the main reasons for the strategy's lack of success. It presents a case study of the "Baixo Limpopo," an agriculturally important area located in the lower reaches of the Limpopo River valley in Mozambique's southern province of Gaza. The case study focuses on the problem of creating the conditions necessary for peasants to enter collective production, and thus make the transition from family to socialized agriculture.

DEVELOPMENT POLICY AND PRACTICE: AN OVERVIEW

The Context

In setting about the arduous task of overcoming a colonial legacy of underdevelopment and dependency, few African countries have had to face difficulties of the magnitude of those faced by Mozambique since independence. In addition to an especially debilitating colonial inheritance,[1] Mozambique's developmental task has from the outset been made more onerous by the effects of a virtual collapse of the colonial economy in the immediate post-independence period and, since then, by the high costs of uninterrupted military conflict and a succession of natural disasters.

With independence, Mozambique inherited a rapidly disintegrating economy. The mass flight of most of the one quarter million Portuguese settlers, who filled most of the key positions in the economy and the state apparatus, and virtually all of those requiring any measure of technical skill, education, or training, produced a generalized crisis in all sectors of the inherited colonial economy and state apparatus. In agriculture, this crisis resulted in a drastic decline in marketed output in all areas of the country (see Wuyts, 1981), with serious implications for the country's food needs, export earnings, and prospects for capital accumulation and national economic development. The decline was due to a number of factors. How the crisis was played out in the region of the Baixo Limpopo is shown below. Its elements were common to most of the country: capitalist settler agriculture disintegrated, the system of trade and commerce collapsed, state administration and support for essential infrastructure and productive activities ceased, sources of essential goods and investment funds were disrupted.

In addition, there were constant military attacks, first by the armed forces of Ian Smith's Rhodesia, and then with the independence of Zimbabwe in 1980, by the South African sponsored anti-FRELIMO armed bands of the "Mozambique National Resistance" (MNR). Though never posing a serious challenge to government authority or stability, these attacks have exacted a high economic price, disrupting development projects and retarding economic recovery. Finally, severe floods and prolonged drought have further weakened an already battered economy and severely compromised numerous government agricultural development projects.

Mozambican Agricultural Policy: 1975 to 1982

FRELIMO sought to stem the economic crisis and overcome the country's colonial legacy of rural underdevelopment, with a fundamental transformation of Mozambican rural society. The strategy of rural development that FRELIMO attempted to implement drew strength, inspiration, and example from the methods, institutions, and experiences of the national liberation struggle (see Saul, 1979, 1984). The theory and practice of self-reliance, of democratic work methods, of collective resolution of problems, and of nonexploitative social and economic relations, which FRELIMO developed in successfully waging a people's war, together with the institutions it created in the liberated areas, such as centralized village communities, production cooperatives, and democratic political structures, all came to be incorporated in the government's initial strategy of rural development.

The first comprehensive formulation of a strategy was provided by the 8th Session of the Central Committee of FRELIMO, in February 1976, in its "Resolution on Communal Villages." In this document, the communal villages were defined as the "backbone" of the country's rural development strategy. The communal village was seen not just as a new habitational arrangement, nor simply as a means for collectivizing peasant agricultural production, but rather as an integrated economic, social, political, and cultural totality to be organized according to "the principles of collective life," and free from "the exploitation of man by man." They are the basic institutional vehicle for reorganizing production along collective lines, for extending basic health, educational, and social services to the rural areas, and for integrating the peasantry into the national life of the country. In short, they are the basic unit for the collectivization of Mozambican rural economy and society.

In conformity with the experience of collective self-reliance of the liberated areas, the resolution stressed that the productive activities in communal villages must rely on local initiative and local resources, and on labor intensive techniques. Although communal villages might have either state farms or cooperatives as their productive base, the resolution gave greater weight to the latter. It failed, however, to discuss the thorny and important questions of the role of peasant family production in communal villages and the way the transition to collective forms of production was to be achieved. It did, however, state that

In view of the political, economic and social objectives of the Communal Village, participation can only involve poor peasants, workers and exploited labourers. Small farmers who own their own means of production may also be accepted if they agree to pool these with those of others for the benefit of the Communal Village [FRELIMO, 1976: 11].

Rich peasants and noncollective forms of production, it appeared, would have no place in the country's communal villages.

The Third Congress of FRELIMO, in February 1977, marked a significant reorientation in agricultural policy away from cooperatives and the spirit of self-reliance and toward state farms and capital intensive agriculture. Though it reaffirmed that "communal villages are our chosen strategy for socialization of the rural areas," and that "state enterprises and cooperatives are the organizational forms in agriculture which are the basis for communal villages," the Third Congress defined the state sector in agriculture as "dominant and decisive" relegating cooperatives to a decidedly secondary status (FRELIMO, 1977a: 46; 1977b: 5). Responding to the acute food supply crisis that beset the country with the collapse of the colonial rural economy noted above, the central committee argued that "the quickest way of responding to the country's food requirements" was to create a state farm sector on the abandoned farms of the departed colonists. In particular, the Limpopo valley, a main area of colonial settlement, was to be transformed into the "granary of the nation."

The government massively increased the level of investments in the state farm sector over the course of the next several years. By contrast, repeated policy pronouncements about the centrality of cooperatives to Mozambique's rural development strategy entailed little material support in practice. As the recent Central Committee Report to the Fourth Congress noted, only 2% of all agricultural investments for the period 1977–1982 went into the cooperative sector (FRELIMO, 1983: 28).

Over this same period, the peasant sector received virtually no state support.[2] On the other hand, peasants were constantly exhorted and mobilized to produce more, to move to communal villages, and to join agricultural cooperatives (see, e.g., Comissão Nacional das Aldeias Comunais, 1980; Assembleia Popular, 1979).

From the Third Congress right up until the latter half of 1982, when preparations for the Fourth Congress began, the direction of rural development practice was one of unambiguous and almost exclusive support for the state farm sector. The verbal ambiguity of official pronouncements may well have been the consequence of disagreement within party and government leadership. The Minister of Agriculture was expelled from his post and from the central committee in August 1978, allegedly for an excessive emphasis on state farms and mechanization in agriculture and insufficient attention to the cooperative and family sectors. There was, however, no corresponding change in the investment practices or priorities of the Ministry of Agriculture.

The first Ten Year Plan launched in 1980, defined as "the decade of victory over underdevelopment," reconfirmed the preeminence of the state farm sector over all others in the country's rural development strategy. And the party's public education booklet of January 1982, "A Situação Actual No Nosso País" ("The Current Situation In Our Country"), emphasized the necessity of limiting consumption in order to provide the large investments that the large-scale projects required. It explained the shortages of foodstuffs and consumer goods in the national economy as a sacrifice necessary in the present phase of development.

By 1982, in fact, shortages of foodstuffs and basic consumer goods had reached a critical level, both in the cities and the countryside. Starting from the crisis levels of the immediate post-independence period (i.e., well below colonial levels), agricultural production had grown a scant 8.8% between 1977 and 1982—well below the rate of demographic growth—and had actually fallen 2.4% between 1981 and 1982 (FRELIMO 1983: 26). In the cities, as store shelves became emptier, more and more of the available goods were channelled into a flourishing black market. In the countryside, consumer goods were all but nonexistent, though the peasantry (climate permitting) was able to grow enough to feed itself in most areas of the country. In town and country, the paucity of food, consumer goods, and basic tools began to breed popular discontent and political demobilization.

It was in the context of an increasingly difficult economic, political and military situation that the Fourth Congress of FRELIMO was held in April 1983. The assembled delegates ratified policy positions that promised a major reorientation in rural (and national) development strategy.

The Fourth Congress

The Central Committee Report to the Fourth Congress made a fairly hardnosed assessment of the performance of the country's rural sector for the period 1977–1982 (the period between the Third and Fourth Congresses), noting that in this period the growth of agricultural production had been "obviously insufficient" (FRELIMO, 1983: 26). The report went on to list the following main problem areas in the country's rural development strategy: the state agricultural sector, "despite the efforts undertaken and the investments made," had "not yet reached the level of organization desired, and the indices of production and productivity are unsatisfactory" (FRELIMO, 1983: 27); the development of the cooperative sector had been "meagre," reflecting "the low level of priority given to it in practice and the inadequate support given by the state structures" (p. 28). The report noted that "[b]etween 1977 and 1982 the number of producer cooperatives rose from 180 to 370," but "their membership grew [only] from 25,000 to 37,000" (p. 28); "the family sector had been relegated to a secondary position," and "[i]n practice, support to the family sector was virtually non-existent, particularly in terms of factors of production" (p. 28); the communal villages, though showing considerable advances and steady growth, continued to face the problem of a weak economic base (p. 28); an excessive emphasis had been placed on complex imported production technologies, for which there existed no corresponding level of technical knowledge and competence among the work force that was to use them (p. 28); agricultural projects had been conceived and implemented in an increasingly bureaucratic and technocratic manner with "no perspective of integrated development aimed at solving the problems of the people, and ensuring the participation of local authorities in their areas of influence" (p. 30).

In light of this assessment of the performance of the agricultural sector, the report proposed a major decentralization of agricultural planning, organization, and implementation; and a corresponding shift in emphasis away from large-scale, capital intensive projects, toward small-scale local projects based on appropriate technologies, both in agriculture and in manufacturing (p. 30). The report went on to state that "in the period from now until the Fifth Congress, actions to promote rural development must therefore be based on wide-ranging support to the cooperative, private and family sectors and on reorganization and consolidation of the state agricultural sector" (p. 30).

The nature of the difficulties that have beset Mozambique's rural development strategy since independence, and that the new orientations of the Fourth Congress are aimed at resolving, are well illustrated in a case study of the government's attempt to socialize agricultural production in the Baixo Limpopo.

RURAL DEVELOPMENT IN THE BAIXO LIMPOPO

The Physical Setting

The southern part of the Limpopo River valley in Mozambique's southern province of Gaza, together with its adjacent hinterland of hilly, dry sandy soils, constitutes a territorial, economic, social, and infrastructural unit commonly referred to as the Baixo Limpopo. The Baixo Limpopo covers an area of approximately 2000 km^2, most of it within the District of Gaza, where the provincial capital of Xai-Xai is located. The rest extends northward and westward into the adjacent districts of Chibuto and Bilene.

The fertile flood plain of the Limpopo, together with that of its tributaries, accounts for about 60,000 ha., or approximately one-third of the total land area of the Baixo Limpopo, and virtually all of the good agricultural land. The adjacent rolling hills on both sides of the valley—locally called the "serra"—have sandy soils of moderate to low fertility. Given the irregularity of rainfall from year to year, the production of marketable surpluses in these soils is severely limited.

By contrast, the flood plain is characterized by highly fertile alluvial soils that, with adequate drainage and appropriate irrigation, have proven to be enormously productive.

The total population of the Baixo Limpopo (including Xai-Xai) is on the order of 240,000 people, giving it a population density of somewhere around 120 inhabitants per km^2, one of the highest in the country. In 1982, about 150,000 people, approximately 80% of the rural population of the Baixo Limpopo, lived in the 30 communal villages then in existence (Direcção Provincial de Obras Publicas e Habitaçao de Gaza, 1982).[3]

The Baixo Limpopo During the Colonial Period

During the colonial period, the Baixo Limpopo was both a major bread basket of the colonial economy and part of the labor reserve of the South African mining economy established in all of southern Mozambique at the turn of the century. By the 1940s, at any given time, an average of 20% of the economically active male population of the province of Gaza was away in wage employment in South Africa (Centro de Estudos Africanos, 1977: 85). The wages of migrant labor were an important source of consumer goods and factors of production for the peasant economy, permitting a certain amount of capitalization of agricultural and, to a lesser degree, craft production.[4]

The Baixo Limpopo was also an area that, since the early part of this century, had been marked for intense agricultural exploitation and Portuguese settlement by colonial planners. Beginning in the late 1930s, the Baixo Limpopo was steadily transformed into a major source of food supplies for the growing Portuguese settler and African proletarian populations of the towns. Marketed rice production, the principal crop of the Baixo Limpopo, averaged about 9000 tonnes per year for the District of Gaza alone. A good year could produce in excess of 12000 tonnes.[5]

The transformation of the Baixo Limpopo into a major commercial agricultural area, however, required the construction and careful maintenance of extensive hydro-agricultural works, for drainage, irrigation, and flood control. Without such infrastructural investments, poor drainage, floods and variable rainfall patterns made agriculture unreliable. Beginning in 1937, the colonial administration, using forced African labor, undertook a phased program of hydro-agricultural development of the Baixo Limpopo, as a precondition for the expansion of capitalist settler agriculture and the development of forced rice cash cropping amongst the local African population.[6]

The system of forced peasant cash cropping in the Baixo Limpopo was closely administered by the colonial state. All the phases of the productive cycle, and initially also of marketing of the product, were subject to the careful control of the colonial administration. The construction and maintenance of the drainage and irrigation canals; the phases of plowing, sowing, cultivating, and harvesting; types of crop rotation; the supply in factors of production (seeds, insecticides, rent of tractors, oxen, veterinary and agronomic extension services, etc.); the obligatory participation of the peasantry; the marketing of the cash crops; and so on, were all carefully controlled and/or supervised by the colonial state. The production of rice in the Limpopo valley, like other forcibly produced cash crops (e.g., cotton) elsewhere in Mozambique, was intimately linked to this central role played by the colonial state in the productive process (see, e.g., Centro de Estudos Africanos, 1980).

Economic forces made the colonial system of peasant surplus production self-reproducing fairly early on. The introduction of forced peasant cash cropping marked a further step in the process of the destruction of an autonomous economy already begun 50 years earlier with the development of migrant wage labor to the mines in South Africa. The considerable level of commoditization of local social relations and reproductive processes caused by the practice of migrant labor, together with the existence of strong market incentives in the form of well-stocked stores, provided a powerful stimulus for the commoditization of the agricultural productive process, and facilitated the rapid "natural" development of a commercial peasant agriculture. As agricultural productive processes became more commoditized, peasant surplus production came to depend increasingly on the growing colonial settler strata of capitalist farmers and merchants as sources of factors of production (tools, tractor rentals, seed, etc.) and as an outlet for marketed surpluses.

The Post-Independence Crisis of the Peasant-Worker Economy

With independence, the agricultural and migrant labor economy of the Baixo Limpopo, like the national economy as a whole, entered into a phase of disarticulation and crisis. In the Baixo Limpopo, this crisis had its basis in two main events: (1) the disintegration of the colonial system of agricultural surplus production; and (2) the drastic decline in migrant labor to the South African gold mines.

The disintegration of the colonial system of agricultural surplus production in the Baixo Limpopo was a multifaceted process. In the first place, the departure of the Portuguese farmers and traders led to a drastic drop in agricultural output and a general collapse in the organization of agricultural marketing and retail trade. In the period 1973–1975, marketed agricultural output of the capitalist agricultural sector for the southern region of the country fell an estimated 54%, and total marketed agricultural production fell 43% (Wuyts, 1981: 48). For the peasantry, the departure of the colonial settlers also meant a loss of an important source of consumer and capital goods, and of an outlet for agricultural surpluses.

The departure of administrators and the dissolution of colonial administration ended the vital coordination and supervision of peasant labor in cash cropping and in maintaining hydro-agricultural infrastructure, and it cancelled the supply of inputs and extension services to cash crop producers. Not surprisingly, in the period 1973–1975 marketed agricultural output for the peasant sector in the southern part of the country fell by 60% (Wuyts, 1981).

Beginning in 1976, the economy of the Baixo Limpopo and of all southern Mozambique suffered a further blow with the sharp decline in levels of migrant labor to South Africa. Between 1975 and 1976, the percentage of the active male population of Gaza Province recruited by WENELA fell from 19% to 4% (Centro de Estudos Africanos, 1977,

1979). This decline further weakened the subsistence base of the peasantry. Unemployment increased dramatically, and the amount of goods and money circulating in the rural economy of the Baixo Limpopo fell, as did the purchasing power of the local peasants for farm inputs and basic consumption goods.

The combined effect of these events gave rise to a profound crisis of material reproduction among the peasantry, and drastically reduced the productive capacity of the Limpopo valley as a whole, transforming many one-time food exporting areas into net food importers. The implications for food supplies to the urban centers and for Mozambique's limited foreign currency reserves were dramatic and far-reaching. It is in the context of this deepening and spreading crisis that FRELIMO sought to implement its socialist policies of rural transformation in the Baixo Limpopo.

Collectivization in the Baixo Limpopo

FRELIMO tackled the agricultural crisis with two main courses of action: (1) the widespread establishment of communal villages, having collective forms of production as their economic base; (2) the formation of a state farm sector out of the abandoned farms of the departing colonial settlers.

The Formation of Communal Villages and Cooperatives 1974–1977. In conformity with the policy of extending the experience of the liberated areas to the rest of the country, an active and extensive program of popular mobilization was launched in the Baixo Limpopo to promote the creation of communal villages and cooperatives in the rural areas, beginning during the period of the transitional government (May 1974–June 1975), and then on a scale much larger after independence. During this initial phase, however, the formation of communal villages proceeded slowly. Though communal villages were "founded" at a fairly steady pace, people moved into them only very gradually. Most of the government's activity around the communal villages at this time was going into mobilization for acceptance of the idea, and into the technical work of locating, surveying and organizing village infrastructure and house lots.

Similarly, although the number of cooperatives kept increasing, levels of popular participation remained low, despite the high degree of popular enthusiasm and good will of the period.[7] By the time of the 1976–1977 campaign, 10 fully formed agricultural cooperatives had been established in the Baixo Limpopo, with an average membership of 100 people, and an average area under production of 100 ha. (Ministerio de Agricultura, 1977).

From the outset, all cooperatives struggled with basic technical and organizational problems, stemming from the illiteracy, inexperience, and lack of technical expertise of the peasant membership, and from the inability of the fledgling revolutionary state to deliver any but the most meager assistance. Serious deficiencies in planning, administration, credit, and supply of machinery and spare parts all prevented the early consolidation and development of the cooperative movement in the Baixo Limpopo.

The Formation of the State Farm Sector 1975-1977. During this same period—from independence to the campaign of 1976-1977—the government took the decision to reorganize the abandoned capitalist farms of the departing Portuguese settlers into a state farm sector. It was argued that this policy was not only the fastest and most effective way of restoring the productive potential of colonial capitalist agriculture—deemed essential to maintaining food supplies to the towns, especially Maputo—but was also a rapid and effective way of initiating the collectivization of peasant agriculture in the Limpopo valley. A state farm sector was also seen as a way of alleviating the growing problem of rural unemployment, caused by the collapse of capitalist settler agriculture, and the decline in migrant labor to South Africa.

The state sector of the Baixo Limpopo was formed in 1976, through the reorganization of numerous abandoned settler farms into four separate production units: one agricultural, one banana plantation, and two dairy and livestock units, jointly totaling some 26,000 ha. In the province as a whole, 25 such production units were formed (Ministerio de Agricultura, 1977: 10).

The immediate material and organizational problems were enormous. The first problem was decapitalization: the departure of the settlers had the immediate effect of producing an acute decapitalization of agricultural production in the Baixo Limpopo. The departure of the settlers, who often destroyed what they could not take with them, resulted in an acute shortage of means of production, transport, animal feed and medicines, breeding stock, and so on, for the embryonic state farm sector.

A further serious difficulty was the patchwork nature of the irrigation system. It was necessary to restructure the existing hydro-agricultural infrastructure, built to satisfy the individual drainage and irrigational needs of individual capitalist farmers.

Furthermore, like the cooperative sector, the formative state farm sector suffered from serious deficiencies in planning and administration, insufficient credit, and lack of machinery and spare parts, all of which stemmed primarily from the limited technical and organizational capacities of the new state apparatus.

The Impact of the Floods and the Third Congress 1977. In early 1977, the difficulties of the formative cooperative and state farm sectors were further compounded by severe flooding, which struck large areas of the Limpopo valley. The floods caused extensive crop losses and widespread destruction of the existing hydraulic infrastructure, thereby further weakening the already fragile productive potential of the cooperative and state farm sectors.

Aside from the setbacks that the floods dealt to the government's first attempts to rehabilitate the Baixo Limpopo through collective forms of production, they also created a civil emergency of enormous proportions, severely taxing the limited resources of the new state apparatus as a whole. Aside from extensive losses to crops, livestock, and infrastructure, the floods also left a large number of people homeless. In the face of the massive popular dislocations caused by the floods, the government stepped up its mobilization campaign for the formation of communal villages, and promptly implemented a rapid program of permanent resettlement of the displaced population into communal villages located on the highground above the valley flood plain. The effort was prodigious, both to convince the peasantry to accept the idea of the communal villages, and to supply technical and human resources needed to help plan, locate, organize, and build the new communal villages. As a result of this program, by the end of 1978, the number of communal villages in the Baixo Limpopo had risen to 18, housing approximately 80,000 people, or just under half of the rural population of the area. In the whole of the province, the communal villages had risen to 91 (Ministerio de Agricultura, 1977, 1978).

The intensified government effort that went into promoting the formation, and especially the occupation, of the communal villages in the wake of the floods, was accompanied by an equally intense government effort to repair the damage caused by the floods in the state farm and cooperative sectors, and to improve their planning and organizational capacity. In this, the government was attempting to implement the orientations of the Third Congress, held in February (1977) at the height of the floods. It had called for an intensification of efforts to increase agricultural output in the Limpopo valley, through the reorganization of agricultural production along collective lines, with priority for the state farm sector.

In a major reform, all state farm production units in the Limpopo valley were brought under two large farm complexes, one in the Baixo Limpopo (UPBL, or Unidade de Producao do Baixo Limpopo), and one further upstream in the Medio Limpopo (CAIL, or Complexo Agro-Industrial do Limpopo). The state farm complex of the Baixo Limpopo was reorganized into 7 subunits of production (known as "blocos"): 5 agricultural and 2 dairy/livestock.

In the cooperative sector, efforts were directed toward improving and standardizing the organizational structures of cooperatives, through the introduction of guidelines and model work schedules, and through courses and seminars to help raise the technical and administrative skills of cooperative leaders.

Government authorities also instituted a global planning process for agricultural production in the province as a whole, to begin with the 1977–1978 campaign. The plan assigned only a minimal role to the peasant sector. In the 1977–1978 campaign, for example, of the 21,216 ha. planned for commercial production, only 8% was to come from the peasant sector. The rest (92%) was all to come from the newly established collective production sectors, with the state farm sector taking the lion's share of the hectarage. The plan for 1978–1979, which was also drawn up at this time, reduced the contribution of the peasant sector still further to 4% of the planned production target, and set the contributions of the state and cooperative sectors at 69% and 27% respectively. In the case of rice production, the plan projected that the collective forms of production would surpass the 1973 colonial level of rice production (the main crop of the Limpopo valley) of 24,388 ha. and 42,400 tonnes for the province as a whole, by bringing 26,216 ha. (with 45,726 tonnes estimated yield) under production. Only 300 tonnes or 1% of this was to come from the peasant sector (Ministerio de Agricultura, 1978).

The intent of the plan was clear: to reestablish colonial levels of production in the Limpopo valley almost exclusively through the newly organized collective forms of production, especially the state farm sector, without relying on the productive capacity of the peasant sector.

Government investments to promote the expansion of collective forms of production went preponderantly to UPBL, with very little going to the cooperatives. Though the government actively promoted the formation of cooperatives, as an adjunct of its communal village campaign, mobilization was not accompanied by any significant corresponding supply of organizational and material assistance. The cooperatives of the Baixo Limpopo, for example, received only modest and tardy help from the state in reconstructing the vital hydraulic infrastructure destroyed by the floods. The machinery needed to redig major canals, build dikes, and so on, was largely monopolized by the state farm sector.

This policy of disproportionate allocation of investments, between the cooperative and state farm sectors, became a central feature of the government's collectivization strategy in the Baixo Limpopo, until the Fourth Congress in 1983. The lack of adequate and efficient investments, and the lack of sustained technical and administrative support and training have, in fact, been two of the major constraints on the growth of the cooperative movement in the Baixo Limpopo in the period between the Third and the Fourth Congresses.

Two other problems that have also retarded the growth of the cooperative movement in the Baixo Limpopo have been (1) the emergence of bureaucratic planning methods within both the national and provincial state structures, and (2) an experiment in obligatory participation in collective production for all communal village members. Though both practices were eventually stopped, they set back the growth of the cooperative movement in the Baixo Limpopo, which has remained weak, with low popular participation. It has nowhere displaced family agriculture as the economic base of communal villages.

In 1982 in the Baixo Limpopo, there were 20 fully formed agricultural cooperatives, with a membership of about 3500, controlling some 3300 ha. of land, but cultivating only 1700 ha. Aside from these fully formed cooperatives, there were numerous embryonic "pre-cooperatives" throughout the area, with a membership of perhaps another 1000 to 2000 people.[8]

In contrast to the paucity of organizational and material support extended to the cooperative sector in the aftermath of the floods, and on up until the Fourth Congress (1983), government support for UPBL was substantial and concerted. Despite the large investments that the state farm received over this period, however, it performed poorly and consistently failed to meet established production targets.

Thus, in the case of rice, the principal crop at UPBL, total yields for each campaign between 1977 and 1982 fell short of planned production targets by the following percentages:[9]

campaign 1977–1978 .... 72%

campaign 1978–1979 .... 79%

campaign 1979–1980 .... 85%

campaign 1980–1981 .... 55%

campaign 1981–1982 .... 83%

A main reason for UPBL's poor performance was the absence of the requisite technical conditions necessary for making a large-scale, highly mechanized, bureaucratically administered state farm work. The lack of sufficient trained personnel proved an insurmountable barrier to successful production. In all campaigns, UPBL struggled with basic technical and administrative problems, which consistently resulted in a gross underutilization of existing production capacity. UPBL simply had no capacity to use efficiently the large capital investments that were made.

Capital intensive investments and increasing mechanization, furthermore, meant a reduction in UPBL's capacity to absorb labor power, and thus did nothing to alleviate the problem of high rural unemployment (and rural-urban migration) made especially acute in the post-independence period by the drastic decline in migrant labor to South Africa.[10] As of 1982, UPBL employed a labor force of some 2700 workers (Serviço Provincial de Habitaçao e Planificaçao Fisica, 1982), in the context of an economically active labor force of some 80000 to 90000 people.[11] In this respect, it is noteworthy that the banana plantation subunit of UPBL, which is far more labor intensive and technically less complicated than rice producing subunits, achieved a stable labor force, and came close to colonial levels of production.

The government continued to pour scarce foreign exchange into UPBL, in the form of imported agricultural technology and expertise, without any significant return, in the hope of turning the state farm around. There was also a trend towards increasing centralization, bureaucratization, and technocratic focus in the rural development institutions in the region. It reached its highest expression in the State Secretariat for the Limpopo-Incomati, SERLI (Secretaria de Estado para a Regiao Limpopo-Incomati). It was formed in 1979 as an outcome of the Third Congress with the mandate to plan and implement a program of "accelerated development" in the whole high-potential Limpopo-Incomati region.[12] The salient features of the SERLI program were (1) an increase in centralized and bureaucratic planning and project administration, with a corresponding decrease in popular inputs and participation by local political authorities; (2) an almost exclusive focus on consolidating the existing state farm sector, with ambitious plans for the construction of more large-scale agro-industrial complexes, and a corresponding paucity of assistance for the cooperative and peasant sectors; and (3) a growing tendency to define the problems of Mozambican agriculture as purely technical problems at the level of productive forces, rather than also as social and political problems at the level of relations of production. Increasingly, government policy saw the peasantry as the object, rather than the subject of the country's rural development strategy.

Though these trends met with considerable criticism within the state and the party, and were finally repudiated in the Fourth Congress— SERLI itself was dissolved (see AIM Bulletin, 1983, No. 82)—they constituted the salient features of Mozambique's rural development strategy, not only in the Baixo Limpopo, but in the country as a whole, in the period between the Third and Fourth Congresses.

The Reproductive Crisis of the Peasant Economy Deepens. The government assumption that the peasantry would simply continue cash cropping as it had before independence, despite an almost total lack of state support and investment, misconstrued the nature and depth of the crisis in the rural economy, especially after the floods. For though the floods accelerated the process by which communal villages became the dominant form of rural habitation in the Baixo Limpopo, they also accelerated the decline of agricultural surplus production by the peasant sector.

The floods severely weakened the productive and reproductive potential of the peasantry. They swept away capital investments and factors of production (oxen, seed, fruit trees, tools, and so on) which could not easily be replaced. The decline in mine labor, and the dissolution of the settler dominated commercial network and capitalist farming sector meant that these once important sources of capital goods were no longer available. By the same token, the considerable commercial and extension services that the colonial state made available to the peasants were no longer there.

The floods also destroyed a large part of the hydraulic infrastructure upon which agricultural surplus production in the Limpopo valley was based. During the colonial period, such reconstruction would have been undertaken as soon as the receding water levels permitted, with the technical assistance of the state and under the direct supervision of the

local colonial administration. Furthermore, the whole coercive apparatus of the colonial state was in place to ensure the prompt and massive
participation of the local peasantry in the reactivation of the hydraulic
works.

With independence, this whole organizational and coercive structure
disappeared. But the new state structures that replaced them lacked the
technical and organizational capacity to carry out such a large-scale
generalized reconstruction of the hydraulic infrastructure of the Baixo
Limpopo. What limited resources were available were channeled
primarily into the reconstruction of the hydraulic infrastructure of the
state farm sector, and, to a lesser degree, into the cooperative sector.
The peasant sector was left largely to rely on its own resources. Efforts
to reconstruct peasant sector infrastructure at the local village community level received only minimal state assistance. Not only did the new
local-level political leaders often lack the organizational capacity to
undertake such a task, but more significantly, the peasantry itself
showed little interest in wanting to do so.

A principal reason for the peasantry's reluctance to reactivate the
hydraulic infrastructure was the growing lack of commercial incentive
for the peasantry to engage in cash cropping. The rapidly declining
supply of consumer (and capital) goods, initially caused by the collapse
of the colonial commercial infrastructure, but increasingly due to the
growing inability of Mozambique's small and struggling industrial
sector to produce them, and the unwillingness of the government to
import them, soon created a situation where demand greatly outstrip-
ped supply, and where money, as a consequence, was itself of
diminishing interest. The peasantry had little incentive to reactivate the
hydraulic works in the valley and recommence cash cropping—the
money it might earn from the sale of its crops was unable to purchase
anything.[13]

In the absence of any material incentive for producing a marketable
surplus, the peasantry continued to retreat into subsistence production.
Thousands of hectares of once intensively cultivated valley land fell out
of production. By the 1978–1979 campaign, peasant rice production,
the main peasant cash crop in the area, fell to a miniscule 11 tonnes of
marketed rice for the whole Baixo Limpopo.[14]

Beginning in 1980, the subsistence base of the peasantry was further
weakened by the onset of severe drought conditions, which have
persisted right through 1983, further reducing levels of consumption
and the peasantry's standard of living.

In village after village visited by the author over the course of 1982, peasants would speak of the time when vast expanses of valley land, now overgrown with wild grasses, were all intensively cultivated. For though peasant food production was adequate to meet basic dietary needs, it was by no means abundant or varied. The decline in the peasant's productive capacity posed a severe constraint on the productivity and output of peasant labor. For the collectivization strategy that the government was pursuing in the Baixo Limpopo, the implications were profound.

Production, Reproduction, and Rural Transformation

The net effect of the declining productive potential of peasant family agriculture was to leave the newly created communal villages with very weak economic bases, capable of supporting very little of the extensive division of labor that they were supposed to facilitate. Though all but the most badly located communal villages gradually stabilized as habitational arrangements and began to show significant degrees of social and political development, the deepening reproductive crisis in the peasant economy prevented the communal villages from becoming the dynamic poles of rural development and socialist transformation that the government had hoped. Communal villages were not only failing to develop collective productive bases, they were also experiencing an acute material crisis. Communal villages increasingly showed themselves to be economic liabilities—net importers rather than exporters of foodstuffs.[15] They were fundamentally blocked in their transformational and developmental functions.

By 1982, the material crisis began to generate a political and ideological crisis. Attendances at local political meetings dropped. Enthusiasm and goodwill began to be replaced by apathy and cynicism. The increasingly difficult economic situation initiated a gradual but growing process of peasant demobilization, which came effectively to block the processes of social, political, and ideological transformation that the creation of the communal villages had set in motion. Though FRELIMO continued to enjoy—and still enjoys—widespread popular support in this rural area, the crisis of reproduction made it increasingly difficult for the party to sustain the level of popular support needed for the social and economic transformations it was seeking to bring about in the countryside. The crisis in reproduction also contributed directly to the production problems of cooperatives and state farms.

In the case of the cooperatives, the economic crisis of the peasant sector gave rise to two main constraints on its growth. First, the reproductively insecure peasantry was unwilling to divert family labor to a form of production that offered dubious reproductive security.[16] Given the serious organizational and material difficulties faced by the cooperative movement, agricultural cooperatives have, by and large, been unable to give a return to labor anywhere nearly as high as family production has. Accordingly, peasant participation has been very low. In short, given its level of development, cooperative production could not offer any but the most marginal producers the measure of reproductive security offered by family production.[17]

Second, cooperative production is in theory essentially surplus production (especially if nonfood crops are grown), and given the lack of market incentive to increase its income, the peasantry has had little desire to engage in surplus production, whether through cooperative or family farm. Despite considerable politico-ideological mobilization by party cadres, popular participation has remained low.

In the case of the state farm sector, the government has not been able to create a stable, socialized rural labor force. That objective hinges on the capacity of state farm employment to guarantee the subsistence of the workers and their families. There are three main obstacles to the capacity of state farm wage labor to guarantee the subsistence of state farm workers.

First, since the wages paid by the state farm sector tend to be quite low (c. 2000 MT. = U.S. $53 per month), and thus unable to guarantee the subsistence of the laborers and their families, in most cases the laborers continue to seek reproductive security in their own fields.

Second, since UPBL practices rice monoculture in the Baixo Limpopo, it requires only seasonal labor, which means that state farm wage labor is incapable of providing a regular income for the peasant families of the communal villages supplying labor to it.[18] Worker-peasants must continue to rely on their own agricultural production to ensure their reproduction. This situation in part accounts for the chronic labor shortages that have plagued UPBL and the state sector everywhere, especially during peak agricultural periods. It is clear that when the peasants must choose between working on the state farm or working on their own fields, they choose the latter, since the yield of their own fields offers greater reproductive security than the seasonal monetary income of wage labor on the state farms. The attempts by UPBL to diversify its production to enable year-round agricultural activity, and thus establish a condition for the creation of a more stable and dependable labor force, has contributed to reducing, if not resolving, the problem of labor shortages during peak agricultural periods.

A third limitation on the process of collectivization through proletarianization of state farm labor has been the virtual disintegration of the market in foodstuffs and consumer goods in the rural areas. From the peasantry's point of view, there is not much incentive to sell labor if there is nothing to be bought with the wages earned. Moreover, if food cannot be purchased, then even year-round, well-paid wage labor on state farms cannot guarantee the reproduction of the peasant family. State farms, including UPBL, have sought to resolve this problem by establishing special shops for their workers. But given the limited quantities of foodstuffs and consumer goods available in such stores, their value in promoting the formation of a stable labor force would seem to be limited.

What is at issue is not simply a question of productive investments, but a question of reestablishing a market in goods and services necessary to the formation of a working class. Short of simply importing the bulk of these goods and services, it is only by providing the cooperative and peasant sectors with the necessary investments and market stimulus to start producing that it will be possible to meet the consumption needs of an emerging rural proletariat. Government policy from 1977 to 1983 failed to grasp the complementary relationship between state farm development and cooperative and peasant agricultural development (on this point, see O'Laughlin, 1981), and it was one basic cause of the poor performance of both forms of collective production in the Baixo Limpopo: the cooperatives were weak because they received no help, and the state farms because their work force lacked local sources of goods and services.

SOME CONCLUDING REMARKS ON THE POLICY SHIFT OF THE FOURTH CONGRESS

It was as a result of a growing realization of this basic contradiction in its agricultural development strategy that the rethinking that culminated in the policy shift of the Fourth Congress was undertaken. There can be little doubt that the shift itself reflects a recognition of the high political and economic costs of concentrating all investments in the state farm sector, while ignoring the much greater productive potential and demographic reach of the cooperative and peasant sectors. The high degree of popular dissatisfaction with existing economic conditions, which was voiced in the thousands of local-level political meetings held to discuss the "Theses"[19] of the Fourth Congress in the period leading up to the actual congress, and conveyed by elected peasant delegates, was not lost on the assembled delegates or the party as a whole.

The Fourth Congress, in fact, concluded that large-scale, capital intensive agriculture is at present beyond the technical and organizational capacity of the country's labor force; and that the state sector in any case can potentially employ only a small percentage of the rural population; and thus to direct all energies into this one sector is to effectively exclude the majority of the rural population from any direct involvement in the main thrust of the development process.

But more than this, the new emphasis on the peasant sector is also an admission that the recuperation and growth of agricultural production cannot be achieved, at the present time, exclusively through collective forms of production. It is recognized that the collectivization of Mozambican agriculture cannot be achieved within the brief period of time initially envisaged, and that the peasant sector must accordingly continue to play a central role in guaranteeing adequate levels of agricultural production. For the immediate future, at least, individual and not collective production will remain the predominant form of agricultural production in the country.

Accordingly, the Fourth Congress decisions to channel significantly more productive investments into the cooperative and peasant sectors, to decentralize planning and administration of agricultural production, especially in the state farm sector, and to send more trained people to work in the countryside, directly in the productive process, rather than leave them in bureaucratic postings in the cities, must together be seen as a significant attempt to overcome production-related constraints on agricultural production of the sort found in Baixo Limpopo. The decentralization of agricultural planning and administration, especially in the state farm sector—which has already resulted in the dissolution of SERLI (AIM Bulletin, 1983, No. 82), and the dismemberment of the Complexo Agro-Industrial do Limpopo (CAIL), the largest state farm complex in the country, into several smaller state farms, and the parcelling out of the remaining land holdings to peasant and petty capitalist producers—is likely to alleviate the limitations imposed by the lack of trained technicians, and by the complexities of large-scale, centralized planning and administration. The decentralization of planning and decision making to the district level is also likely to minimize a constraint and danger of a more political nature, namely the trend toward technocracy and bureaucratization in rural development practice.

Increased capital investment in the cooperative and peasant sectors also offers a possible way of providing state farm workers with a secure source of food supplies sufficient to guarantee their reproduction as wage laborers. The channelling of productive investments into the cooperative and peasant sectors, therefore, would assist in transforming the peasantry from a simple labor reserve for state farms into a stable rural working class.

Increased capital investment in the cooperative and peasant sectors, however, is unlikely to result in any significant increase in agricultural production (and the productivity of peasant labor), unless some concerted action is taken to reverse the decline in the level of real consumption by the peasantry through a substantial increase in the supply of basic consumer goods. For the central problem of the low productivity and growth of Mozambican agriculture is not simply one of low productive capacity, but perhaps more significantly (in the short term) one of decline in real consumption by the peasant producers to the point where reproduction is threatened. If new productive investments are not to be underemployed, and if the peasants' retreat into subsistence production and passive resistance is to be overcome, and agricultural growth fostered, an increase in the rate of supply of consumer goods to the peasantry may be necessary, even at the cost of a reduction in the rate of accumulation.

The documents of the Fourth Congress reflect FRELIMO's attempts to grapple with this whole issue. The importance placed on the necessity of promoting the "commercialization" of peasant surpluses, and on developing small-scale local industries, as sources of manufactures for local consumption, reflect an awareness of the necessity of overcoming not only productive constraints on agricultural surplus production, but also constraints of a reproductive character. These initiatives constitute a significant attempt to address both the basic reproductive issue of increasing existing consumption levels, and the question of linking industrial and agricultural development strategies. These positive steps, however, may in the short term have to be accompanied by the importation of manufactures, until such small-scale industries become sufficiently established, if the hoped for expansion of agricultural production is not to be delayed any longer.

NOTES

1. See Mittleman (1978), Isaacman (1978), Wield (1983).

2. For purposes of this discussion, the term "peasant sector" is understood to include also the rich peasantry/petty capitalist producers, which in official Mozambican government discourse are usually categorized separately as the "private sector."

3. The Baixo Limpopo is not an administrative unit, and thus no official statistics are available for this area as such. All statistical data for the Baixo Limpopo presented in this chapter, unless otherwise indicated, are estimates and calculations made by the author on the basis of available census figures and statistics for existing administrative units.

4. The growth of an African capitalist agriculture was severely restricted by racist colonial legislation and practices, which favored the development of Portuguese settler agriculture; and by the competition of this latter and the South African mining economy for available labor power. I owe this latter observation to Marc Wuyts.

5. These figures are based on interviews with long-time employees of the rice hulling and storage plant in Xai-Xai, formerly known as the Fabrica de Descasque Santos Gil, now owned by the state.

6. For an official colonial administration account of the (latter day) phases of this process, see de Sousa Monteiro (1955).

7. In the context of the post-independence euphoria, FRELIMO's mobilizational efforts met with a high degree of positive popular response, which led to the formation of dozens of "collective fields," or "machambas colectivas," throughout the province of Gaza. The collective fields, sometimes also called the "people's fields" (machambas do povo), were ad hoc, loosely organized, community-based forms of collective agricultural production, which sprang up with minimal mobilizational effort throughout the country in the immediate pre- and post-independence period. They were, to a large extent, expressions of the high levels of popular support for FRELIMO and enthusiasm over independence, and in nearly all cases served as precursors for agricultural cooperatives proper. But as these collective fields began to be organized more formally as agricultural cooperatives proper, thus demanding regular and consistent labor inputs from the peasantry, levels of popular participation in collective production dropped, as the peasants took a wait-and-see attitude.

8. These figures are an estimate based on data contained in Serviço Provincial de Habitação e Planificação Fisica 1980, 1982.

9. These percentages are based on calculations from statistics contained in Secretaria de Estado Região Limpopo-Incomati (1982).

10. This is a point that has been repeatedly made by the Centro de Estudos Africanos, and by its staff members individually, in various publications: e.g., Centro de Estudos Africanos (1977), Wuyts (1979, 1981).

11. This figure is an estimate derived from calculations based on available census data.

12. The Limpopo-Incomati region is a large, potentially very rich agricultural area bounded by the Limpopo and Incomati rivers and their tributaries.

13. It is noteworthy that in many areas of the country, the government has had to resort to a system of direct exchange of agricultural produce for consumer goods in order to gain access to peasant agricultural surpluses.

14. Based on statistics supplied by the Fabrica de Descasque de Arroz de Xai-Xai (1982).

15. There is strong evidence to suggest that the peasantry has been relying on its monetary savings and the occasional sale of produce to pay for the purchase of basic foodstuffs they themselves cannot produce. Given the shortages in the supply of such foodstuffs, and all consumer goods generally, even modest monetary resources have been sufficient to purchase what goods have been available for extended periods of time. Clearly, when such savings are finished, the peasantry is forced either to resume surplus production, despite the unfavorable economic conditions for doing so, or to retreat further into subsistence production and accept a further drop in consumption and standard of living.

16. This point has been repeatedly made by the Centro de Estudos Africanos (1979).

17. The membership of nearly all cooperatives, in fact, is overwhelmingly female, of whom a large percentage are widows or persons lacking a secure agricultural productive base.

18. See Note 16.

19. The theses of the Fourth Congress were a series of six statements on main economic and political issues to be addressed by the Fourth Congress. They were widely circulated and discussed in schools, work places, and villages throughout the country, and provided an important channel for mass popular input into the proceedings of the congress.

REFERENCES

Agencia de Informaçao de Moçambique—Bulletin (1983) Special Issue: Fourth Congress of the FRELIMO Party. No. 82.

Assembleia Popular (1979) Quarta Sessão. Resolução sobre agricultura e aldeias comunais. Maputo.

Centro de Estudos Africanos (1980) A transformação da agricultura familiar na provincia de Nampula. Maputo.

—— (1979) Problemas de transformação rural na provincia de Gaza. Maputo.

—— (1977) The Mozambican Miner: A Study in the Export of Labour. Maputo.

Comissão Nacional das Aldeias Comunais (1980) Primeira reuniao nacional das aldeias comunais. Maputo.

DE SOUSA MONTEIRO, J. (1955) Relatorio sobre o resgate dos "machongos" do sul do Save. Maputo: Imprensa nacional de Moçambique.

Direcção Nacional de Habitação (1981) Estatistica sobre as aldeais comunais. Maputo.

Direcção Provincial de Obras Publicas e Habitação de Gaza (1982) Aldeais comunais e ocupação territorial do vale do Limpopo no Distrito de Xai-Xai. Xai-Xai.

—— (1980) Aldeias comunais e ocupação territorial do vale do Limpopo no Distrito de Chibuto. Xai-Xai.

Fabrica de Descasque de Arroz de Xai-Xai (1982) Estatistica. Xai-Xai.

FRELIMO (1983) "Out of underdevelopment to socialism." Fourth congress. Central committee report.

—— (1982) A situação actual no nosso pais. Maputo.

—— (1977a) Central Committee Report to the Third Congress. London: Mozambique, Angola and Guinea Bissau Information Centre.

—— (1977b) Economic and Social Directives of the Third Congress: Summary. Maputo: CEDIMO.

—— (1976) 8ª Sessão do comité central. Resolução sobre as aldeias comunais. Maputo.

—— (1975) Primeiro seminario nacional de agricultura. Comunicado final e recomendações. Marrupa.

HANLON, J. (1978) "Does modernization=mechanization?" New Scientist, 28 August.

HARRIS, L. (1980) "Agricultural cooperatives and development policy in Mozambique." J. of Peasant Studies 7, 3.

ISAACMAN, A. (1978) "A luta continua: creating a new society in Mozambique." Fernand Braudel Center for the Study of Economies, Historical Systems and Civilizations. Binghamton: State University of New York.

Ministerio de Agricultura (1981) A situação agraria do pais. Maputo.

—— (1978) Conselho agrario provincial por ocasião da realização da III reunião do conselho agrario nacional. Xai-Xai. Provincia de Gaza.

—— (1978) III reunião do conselho agrario nacional. Maputo.

—— (1977) Conselho agrario provincial por ocasião da realização da II reuniao do conselho agrario nacional. Xai-Xai. Provincia de Gaza.

—— (1976) Primeiro seminario nacional de cooperativas. Maputo: CEDIMO.

O'LAUGHLIN, B. (1981) "A questão agraria em Moçambique." Estudos Moçambicanos 3: 9-32.

SAUL, J. (1984) A Different Road: The Transition to Socialism in Mozambique. New York: Monthly Review.

—— (1979) The State and Revolution in Eastern Africa. New York: Monthly Review.

Secretaria de Estado da Região Limpopo-Incomati (1982) Estatistica. Xai-Xai.

SKETCHLEY, P. (1980) Casting New Moulds: First Steps Toward Worker Control in a Mozambique Steel Factory. San Francisco: IFDP.

WIELD, D. (1983) "Mozambique—late colonialism and early problems of transition," in G. White, et al. (eds.) Revolutionary Socialist Development in the Third World. Lexington: Univ. of Kentucky Press.

WUYTS, M. (1981) "Sul do Save: estabilização e transformação da força de trabalho." Estudos Moçambicanos 3: 33-44.

—— (1980) "Economia politica do colonialismo em Moçambique." Estudos Moçambicanos 1: 9-22. Maputo.

—— (1979) "On the question of mechanisation of Mozambican agriculture today: some theoretical comments." Centro de Estudos Africanos, Universidade Eduardo Mondlane. Maputo.

About the Contributors

TAISIER ALI teaches political science at the University of Khartoum. His Ph.D. dissertation, based on extensive field research in Sudan and completed in 1982 at the University of Toronto, is on the state and agricultural policy in Sudan. His publications include articles on Sudan and on the theory of dependency.

JONATHAN BARKER teaches in the Department of Political Science at the University of Toronto. In 1964–1965, he conducted research on rural change in a district in the groundnut region of Senegal. He taught at the University of Dar es Salaam in 1970–1972 and did research on the 1970 elections and on ujamaa in the regions of Iringa and Mbeya. He has published a number of articles on local politics and rural change in Africa.

BONNIE K. CAMPBELL teaches at the Department of Political Science at the Université du Québec à Montréal, and has done extensive research on the political economy of the Ivory Coast. Her work on this subject is published in a wide variety of journals and in the form of an essay in *West African States* (edited by John Dunn, Cambridge University Press, 1978). She is the author of *Libération nationale et construction du socialisme en Afrique. Angola/Guinée-Bissau/Mozambique*, (Eds. Nouvelle optique, Montreal, 1977), and *Les enjeux de la bauxite. La Guinée face aux multinationales de l'aluminium*, (Presses de l'Université de Montréal and Institut Universitaire des Hautes Etudes Internationales de Genève, 1983).

WILLIAM COWIE is a consultant on development matters, now living in Toronto. He has lectured in the Department of Geography at the University of Toronto. His Ph.D. research for the London School of Economics was on "Changing Settlement Systems and Economic Development in Eastern Province, Zambia." He has also done research in Kenya's Central Province. His published articles analyze agricultural strategy, nationalist politics, and the migrant worker system of Zambia.

WILLIAM DERMAN teaches in the Department of Anthropology at Michigan State University. His Ph.D. research in the mid-1960s was reported in his book *Serfs, Peasants, and Socialists. A Former Serf Village in the Republic of Guinea* (Berkeley: University of California Press, 1973). He has published articles on rural class formation and drought in the Sahel. He is currently engaged in a research project on the implications of dam construction and development projects in the Gambia river valley.

LINDA FREEMAN is Assistant Professor in Political Science at Carleton University, Ottawa, Canada. She has authored studies on the political economy of Canada's relations with Africa, particularly Canadian aid programs, patterns of trade, and involvement in white Southern Africa.

MYRIAM GERVAIS is a Ph.D. Candidate in political science and a Teaching Assistant at the Université du Québec à Montréal. She has done extensive research in Upper Volta and Mali, and is currently preparing her dissertation on peasants, capital, and state in the Sahel.

MOHAMED S. HALFANI is on the faculty of the Institute of Development Studies at the University of Dar es Salaam. He is completing a dissertation in political science at the University of Toronto on foreign-financed projects for housing the urban poor in Tanzania.

JOHN LOXLEY is Associate Professor of Economics at the University of Manitoba, Canada. He was the Research Manager of the National Bank of Commerce, Tanzania, and taught economics at the University of Dar es Salaam. He was the first Director of the Institute of Finance Management, Tanzania and has recently acted as an Economic Advisor to the Government of Tanzania on its structural adjustment program and on its negotiations with the International Monetary Fund. He is currently writing a book for the North-South Institute, Ottawa, on external indebtedness and structural adjustment in the Third World.

JOTHAM MOMBA teaches in the Department of Political and Administrative Studies at the University of Zambia. His Ph.D. thesis at the University of Toronto, "The State, Peasant Differentiation and Rural Class Formation in Zambia: Case Study of Mazabuka and Monze Districts," was completed in 1982. It reports the results of his local-level research.

JAY O'BRIEN teaches in the Department of Anthropology and Sociology at Lawrence University in Appleton, Wisconsin. His Ph.D. thesis (University of Connecticut, 1980) is on "Agricultural Labor and Development in Sudan." From 1974 to 1979, he conducted research in Sudan and taught at the University of Khartoum and the University of Gezira. He has published a number of articles and book chapters on agriculture and labor in Sudan.

OTTO ROESCH is completing a Ph.D. dissertation on problems of rural development in Mozambique in the Department of Anthropology at the University of Toronto. He is also an active member of the Toronto Committee for the Liberation of Southern Africa (TCLSAC).

BROOKE GRUNDFEST SCHOEPF has taught at the University of Zimbabwe, Tuskegee Institute, National University of Zaire at Lubumbashi, University of Connecticut, and Tufts University. She has published numerous articles on the social relations of medical care, research in women's studies, politics and ethics in anthropology, and farming research.

ROBERT SHENTON received his Ph.D. from the University of Toronto in 1981, and is now a postdoctoral fellow of the Social Sciences and Humanities Research Council of Canada at the University of Guelph. He has published articles in the *Review of African Political Economy* and the *Journal of Peasant Studies*. His current research interest is on the history of agricultural development in Africa.

MICHAEL WATTS has been Assistant Professor in the Department of Geography at the University of California, Berkeley, since 1979. He is author of *Silent Violence: Food, Famine and Peasantry in Northern Nigeria* (University of California Press, 1983), which details his work on agrarian change in northern Nigeria, his principal research and writing focus. He recently returned from 10 months in Senegambia where his work focused on irrigation systems and local accumulation among Serrahuli peasants in eastern Gambia.